# FRANCE, SPAIN AND THE RIF

# FRANCE, SPAIN AND THE RIF

## BY

### WALTER B. HARRIS

F.R.G.S., F.S.A., F.S.A. (SCOTLAND)
MEMBRE DE L'ACADÉMIE DES SCIENCES COLONIALES (PARIS)
OFFICIER DE LA LÉGION D'HONNEUR
COMMANDEUR DE L'OUISSAN        UITE DU MAROC
AUTHOR OF
"TAFILET," "MOROCCO THAT WAS," ETC

## The Naval & Military Press Ltd

Published by
**The Naval & Military Press Ltd**
5 Riverside, Brambleside, Bellbrook
Industrial Estate, Uckfield, East Sussex,
TN22 1QQ England

Tel: +44 (0) 1825 749494
Fax: +44 (0) 1825 765701

www.naval-military-press.com
www.military-genealogy.com

## NOTE

Two chapters of this book (Chaps. I and VIII) appeared in much their present form in 'Foreign Affairs' (America), June, 1925 and in 'The Round Table,' March, 1924. They are republished here by the kind permission of the Editors. I'desire also to express my thanks to Señor Diaz Casarieqo, of Madrid, and to 'Photo Coutanson,' and to Messrs. Gillot and Rabel, of Casablanca, for the facilities accorded me for the reproduction of their excellent photographs.

W. B. H.

# PREFACE

With the opening of a New Year it may be hoped that an end has come at last to the long period of war in the Rif—a war that has caused almost unimaginable suffering to all concerned.

Like all wars it has been marked by acts of cruelty and barbarism. On the one hand every modern method of destruction, the outcome of man's intelligence and ingenuity, has been employed. On the other, the innate cruelty of primitive race has been let loose. On both sides there have been reprisals. All have paid, and paid dearly, the price of war, the luxury of bloodshed.

War anywhere and everywhere is horrible—this war in Morocco was doubly so. The Rifis were deprived of all medicaments and surgical aid; yet the imposition of this unnecessary addition to their sufferings did nothing to shorten the campaign, and probably nothing to lengthen it. The agony of Spain was little, if any, less. The youth of the Peninsula has died, massacred, tortured, mutilated, in its thousands. For the French the period of war was shorter. They were prepared for the encounter, but even for them the campaign was a bitter one. There were rude awakenings and cruel experiences.

There were acts of great endurance and courage, as there always are when men, whatever their race or religion, are called upon to slay one another. But there is no Glory in War, however noble and self-sacrificing individual acts may be.  It is cruel, devastating, hideous.  It leaves behind it a track of corruption.  Its remembrance is a cup of bitterness.

That the war in the Rif is over is a cause of thanksgiving at the opening of this New Year.  That it will never occur again must be our prayer.

W. B. H.

Tangier,
  1 *January*, 1927.

# CONTENTS

# LIST OF ILLUSTRATIONS

## MAPS

# FRANCE, SPAIN AND THE RIF

## CHAPTER I

## THE STATUS OF FRANCE AND SPAIN IN MOROCCO

The modern history of Morocco may be said to have begun in 1904 with the Anglo-French Agreement of that year.  For some time previous to that date the Moorish Empire had been breaking up.  A strong Sultan, Mulai Hassan, had died in 1894, leaving as heir to his throne one of his younger sons, Mulai Abdel Aziz, a mere boy. For several years the power lay in the hands of the Grand Vizier, and it was not till his death in 1901 that the young Sultan emerged from the precincts of the secluded palace to take over the reins of Government.  Well-intentioned, weak, misled and shockingly robbed, Mulai Abdel Aziz was incapable of maintaining order over the turbulent tribes whom a long period of repression and extortion had rendered only too ready to revolt.  His plight was not rendered any the happier by the fact that the two Powers most interested at that period in Morocco—England and France—were united by no ties of friendship.

France, intent upon rounding off her great possessions in North Africa, coveted the rich but almost unknown country that lay between the Algerian frontier and the

Atlantic Ocean.   England, desiring nothing for herself in
Morocco—unless it was Tangier, which she knew could
never be hers—was firmly determined to combat all
France's schemes to obtain a preponderating influence
in the country.   Accordingly the British Government
strongly supported the young Sultan in resisting the
constant strain of French pressure.   Germany and
Spain, jealous of France's African possessions, gave
England a moderate measure of support.   But the
bolstering up of the decaying Moorish Government
could not save the situation.   Tribal revolt, misgovernment, corruption, disturbances on the Algerian frontier
and near the Spanish ' Presidios ' on the Mediterranean
coast, indicated the end of Moorish independence.   The
British Government realized at length that no assistance that it was prepared to give—and the assistance
had always been more in advice than in substance—
could prolong for any but a very short period the life of
the decaying empire.   There remained but one purpose
that Morocco could serve—that of a pawn on the chess-
board of Europe.   It is possible that active intervention might have been a remedy, but active intervention
was exactly what Great Britain was determined to
avoid, and under no circumstances, less perhaps than
the seizure of Tangier by a Foreign Power, would she
have taken the risk.

Only lately emerged from the throes of the South
African War, England required a long period of peace.
The death of Queen Victoria and the accession of King
Edward VII had awakened a desire for a new foreign
policy, and for new friends in Europe.   It had long been
King Edward's wish to see an improvement in the rela-
tions between England and France.   His arrival on the

throne rendered this possible. He enjoyed great popularity in France. He was esteemed and trusted in England, where his great ability was fully recognized. Under his influence the attitude of the two peoples toward each other changed and an exhibition of goodwill on both sides rendered an Entente feasible. The first step was the elimination of the points of friction which existed between the two countries, and there were no more serious points of friction than Morocco and Egypt. It was realized that before any permanent entente could be reached these two disturbing elements must be got rid of. A single formula was devised—the withdrawal by England and France of their political interests in Morocco and Egypt respectively. England was to have a free hand in Egypt to continue her work in that country, while the closed doors of Morocco were to be opened to France. The withdrawal of British political interests in Morocco, where they were paramount at the Court of Mulai Abdel Aziz, practically left Morocco in the hands of the Power against the intentions of which the British Government had never ceased to warn the Sultan. It was only when the Anglo-French Agreement was signed that the Sultan learned that the staff on which he had always leaned had proved to be a broken reed.

It is to this Anglo-French Agreement of 1904 that the existing situation in Morocco owes its origin, for it contains the basis of all the subsequent arrangements, treaties and conventions which in any way confirm or modify the spheres of influence of France or Spain, or determine the status of Tangier. It is therefore essential, in reviewing subsequent events and the existing situation in Morocco, that the terms of this original

agreement should be borne in mind. Briefly, as far as
lay in the powers of the contracting parties, with certain
non-political and commercial exceptions, it gave England
in Egypt and France in Morocco full liberty of action.
The benefits that accrued to England in Egypt are
outside the scope of this work.

By Clause II of the Agreement the British Government recognizes that it pertains to France to watch over
the security of Morocco and to furnish the Moorish
Government with all such assistance in administrative,
economic, financial and military reform as it may
stand in need of. No hindrance will be put in the
accomplishment of France's duty in this respect by the
British Government, provided the existing rights of
Great Britain are not interfered with. In Clause IV the
two Governments mutually guarantee that in Egypt and
Morocco respectively there shall be maintained an
equality of treatment in the Customs Houses, and under
all other forms of taxation, and in the transport of
merchandise on the railways. In Clause VII the two
Governments undertake that they will allow the construction of no fortifications on the Southern shore of
the Straits of Gibraltar, or along the coast of the Atlantic
Ocean as far South as the mouth of the Sebu River, or
on the Mediterranean as far East as the Spanish 'Presidio' of Melilla. Exception is of course made of such
fortresses and positions as Spain holds along the latter
coast.

So far the Agreement was limited to the two contracting parties, England and France; but it was
evident, and only just, that Spain's geographical position, and the fact that she possessed territory on the
Mediterranean coast of Morocco, gave her an indisput-

able right to be a party to any such arrangement. Ceuta, Peñon de la Gomera, Alhucemas and Melilla had been Spanish territory for centuries, and in the far South, opposite the Canary Islands, she claimed a long-abandoned possession, Santa Cruz de Mar Pequeña.

Clause VIII states that the two Governments, inspired by sincerely friendly sentiments toward Spain, take into particular consideration the interests that Spain has acquired by her geographical position and her territorial possessions on the Mediterranean coast. On this subject, it is stipulated that the French Government will concert with the Spanish Government, and will communicate to the British Government the terms of the arrangement which may result between France and Spain. In the last Clause the British Government undertakes to give the French Government its diplomatic assistance in the carrying out of the terms of the Agreement.

Such are briefly the contents of the Anglo-French Agreement of 1904. A separate and secret Convention accompanied it, in which the proposed extent of the Spanish zone was specified, but which at the same time gave the French Government entire liberty to negotiate this question of delimitation. So successful were the French in these negotiations that Spain was satisfied with a very much smaller sphere of influence than France was prepared to grant. The original proposition included not only the rich Gharb plains North of the Sebu River, but even Fez itself. It was a disappointment to the Spanish Government to learn, after their Agreement with France was signed, that they might have included in their sphere of influence these valuable assets.

France and Spain having come to terms, the Spanish

Government gave its formal adherence to the Anglo-French Agreement on October the 3rd, 1904. This recognition by Spain was followed by a secret arrangement with France, which was signed on October the 30th, and the next year (1905) a second secret Franco-Spanish Convention was signed on September the 1st.

The following year (1906) a Conference on the subject of Morocco was held at Algeciras, summoned by the Sultan at the instigation of the German Government, which had become anxious as to the intentions of England, France and Spain in regard to that country. The attitude adopted by the Governments of those three Powers, however, successfully prevented the introduction of any question that threatened the eventual operation of the terms of the Agreements which had been signed between them during the previous two years. Certain reforms were introduced on an international basis, and the equality of treatment in commercial industrial matters was guaranteed to the subjects of all the signatory Powers in Morocco. The question of spheres of influence never arose, and the Germans and their supporters, who had hoped to raise the entire subject of Morocco's future, failed in their endeavours to do so. The ultimate results of Algeciras were to strengthen the position of France and Spain in Morocco.

In 1911, the German Government having in the meantime left no stone unturned to hamper France's Moroccan policy, even to the sending of a warship, the *Panther*, to Agadir—and having at last realized that its efforts were in vain—proposed a deal. In return for territorial concessions in West Africa, Germany signed a treaty with France on November the 4th, 1911, by which she bound herself to adhere to the Anglo-French

Agreement of 1904. There were a few modifications, but none which affected the spirit of that Agreement. The German Government formally recognized the right of France to extend her control in, and her protection over, Morocco. This treaty also confirmed to France the privilege of the diplomatic representation of Morocco both in that country and abroad.

By this Franco-German treaty France's position in Morocco was greatly strengthened. Her predominance and liberty of action had now obtained the support of all the Powers whose consent was of importance—England, Spain and Germany. With regard to the other Powers, the interests of which were economic and commercial, the Act of Algeciras gave a sufficient guarantee of equality of treatment. France found herself authorized to introduce into the country all such ' administrative, judicial, economic, financial and military reforms' as she might think fit, provided they did not affect the status and rights of the subjects of other Powers. In short, France became the recognized collaborator with the Sultan and the Moorish Government in every branch of the Administration.

It was the course of events in Morocco itself as much as this series of political arrangements outside of it, that brought about in 1912 the negotiation and declaration of a French Protectorate over Morocco.

The Sultan, Mulai Abdel Aziz, whose authority at the moment when the British Government in 1904 had abandoned the task of trying to prop up the decaying Moorish Government had already become greatly diminished, lost the throne in 1908. His brother Mulai Hafid, egged on and supported by the influential Chiefs of the South, had raised the standard of rebellion.

After a long campaign, in which an intense desire never
to come to decisive action seems to have been the
common aim of both parties, Mulai Hafid gained the
day.   Both Sultans—for at one period they both reigned
in different parts of the country—were without adequate
means to finance the campaign.   The war was desultory
and uneventful.   Both were dependent upon the
deserters from the other's army for troops, and the
soldiers fought for whichever side could afford to pay
them.   On French advice and with French financial
assistance Mulai Abdel Aziz set out from the coast with
an expedition in August, 1908, for the reconquest of his
Southern capital, Marrakesh.   Within a day or two's
march of the city, owing to a rising of a supposed friendly
tribe against him, he was defeated.   His camp was
pillaged and he returned to the coast a fugitive.   There
he abdicated in favour of his brother.   Mulai Hafid was
proclaimed at Fez and at Tangier, and all Morocco
recognized him.   He reigned for four years (1908–1912),
and though at first he showed signs of a desire to restore
the fortune of his country, it was too late.   Chaos and
corruption had done their work.   Wearying of the
struggle, at war with his tribes, at the mercy of the
Foreign Powers, his treasury empty, Mulai Hafid
abandoned hope.   From month to month the situation
became more difficult.   At length, in 1911, besieged in
his capital by the tribesmen of the surrounding districts,
he appealed to the French Government for assistance,
and troops were dispatched to Fez.   It was the beginning of the end, and in March, 1912, he signed a treaty
by which he recognized a French Protectorate over
Morocco.   It was the end of Morocco's centuries of
independence.

As in the case of the Agreements with England in 1904 and with Germany in 1911, France's treaty of Protectorate with the Sultan of Morocco included the whole of that country with the exception of Tangier. The French Government was charged with the foreign relations, and the Sultan undertook to conclude no act of international character without the consent of France. The status of the French Résident-Général, whose powers are most extensive, was outlined ; the control of practically the whole administration rested in his hands. To this there was only one exception. Tangier had been carefully eliminated from all these treaties and agreements, that is to say there had been inserted a Clause in each of them by which it was agreed that the status of Tangier should be determined by a separate arrangement. It was clear, therefore, and undisputed, that Tangier and its little zone fell neither in the French Protectorate nor in the Spanish sphere of influence. An exception to France's complete control of Morocco, though not mentioned in the Protectorate Treaty, was the Spanish zone, which the French Government had by the Anglo-French and Franco-Spanish Agreements of 1904 definitely engaged itself to recognize. On the subject of her zone of influence Spain had not, and has not to-day, any direct treaty with Morocco. She has merely the Agreement with France that she was to occupy and administer a section of Northern Morocco extending from the Algerian frontier to a spot a little South of the town of Laraiche on the Atlantic coast, including the whole Northern coast-line with the exception of Tangier. To this transaction the Sultan and Moorish Government were in fact not parties. The situation was briefly as follows : France had negotiated

with the Sultan of Morocco a treaty of Protectorate over
the whole of Morocco, excluding Tangier ; but France
had, at the time of the signature of this treaty, already
pledged herself to sublet to Spain the northern section
of this country and a zone in the desert regions of the
South.   Spain's position in Morocco is based  solely
upon her treaties and agreements with France.

The moment had now arrived to study in detail the
terms upon which the Spaniards were to administer their
sphere of influence, and for a more definite delimitation
of its frontiers.  The French Government, once the
Treaty of Protectorate was signed, immediately opened
negotiations with Madrid, and the result was the
Franco-Spanish Treaty of November, 1912.  By the
first Clause of this Treaty the French Government
formally recognized that it pertained to Spain to keep
watch over the security of the Spanish zone and to grant
the Moorish Government within the limits of the zone
all such administrative, economic, financial, judicial and
military assistance as might be needed.   In fact by this
first Clause of the Treaty France transfers to Spain the
rights and responsibility of fulfilling the same functions
in the Spanish zone as Great Britain had recognized as
pertaining to France over the whole of Morocco by the
Agreement of 1904.  Spain, by signing this Treaty,
accepted responsibility for the maintenance of order and
the introduction of reforms.  Clause II confirms the
civil and religious authority of the Sultan over the
Spanish zone, and agrees that it shall be administered,
under the control of a Spanish High Commissioner, by a
Khalifa chosen by the Sultan from two names to be
submitted by the Spanish Government.  The Khalifa
was to reside in Tetuan and would be invested by the

Sultan with full powers. The Spanish High Commissioner should be the sole intermediary between the Khalifa and the local agents (Consuls) of the Powers in the Spanish zone, but the Spanish Government recognized Clause V of the French Treaty of Protectorate by which all relations with the diplomatic representatives of Foreign Powers are vested in the French Résident-Général, who is the Minister of Foreign Affairs for all Morocco. The authority of the Spanish High Commissioner in his relations with the Foreign Consuls is therefore strictly limited to questions of local interest.

The Treaty, after stating the geographical limits of the Spanish Northern and the Southern desert zones, stipulates that the Spanish Government shall under no circumstances alienate or cede even temporarily her rights over any part of these zones. Spain undertakes, as England and France had already done by the Agreement of 1904, to allow no fortifications to be erected on the coast of her zone—with the exception, of course, of her ' Presidios,' which are Spanish territorial possessions. The Franco-Spanish Treaty also delimits the frontier of the little Tangier zone and confirms the liberty of education and cults. Spain's right to spend on the upkeep of her sphere all such taxes as she may collect, together with the mining royalties, etc., is recognized, and there are various further Clauses which affect the functions of the Moroccan State Bank, the Tangier-Fez Railway and the protection of natives at home and abroad.

Spain, though possessing full powers to administer her sphere as she may deem fit—provided Treaty rights are not affected—has legally no Protectorate over her zone of Morocco. Her powers are delegated by France,

whose Protectorate extends over the whole of Morocco.
But in the interests of practical Government Spain's
position in Morocco has been recognized as amounting
to a Protectorate. With the exception of the diplomatic relationship with the Foreign Powers the Spanish
High Commissioner enjoys in Spanish Morocco practically the same almost unlimited powers as does the
French Résident-Général in the French Protectorate.
In the same way the Khalifa in Tetuan plays the part of
a Spanish protected Monarch, and is invested with all
the paraphernalia of an Oriental Sultan. Even the
imperial parasol is carried above his head on state
occasions, and except in name he is a sovereign. It has
been the policy of both France and Spain to dissociate
in fact, while preserving in form, the two Governments
of the French Protectorate and of the Spanish zone.

This system of splitting up into spheres of influence a
country which, while nominally one, forms as a matter
of fact different political and administrative entities, is
not one that can be recommended. More especially is
this the case where, as in Morocco, it was done without
consultation with the ruler or the people of the country,
and introduces frontiers that only to a very small extent
are based upon natural or physical features—frontiers
that pass through unexplored and unknown districts.
An imaginary line was drawn from point to point, often
varying with the supposed contour of the country, and
the tribes through whose territory this arbitrary frontier
passed were told that the inhabitants who lived to the
North were subject to Spanish administration, while
those to the South fell in the French Protectorate.
Naturally this delimitation required, as the country
became better known, considerable readjustment ; but

*Photo. Alberto.*

THE SULTAN GOING TO THE MOSQUE

even to-day there are districts on both sides of the frontier which are still unoccupied by the French or the Spaniards, and which are still almost unexplored, though the campaign of the spring and summer of 1926 has done much to open up the country in question.

Had the Spaniards in the past shown in their administration of the Moslem population of their zone a skill equal to that of the French, the situation in their zone would have been solved long ago. There is no need to describe here the admirable work that the French have accomplished under Maréchal Lyautey. It is an achievement that is perhaps unrivalled in the annals of African administration. The Spaniards have until lately been less fortunate. Their intentions have been of the best, but they have been hampered by want of previous experience, by sacrificing practical results to an exaggerated sentiment of *amour propre*, by disorganization and by lack of imagination. But the events of this year (1926) have entirely changed the situation, and Spain to-day, after a great effort admirably performed, can look forward with justifiable hope to a period of peace and prosperity.

No chapter that deals with the situation of France and Spain in Morocco would be complete without some mention of Tangier, which, with its little hinterland of about 200 square miles, forms the third zone of Morocco. It has already been pointed out that in the various treaties and agreements that had been come to between the Governments of the various Powers interested in Morocco, and in the Treaty of the French Protectorate itself, there had been inserted clauses which determined that the status of Tangier was to be settled by ulterior arrangement.

Tangier for a century or more has been the diplomatic capital of Morocco in that it was the residence of the Representatives of the Foreign Powers accredited to the Sultans, whose policy it has always been to close the interior of their country to all foreign influence. Force of circumstances arising from questions of public order and hygiene, and from other causes, had not only brought about the régime of the ' Capitulations '—by which the subjects of the Powers enjoyed the privilege of being under the jurisdiction of their respective Consular authorities all over Morocco—but also special Concessions in Tangier itself. The Sultans from time to time had delegated to the Foreign Representatives at Tangier certain rights of participation in the local Government. From this there grew up a sort of international régime, always, be it understood, under the sovereignty of the Sultan. It was on the existence and recognition of this régime that the British Government, basing its policy on the great importance of the strategic position of Tangier, demanded its neutrality and its internationalization—under a special status.

It can be realized that the position of the population of Tangier while awaiting the settlement of their fate was no enviable one. Friction and obstruction reigned supreme and the interests of its inhabitants, and of the place itself, were sacrificed to the pettiness of local jealousies. In 1913, however, a Conference of the delegates of England, France and Spain met at Madrid, but the resulting Convention was still unratified when war broke out in 1914. It was not until 1923 that the question was reopened, and in October of that year a Conference met at Paris. On December the 18th a

Convention was signed and in due time ratified by the British, French and Spanish Governments.

It was scarcely disputed at the time that this Convention was more political than practical, and that its object was rather to rid the interested Governments of a difficult and possibly dangerous question than to discover a solution that would ameliorate the unhappy condition of Tangier and its population. A sufficient measure of good-will and conciliation was exhibited in Paris to facilitate an arrangement, within the limits of political exigencies. The three Governments concerned considered that they could count upon the acquiescence and the support of the other Signatory Powers of the Algeciras Act in any decision that they might themselves arrive at. The Italian Government had expressed a desire to participate in these deliberations, but its request was refused for reasons which, even if their legitimacy was evident, were neither quite reasonable nor quite wise.

The Convention signed in December, 1923, was only officially brought into force in Tangier in June, 1925, for many supplementary questions, such as the drawing up of the Sultan's ' Dahirs ' and of the legal codes, had to be undertaken, matters of considerable labour.

There is no need to do more than recall the outline of Tangier's status. The town and its zone of little more than 200 square miles in extent remain under the sovereignty of the Sultan of Morocco, who is represented in Tangier by the Mendub. The Mendub and his assistant officials have all but complete control of the native population, while the administration of the Islamic law is also placed under the Sultan's authority. The native population, both Moors and Jews, who form

a large majority of Tangier's inhabitants, are thus to all
intents and purposes withdrawn from the jurisdiction
of the international administration and subjected to the
government of the Sultan and of the French Protectorate,
over which the Tangier Administration has, of course,
no control.

The Moors and Jews have their Islamic and Rabbinic
Courts, entirely apart from the Tangier Government.
The international civil and criminal codes are administered in Mixed Tribunals by Judges of British, French
and Spanish nationality.   The executive government of
Tangier lies in the hands of an Administrator and two
Assistant-Administrators.   They are of French, British
and Spanish nationality.   The Public Works are under
the charge of a Spanish engineer, and the staffs of the
various Government offices are recruited from the many
nationalities and several religions of Tangier, chosen for
their qualifications.

There is an International Representative Assembly
which is responsible for local legislation.   This Assembly
is in turn subject to a Committee of Control—consisting
of the Consuls-General of the adhering Powers—whose
duty it is to confirm the Assembly's decisions, provided
they are in accordance with the terms of the Convention.
The Legislative Assembly should, if fully constituted,
consist of twenty-six members representing eight nationalities, elected by their compatriots or nominated by
their Consuls-General.

As a matter of fact the two Italian members and the
American member have never been elected or nominated,
as the respective Governments of these countries have
not yet recognized the new status.   It is this refusal on
the part of these two Governments to acquiesce in the

change of régime that is one of the principal obstacles to the success of Tangier's internationalization. There are, it is true, many other and serious drawbacks in the status itself, sufficient to retard the smooth working of so complicated a machine. One, and a very important one, though perhaps it was inevitable, is this isolation of the Moroccan subjects of Tangier under what amounts to the foreign control of the Sultan and of the French Protectorate Government.

The result of the abstention of Italy and America is this—that while the Governments of Great Britain, France, Spain, the Netherlands, and Belgium, which are all represented to-day in Tangier by Consuls-General, have recognized the new status and taken the necessary legal steps to place their nationals at Tangier under its jurisdiction, the subjects of Italy and of America, on the contrary, are not amenable to the new laws, and still enjoy the privileges—if such they can be described—of the old régime. That is to say, they have the benefit of the Capitulations and remain, as formerly, under the jurisdiction of the laws and Consular Courts of their respective States. The result, as can be realized, is one that cannot fail to cause difficulties, while it may at any moment cause danger, and it does away with all principles of equality of treatment.

It had been argued, and with reason, that, quite apart from the abstention of certain Powers, the difficulties with which Tangier's new Government finds itself confronted arise more largely from the situation which existed in Morocco when the Convention was drawn up and the restrictions that this situation imposed upon the negotiators than from imperfections in the status itself. There were acquired rights which could not be disre-

c

garded; there were claims justified and unjustifiable; there were political, strategical, and commercial requirements—and above all, the foundation on which the new structure had to be raised was the corrupt system already in existence.

Again, the whole question of Tangier had already been greatly influenced by its geographical position. The situation of the town on the narrow straits that unite the Mediterranean and the Atlantic is almost unique in its advantages, lying as it does on the high road of shipping at the point where Europe and Africa are nearest. Yet it has been largely this natural advantage that has done so much to ruin Tangier, for it has given the place a strategical value of such importance as to awaken the jealousies and suspicions of the European Powers. Its possession by such a weak authority as was the Sultan of Morocco before the introduction of the French Protectorate gave certain Governments of Europe a wonderful opportunity for protracted intervention, and they were not slow to seize it.

From 1912, when Morocco was definitely split up into French and Spanish spheres, Tangier and its little zone have been isolated, and they remained on under the corrupt Moorish régime rendered still more injurious by constant diplomatic obstruction to all improvement. Geographically, Tangier is part of the Spanish zone, and geographically, the two should have remained inseparable. There were practical and political reasons why this was not possible, just as there were reasons why Tangier could not have been attached to the French Protectorate. Nevertheless, the stroke that rendered Tangier independent of the Spanish zone deprived it of its hinterland and its means of livelihood, and Spain of this most valuable outlet to the sea for her African sphere.

It has often been asked why Tangier was not included in either the Spanish or French zones, or a mandate given to England for its administration. The answer is simple. Neither England nor France could afford to see the other installed there. The same difficulty did not exist in the case of Spain, for she already owned the Northern shore on the Straits, with the exception of Gibraltar, and was already destined to command most of the Southern shore. It was considered, however, expedient that Spain should not be permitted to include Tangier within the limits of her zone. The reason was that, although Spanish possession of the place was not in itself a menace to England or to France, a combination of Spain and Germany was always possible as a set-off to the, at that date, newly-formed Entente between England and France. Happily, Spain is to-day a firm and valuable friend to the two Entente Powers.

In the autumn of 1926, when the conclusion of the Rif War had brought peace in all the region of the Spanish zone that is in touch with Tangier, General Primo de Rivera, Marqués de Estella, President of the Spanish Council, claimed from the French and English Governments the incorporation of Tangier in the Spanish zone, or failing that solution, a mandate for its administration from the League of Nations. Neither claim was acceptable to the two Governments concerned, but it was allowed that Spain's position justified a certain predominance in Tangier and its zone, and preliminary conversations were proposed between Paris, London and Madrid for the purpose (1) of obtaining Italy's adherence to the 1923 Convention, which it was at the same time proposed to modify, and (2) to discuss in what form certain privileges in the Administration could be delegated to Spain within the scope of existing treaties. Such was the situation at the date of the writing of these words (September the 26th, 1926).

# CHAPTER II

## THE RIF

No description of the Rif, no account of recent events in that country, would be complete without some reference to the Berber race to which its inhabitants belong and of which they form so characteristic and so typical an example. Recent studies, though still in their infancy, have done much to throw light upon these most interesting people who have played and will continue to play in the history of Morocco so important a part.

It is only lately that it has been generally realized—if in fact it is generally realized—that the majority of the population of Morocco is not of Arab origin. In certain districts, and those the most accessible, there are found tribes of Arab descent, though, even there, seldom unmixed with Berber blood. They are the offspring of the invaders of A.D. 681 and 707, or of the later Arab immigrants of the eleventh century. There are, and can be, no precise estimates of the relative importance of the natives of Berber and Arab origin respectively ; but the latest to hand, drawn up with care and after much inquiry, gives the following numbers :

| | |
|---|---:|
| Population of Morocco . . . . . | 4,000,000 |
| Pure Berbers . . . . . | 1,750,000 |
| Slightly Arabicized Berbers . . . | 1,000,000 |
| Arab origin . . . . . | 1,250,000 |

That is to say, a total Berber stock of 2,750,000 against

1,250,000 natives of Arab origin.   In the Spanish zone
of Morocco, of which the total population is estimated
at 766,000, the numbers, included in the above, are
as follows :

| | |
|---|---|
| Pure Berber (the Rif 250,000)   .   .   . | 397,000 |
| Arabicized Berbers   .   .   .   .   . | 369,000 |

The ignorance which formerly existed on the subject
of the vast numerical superiority of the Berber race in
Morocco was no doubt largely owing to the fact that these
tribes had been driven, or had retired, into the remoter
districts of the country and that they were inhospitable,
refusing all intercourse with the stranger or foreigner, as
in the Sus and the Rif.   It must not be forgotten that
until very recent years Morocco closed its doors to almost
all outside influence, and that it was the policy of the
Sultans and of the Maghzen—and not only that of the
tribes—to hold themselves aloof from the world.   Thus
information as to the population of the country was
scant.   The Moors themselves had no interest in statis-
tics, and no system of controlling information.   They
were generally as ignorant of the details of their territory as they were of the geography of other lands.   They
had some general idea of direction and distances, mea-
sured by time, but what lay between the caravan
tracks they neither knew nor cared much.   It was sufficient that as a rule the state of security on the roads left
much to be desired, while away from them, as often as
not, there was none.

The Berber tribes were often almost as inhospitable to
the Arab as they were to the foreigner.   Even in Europe,
beyond a vague outline of tribal geography, and the
itineraries of certain travellers, there was a complete lack
of detailed information about any but the most accessible

regions. To the coast towns the Berber came in search of work or, in the case of the Susis, as petty shopmen, but as a rule he spoke Arabic and became merged in the town population. The foreign resident at least scarcely distinguished the two races, except perhaps that the Berber was the better workman. Even the early geographers and historians, Ibn Khaldun and Leo Africanus, do not seem to have fully appreciated the dissimilarity of the Berber and Arab races. As early as those days the inaccessibility of the country the Berber tribes inhabited, their mistrust of the stranger, their desire to maintain their independence—and this has been the determining feature in all their history—and the constant state of intertribal warfare in which they have existed, have all tended toward ignorance of their status and of their country.

Until a very few years ago the Europeans who had succeeded in penetrating into the Berber regions of Morocco were few and far between. One or two had been able to visit the cedar forests that lie to the South of Fez ; a few had travelled in the Southern Atlas and pushed on into the Sus or to Tafilet—and that was almost all. This refusal to receive strangers into their country was not, as was often thought, due to religious fanaticism but to political distrust, to vague traditions of past invasions and of wars with European peoples, and to fears for the future. The Berber mentality is closely allied to that of European races, and they seem always to have realized that once their resistance to exterior influences was broken down their independence would be lost. They held, and hold, their independence very dear, not perhaps from any spirit of racial patriotism—for Berber patriotism seldom extends beyond tribal limits—but

from a rooted and innate detestation of all authority outside that exercised by their own democratic and local
organization. While the Arabs have turned toward
autocracy the Berbers are democrats in spirit and in
practice.

Before, however, the subject of Berber organization is
touched upon—and some words on that question are
necessary to explain the progress of Abdel Krim's campaign in the Rif—mention must be made of what is
known, or surmised, as to the origin of the Berber race
of Morocco.

Many theories have from time to time been put forward on this subject, but that which is now most generally accepted, and which recent investigations seem to
warrant, is that the Berbers of Morocco are the descendants of a white Mediterranean people who were in all
probability also the ancestors of the Celts with whom
they have much in common. The type, often described
elsewhere as the Celtic type, is still found amongst a
number of the Berber tribes. Red-bearded and light-
eyed natives are common in the Rif and amongst the
Jibala tribes, and even in the Middle Atlas' to the South
of Fez and Taza. But this type is not by any means
universal, for there exists alongside it, but curiously distinct, another and quite different one. This is represented by the darker Berbers, with their curious fringe
of beard and more sturdy build. Yet to-day so closely
are these two types allied in custom, habits, language
and religion that except for the marked dissimilarity of
feature they would be undistinguishable. It is clear that
the origin of this latter type is other than that of the
white Mediterranean race, and it is generally supposed,
not without adequate reason, that they are the descend-

ants of an Oriental Semitic people who at some early period immigrated into Morocco. Their resemblance to the Early Assyrian has often been remarked.

Until further researches have been made—and the want of monuments renders research arduous—little more can be said at present as to the origin of the Berbers. Even when an historical period is reached there is a great scarcity of sources of information, owing not a little to the fact that, just as is the case to-day, these people held themselves aloof from intercourse with the foreigner and in a state of complete independence. This secluded existence has, however, helped to preserve their customs and traditions which even the various religions they have at times adopted and discarded have but little affected. While want of contact with the outside world has retarded progress amongst them, it has at the same time preserved many of their original characteristics, with the result that to-day the Berbers exhibit traces of a highly organized tribal administration mingled with every form of superstition and many relics of barbarism.

Attempts have been made to arrive at a conclusive opinion as to the original grouping of the Berber tribes of Morocco. Although owing to intermarriage and migration, and probably also to warfare, this grouping can no longer be said to exist, there is little doubt that there were in Morocco three divisions of the Berber race. They are (1) the Masmuda, including the Ghomara, (2) the Zenata and (3) the Sinhaja. The tradition of their descent from one or other of these sections is still current amongst the tribes. The Rifis, with whom we have principally to deal, trace their origin as follows: The Eastern Rifi tribes claim to be the descendants of the Zenata people, and still speak a dialect that points to that origin. The Central and Western tribes state that they are of Ghomara (Masmuda) descent, while certain mountain districts of the Rif and probably the whole of the Jibala are of Sinhaja stock.

What was the reason, or origin, of those great divisions of the Berber people ? It is more than probable that they originated in a political instinct of balance of power, rather than in any racial separation. We find even to-day amongst the tribes a system of federation and on a larger scale of tribal alliance, which undoubtedly exists for this purpose. These are the ' sofs ' and the ' lefs,' of which some mention must be made. While the word ' sof ' is applied to each of the two politically rival parties existing in the same village or district, the ' lef ' has a larger extension and signifies an *entente* between tribes or portions of tribes, for the purposes of common association, protection or even aggression. There is usually an oath of fidelity demanded and given. On the whole they tend toward the maintenance of peace. The ' lef ' can under certain circumstances be abandoned but is generally of a certain duration. A number of the original ' lefs ' of the Berber tribes disappeared on the occupation of Morocco by the French, to reappear in a vastly larger form as an anti-French ' lef '—an alliance for the purpose of protecting themselves against foreign aggression. In the formation of these new ' lefs ' old quarrels and blood feuds disappeared and tribes from time immemorial at enmity joined the new Entente.

In course of time intermarriage and association between the three great divisions of the Berbers—Masmuda, Zenata and Sinhaja—may have destroyed their individuality. It may have been, too, that the political situation no longer necessitated the maintenance of this balance

of power, and that in the face of a common enemy—the
Arab invader and to a certain extent the European—
they broke down the barrier of their separatism and
merged into a larger federation.

It must not be forgotten that since the early immigration of an Oriental Semitic race and its intermarriage
with the white Mediterranean people who then inhabited
Morocco, there have been other but less important intro-
ductions of foreign blood. The Romans are known to
have mixed freely with the inhabitants of the country.
It was they who introduced Christianity amongst the
Pagan and Jewish Berber tribes, with such success that
as late as the eleventh century of our Era there were
still Christian communities existing in the Rif, no doubt
either descendants of the Romans themselves or of the
Berbers they converted. On several occasions while
travelling amongst Berber tribes I have heard the natives
claim, with some show of pride, Christian origin. It
would appear that, converted as they undoubtedly were,
they were never slow to lose an opportunity to adopt
unorthodoxy and were readily persuaded to become
adherents to any new sect or schism that might arise, a
propensity arising from their rooted dislike to authority,
even on matters of faith.

The same inclination is clearly apparent to-day,
although they are now of course professed Moslems.
Hesitating to seek another God they stray far and wide
in the search of other manifestations, which accounts for
their predilection for a multitude of saints, dead or alive,
and their readiness to embark on mysticism by becoming
members of religious brotherhoods. This is especially
remarkable in the Rif. It is more than possible that in
this manner they have been able to maintain their mani-

festly pagan traditions by decking them out in Moslem raiment, even though thoroughly unorthodox. The tomb of the Mohammedan saint merely covers for them some sacred spot, holy by tradition and dating far earlier than Moslem times. The hollow rock, the tree covered with its ex-voto rags, the sacred pool full of fat fish or water tortoises, known to-day as dedicated to the memory of some Moslem divine, is still to the Berber the haunt of the spirits which his ancestors worshipped and which he still reverences. His words invoke the Moslem saint; his heart implores the aid of the pagan spirit. There is no doubt that where Islam was forcibly spread amongst them they purposely chose as the place of sepulture of the doctors of the law, and of the descendants of the Prophet, the spots which in their eyes were already hallowed—the dwelling places of their pagan gods. The introduction of all new faiths has required the construction of mental bridges to lead the faithful across.

The Jewish conversion of the Berbers, dating from the second century A.D., preceded the introduction of Christianity, and appears to have been largely successful. It began by an important movement of immigration, which was repeated in the fifth century, when a large number of Jews accompanied the Vandals on their invasion of Morocco. They settled and proselytized amongst the Berbers. Although, under the influence of Islam, Christianity entirely disappeared amongst the tribes, Judaism held its own, and there still exist in the Southern Atlas little Israelite communities, which except for a few details of dress cannot be distinguished from their Islamic Berber neighbours. It is interesting to know that the Berber tendency toward unorthodoxy in very faith they have ever adopted is still to be found

amongst these Jews, and that their doctrines are looked
upon askance by the learned Rabbis of the Moroccan
cities, in all of which there are Jewish communities. In
the towns of the interior many of the Jews are also of
Berber origin, while those of the Coast, and to a certain
extent of the large interior cities, are the descendants of
the exiles from Spain and Portugal.

Roman blood must still flow in certain districts and the
tradition of Roman descent is still found in those regions.
It has left, however, no distinguishable trace, though
Roman features are not uncommon. Not so the negro
blood, which from the introduction of slaves has tainted
certain Berber regions ; for example, the tribes of the
far South. Even in the Middle Atlas and, though much
more rarely, in the Rif itself, the presence of black origin
is apparent in individuals and even in families. The
Berbers, however, seem to recognize it as a disparage-
ment, and as a rule avoid intermarriage with slaves.

In many respects the Berbers of Morocco are more
pagan than Moslem, though they would be shocked if
told so. They have adopted but little of the Koranic
law in spite of the divine origin of that sacred book in the
eyes of Mohammedans, and they depend for their legislation, administration and customs upon oral traditions.
In many cases, such as the refusal to admit the inheritance of property by women, they deliberately ignore the
Islamic law. It is a curious fact that, although their
women-kind are deprived of this right of inheritance, in
other respects they enjoy privileges quite unknown
amongst the Arab inhabitants of the country. The Berber women go unveiled and mix and converse on terms
of equality with the men. Often the influence of individual women is very great in the family, and even in the

tribe.  During one of my visits to the Beni Mtir tribe,
before the introduction of the French Protectorate, their
Kaid, Akka, was called away to visit some other tribe
to which the Beni Mtir were united by ' lef.'  In his
absence his mother, an old Berber woman, took his place
and governed the tribe, sitting in justice in the great
black tent of her son.  Her word was law.  It is seldom,
too, that the Rifi marries more than one wife,—in fact
monogamy is general throughout the Berber tribes.  The
Rifis themselves have a proverb which states that
' The wife is the beam which supports the roof of the
house.'

The relatively superior position which women enjoy
amongst the Berbers is but one of the many examples of
the manner in which heredity, custom and tradition have
impeded the introduction of Islamic tenets.  In certain
things the precepts of the Koran are observed.  Most
Berbers keep the Fast of Ramadan.  It would seem that
the distinction between what they accept and what they
refuse is based upon the following principle : Ordinances
which are religious only and are not in opposition to
inherited custom are observed, while those which are
contrary to tradition are disregarded.  Yet to all outward and visible appearance the Berber appears more
devout than the Arab.  There are more mosques in the
Jibala region than in any other in Morocco ; there is not
a village that does not possess one.  There is not a ham-
let where at the regular hours the call to prayer is not
heard.  Generally consisting of thatch huts resembling
the humble cottage of the mountaineer or villager, without a minaret or any sign of their religious dedication,
these little country mosques are respected and kept in
repair by the village community.  They serve not only

as places of prayer but also as village schools, and from far and wide boys are sent to the mountain districts for their education, that is to say, to acquire a more or less proficient knowledge of the Koran.

It requires, however, only a short visit to any of those regions, more particularly if that visit is made in summer, to discover that parallel with strict religious observance there is a strain of undisguised paganism which in many cases the inhabitants do not even attempt to disguise under the cloak of Islam. Pilgrimages to holy springs and to groves of trees are of common occurrence. Women who are barren pass through a narrow passage between rocks ; persons who are bitten by a mad dog swallow a hair from its tail in a glass of water drawn from a sacred spring ; children who are sick are held in the branches of mystic trees. Often enough the name of a Moorish saint is invoked, but these rites are far removed from the tenets of orthodox Islam. Besides these local places of pilgrimage there are also the tombs of important personages, who either from the rôle they played in the history of the country, or from their religious prestige, have been raised to a state of sanctity. Some have been the founders of the many sects that exist in Morocco, which, though quite unorthodox in teaching and in practice, are reverenced by large numbers of the people. Their ' Zawias '—centres of their religious teaching—are sanctuaries for the criminal, as well as places of pilgrimage and instruction. The Rif has been particularly under the influence of these sects, and throughout their country there are found a large number of ' Zawias,' representing for the most part either the Taibiya sect of the Shereefs of Wazzan or the Shereefian family of Akhamlich, both of which

cults have played an important political part in Rifian
affairs.

But the pagan rites still practised in the Rif and Jibala
districts are not limited to these pilgrimages to saints'
tombs and holy places.   The tribes still retain without
any glamour of Islamic disguise many of their primitive
customs and traditions.   Their pre-Mohammedan origin
is clearly demonstrated by the fact that the seasons of the
year at which these rites are practised depend upon the
Julian, or solar, calendar, whereas all Islamic feasts and
functions follow the lunar system.   The state of inaccessibility in which the tribes have maintained themselves has prevented any intensive study of their folklore
and customs, but it seems clear that their original religion
consisted, like that of nearly all primitive peoples, in the
worship of the spirits of nature.

The superstitions and traditions of the Berbers of
Morocco can be traced to two origins—the earlier, the
very primitive cult of magic, by the practice of which
they sought desired results ; and secondly, the cult of
spirit worship.   In the former there are a number of surviving examples in ceremonies and acts which are still
performed for the obtaining of rain.   In the Rif, a large
wooden spoon, the Tahonja, is decked out as a female
doll and led in procession to Anzar, her fiancé, who however seems to be allowed no material representation.
This is but one example of the many rites practised for
this purpose.   Nearly all the ceremonies are agrarian, as
might be expected in an agricultural country, and are
seemingly based upon the belief that the benefits of
heaven showered upon the earth depend upon figurative
marriage—the law of creation.   Sacrifices and proces-
sions for the same purposes are common, and cultivated

fields, newly dug wells and the foundations of buildings are sprinkled with blood, preferably that of a black he-goat or a black cock.

The ' Jinun,' a vast race of spirits, are feared or respected by the people, and acts dedicated to their propitiation are in constant practice. Their leaders are often mentioned by name, and a certain Ali el-Ghiaut is said to be their king. The grottos and caves which give ingress to the kingdom of the ' Jinun ' are often visited for purposes of sacrifice or consultation with the inmates. There are good and bad ' Jinun,' and they even profess different religions—believers and infidels—Moslems, Christians and Jews. To the Berbers the ' Jinun ' have a very real existence and enter into constant contact with mankind.

While there are nomad and semi-nomad Berber tribes in Central Morocco and across the Atlas, and in the region of Ujda to the East, the population of the Rif and Jibala country is sedentary. The nature of the land inhabited would prevent their being anything else, even had they a propensity to wander. Their villages usually consist of clusters of thatched houses, many only of one room, others of several rooms built round an open court. The walls are low and the thatch overhangs them, so that little of the masonry is visible. To enter, one must stoop. Inside, however, there is at times a measure of comfort and, where means allow, even of comparative luxury ; for the Berber is a lover of his home, which he decorates as far as his scanty means allow, and the rude exterior of these roughly-thatched huts, for they appear as little more, is often in astonishing contrast to what is found within. Cleanliness is nearly universal in these interiors.

D

In the Rif, particularly in its Eastern part, the villages consist of detached flat-roofed buildings scattered amongst the fields and orchards, but these it would appear are inhabited only by the richer class, the owners of agricultural land. For the rest their habitations are poorer than amongst the Jibala, and their dwellings inferior in construction, cleanliness and comfort.

The Rifis are certainly less civilized than the Jibala. They have lived in a perpetual state of war, now and again against a common enemy—the Sultan at times—but more often amongst themselves—tribe against tribe and family against family. The Rifi will abandon everything in the pursuit of vengeance, just as he will sacrifice everything to have the wherewithal to buy a rifle. Peace seldom reigns for more than a few months at a time. If a quarrel does not exist a pretext is found for instituting one. The 'Bloodfeud' is universal. There is no pardon and no mercy—nothing but hate and treachery and death in the pursuit of revenge. Even religious ceremonies and tribal festivities are often interrupted by murder. I have known whole families treacherously massacred at a feast of 'reconciliation.' The Sheikh Duas of Anjera murdered his rival Deylan and his four sons while seated partaking of his hospitality in his own guest-room. A volley was fired by his retainers from without the door and windows, and the deed was accomplished. A nephew of Deylan alone survived. He took to the mountains and from time to time waylaid the members of the enemy family. He shot Sheikh Duas himself on his way to market, and one by one he wiped out his sons and relatives. Alone, lying long in wait, he killed eight members of the hated class before he himself fell a victim to the rifle of a member of the Duas

VICTIMS OF THE WAR.

TYPICAL JIBALA VILLAGE.

family. The Rifis boast that few of their countrymen grow old, and that not many reach middle age. And yet away from their own country they are quite docile workmen, trusting and trustworthy, full of sentiment; and if treated with sympathy, they become devoted servants and friends. But often the spirit of revenge will return; a duty has to be performed, a vengeance to be carried out. Armed with his rifle the Rifi, full of apologies, goes off. Sometimes he returns; often nothing more is heard of him. Never probably in the history of their country have the Rifis abandoned their quarrels and stayed their vengeful hands as they have done during this late campaign against France and Spain. Tribes whose animosity was a byeword, whose hatred was proverbial, made peace in order to obey, and to obey blindly, the first Rifi who has ever been able to unite them—Abdel Krim.

Generally speaking, the Rifi is extremely poor. In no part of Morocco is life more difficult. Hard and inured to suffering, by nature cruel, poorly and insufficiently clad, ill-nourished, lacking even the most modest comforts of life, the Rifi has nevertheless maintained his independence, and by undoubted force of character and of dogged determination has kept the foreigner and the stranger from his door. He has never until to-day been conquered, and to-day it has taken the armies of two great Powers, France and Spain, to invade his country— and at what a cost in life and money! Cruel, stubborn and courageous, the Rifi has for centuries resisted all foreign influence. Has he benefited by it? It is very doubtful, and it is not difficult to imagine his lot a far happier one in the future than it has been in the past. The only peace they have ever known has been outside their own country. From childhood the Rifi boy is taught to make war and to hate. The children have the look of frightened eaglets, suspicious but ' out for blood.' The first thing a boy learns is who are his father's enemies—and to handle a knife and rifle. He has no chance of cultivating finer feelings, though they are not absent from his nature. They come of a white race ; they have many of the sentiments of white men, warped by generations of suffering and hate. They are lovers of poetry and music, and romance plays no little part in their lives. Their outlook toward womankind is that of Europe rather than that of Africa. Hard as the women have to work in the Rif, they are respected. The standard of morality is high. The punishment of adultery is death. By instinct honest and moral—though treacherous when in search of revenge—they seek, once away from their country, opportunities to prove their fidelity. They settle down to the most modest situations and remain long in the same service. They have no spirit of fanaticism and are more trusting of Christians and Jews than they are of their own people. The question of divergence of faith means little or nothing to them. They one and all deprecate the manners and customs and the cruelty of their countrymen ; yet, when the call comes they go back. Tradition and the honour of the tribe or family is too deeply embedded to be cast off so easily.

The language spoken by the Rifis is Thamazirth—the Berber tongue—though the Rifi dialect differs in many respects from those spoken in Central and Southern Morocco. It is no doubt the language of the Semitic race which at some very early period migrated from the East and intermarrying with the white Mediterranean people of Morocco formed the Berber stock. The language of the earlier inhabitants has entirely disappeared without leaving any discoverable trace. How came it that the tongue of these immigrants of new blood so entirely replaced that of the white people ? The resistance of the fair type, still so common amongst the Rifis, would appear to prove that numerically the invaders were in a minority. Possibly the new-comers brought with them a new civilization and new religious beliefs, the adoption of which, and of words to express them, necessitated the introduction of new terms and new expressions. All that remains to-day of the original race is its type and the cromlechs they no doubt erected.

The Berber language is not to-day written in any part of Morocco, nor have inscriptions yet been found in that script. In order to express themselves in writing, they have to adopt the Arabic characters.

Of the ancient history of the Rif very little is known. The tribes which inhabited it probably were much as we know them now, determined to prevent the installation of the foreigner in their country, distrustful and treacherous. Neither the Phœnicians nor the Romans seem ever to have succeeded in penetrating inland, though they had settlements on the coast. Of this the earliest was Rusadir, the modern Melilla, renowned for the export of honey, which, till modern times, replaced sugar, and was an important article of commerce. The Rif honey has always been celebrated and is still exported in small quantities to other parts of Morocco. The town of Badis, of which the ruins still exist on the Ghomara coast, was at one time in Roman occupation, and reached a certain importance in Arab history.

When in the seventh and eighth centuries of our Era

the Arabs invaded Morocco they found the Rif peopled
by the two Berber stocks of Ghomara (Masmuda) and
Sinhaja, for it was not until the thirteenth century that
the Zenata incursion took place.   The first Islamic state
that existed in Morocco was in the tribe of Temsamen
in the Rif, where a lieutenant of Musa ben Noseir, by
name Salih Ben Mansur el-Himyari, of the Yemen,
installed himself and obtained a charter of his rights from
the Omeyad Sultan of Damascus in the year 710.   El
Bakri refers to the population of that region as having
been converted at that period to Islam.   This small independent kingdom lasted fifty years and its collapse
seems to have immediately followed the pillage of its
town of Nekor by the Normans in 760.   In 1015 the
Fatimides took the place by storm and it was eventually
destroyed by Yusef ben Tashfin in 1084 during his conquest of Northern Morocco.   He was the first ruler who
can claim to have brought the Rif into the Empire of
the Sultans of Morocco.   In 1142 the Rifi tribes recognized the Almohade Sultan Abd el-Mumen ben Ali, but
in the following year they rebelled and the Sultan was
forced to lead an expedition in person to crush the revolt.
The reconquest of the Rif took several years.

A large number of Rif tribesmen took part in the invasion of Spain.   They were present at the victory of
Alarcos in 1195 and at the defeat of Navas de Tolosa in
1212.   But their attention was soon turned to events
nearer home, for in 1216 the invasion of their country by
Abd-el-Haqq ben Marju, a Zenata Chieftain, and a crushing defeat of the tribesmen in Bottioua near the Wad
Nekor, brought them under the domination of the Merin-
ides (Beni Merin).   Their rule, however, was no easy
one.   Revolts were common, and in 1287 Badis, the

principal town and port of that part of North Morocco, was sacked by a revolted tribesman and his bands. His rebellion was suppressed and the rebel's head was exhibited in all the towns of Morocco as far South as Marrakesh.

It was the arrival of the Christians upon the coasts of Morocco that brought the Rif into historical prominence. In 1415 the Portuguese had taken possession of Ceuta. In 1458 they had landed at Alcazar Soreir on the Anjera coast of the Straits of Gibraltar, and in 1471 Tangier and Arzeila had fallen into their hands. Stirred by the successes of their neighbours, the Spaniards in turn sent expeditions across the Mediterranean. In 1496 they took Melilla, and in 1508 they occupied the Peñon de Velez opposite Badis on the Ghomara coast.

In 1664, after more than a century of anarchy, the throne of Morocco passed into the hands of the present Alaouite dynasty, and Mulai Reshid became the first Sultan of that line. By 1680 the Rif seems to have entirely passed under the rule of the new dynasty and furnished the main part of the troops with which Mulai Reshid in 1684 occupied Tangier after the departure of the British, who had been for twenty-two years in possession of the place which formed part of the dowry of Catherine of Braganza on her marriage to King Charles II. Laraiche was wrested from the Portuguese in 1689 and Arzeila in 1690, and Mulai Reshid's authority was sufficiently established to allow him to turn his attention to other parts of Morocco. A revolt of the Rif occurred during the lifetime of his successor, Mulai Abdullah ben Ismail, and was not repressed until 1743, when the rebel leader, the Basha Ahmed ben Ali, who had succeeded in raising all the Northern Jibala tribes, was defeated and killed at Alcazar. But the Rifis could not long remain tranquil; their hate of all authority was unquenchable, and more than once in the succeeding years the Sultans had to send expeditions into the country. In the opening years of the nineteenth century on no less than four occasions the Sultan, Mulai Suliman, was forced to invade the Rif, in 1802, 1810, 1812 and 1813. The last of these expeditions he commanded in person. It was entirely successful and the Rifis were severely punished. For nearly a century they remained quiet, recognizing the authority of the Sultans, but at the same time asserting to a large measure their own independence. It was an incident which occurred in 1893—the reported desecration of the tomb of Sidi Uariash by the Spaniards—that set the Rif ablaze once more and necessitated the presence of an army of 20,000 Spaniards at Melilla.

' The Rif ' is in its origin a geographical term, although in Morocco in process of time it has acquired a wider signification in that it is now applied to all the country inhabited by the so-called Rifi tribes. The Arabic word Rif in its literal form implies ' an edge ' or ' a border,' and is still in use in other parts of Morocco in that sense ; for instance, the outer circle of tents of the Sultan's camp was always known as ' er-Rif.' As is so often the case amongst Arabic-speaking peoples, the word has taken different meanings in different countries. Whereas in Arabia the term Rif infers cultivated land, though not losing the significance of a strip or border, in Egypt it is used to describe the banks of the Nile. In Morocco its geographical origin was its application to the seaboard of the Mediterranean without any reference to cultivation or fertility. From being originally a geographical expression it gave its name in time to the Berber tribes who inhabited that region, who in turn passed it on to a far larger district than its original significance warranted. As the groups of coast tribes increased or migrated or federated, they carried with them their acquired title of Rifis. Thus the Rif to-day is best, though perhaps unorthodoxly, described as being the country held by a group or groups of Berber tribes speaking the Rifi dialects of the Thamazirth language. Though technically fault may be found with this definition, it is undoubtedly the best suited for all ordinary purposes, and politically, if not geographically, correct.

The name Rif as applied to this region of Morocco has no great antiquity. Neither Ibn Haoukal nor El-Bakri, who wrote in the tenth and eleventh centuries respectively, mention it, though the latter gives a list of the towns therein situated, and it was probably not till the advent of European invaders and pirates that the name was introduced. It has been suggested that it was applied in its military significance, the Rif coast being considered an outer line of defence for the interior of the country, the Northern point of resistance against any attack on Fez. In any case no Berber origin can be given to the name Rif, for it is an Arabic word and could only have been introduced at the earliest in the first Arab invasion of Morocco in A.D. 707.

El-Bakri, though not mentioning the Rif, writes of the neighbouring country of the Ghomara, confusing them in a common origin. He gives the limits of the Ghomara federation as extending from a few miles to the East of Tangier to Taguisas on the Mediterranean coast about 40 miles South-East of Tetuan.

The first mention of the name Rif is in a book written

in the fourteenth century by Abdel Haqq el-Badisi, who as his name implies was a native of Badis, a town on the Ghomara coast. He included in the Rif the entire coastal region between Ceuta and the present Algerian frontier. The Raoudh el-Qirtas, which dates from the same period, extends the Rif Westward as far as Tangier. The author of this work does, however, make certain, though rather vague, distinctions between the Rif and Ghomara. Ibn Khaldun, writing a century later, is still less definite, and Leo Africanus, at the end of the fifteenth and beginning of the sixteenth centuries, scarcely distinguishes between them. He writes :

['A DESCRIPTION OF ERRIF, ONE OF THE SEVEN REGIONS OF FEZ.]

'Westward this region beginneth neere unto the Straites of Gibraltar, and extendeth eastward to the river of Nocor, which distance containeth about an hundred and fortie miles. Northward it bordereth upon the Mediterran sea, and stretcheth fortie miles Southward unto those mountaines which lie over against Ouarga and the territorie of Fez. This region is very uneven, being full of exceeding cold mountaines and waste deserts, which are replenished with most beautifull and straight trees. Here is no corne growing, they have great store of vines, figs, olives and almonds. The inhabitants of this region are valiant people, but so excessively given to drinking, that they scarcely reserve wherewithall to apparell themselves. Head-cattel they have but fewe : howbeit upon their mountaines they have great plentie of goats, asses, and apes. Their townes are but few : and their castles and villages are very homely built without any plancher or stories, much like to the stables of Europe, and are covered with thatch or with the barke of trees. All the inhabitants of this region have the balles of their throatpipes very great, and are uncivill and rude people.'

It will be noted that Leo Africanus in the above description includes not only Ghomara but also some of the Jibala tribes inhabiting the region of Tetuan.

El-Bakri, who wrote in the eleventh century, gives a

list of the tribes and towns, though as already stated he does not mention the word Rif. Of the places he describes, little but ruins remain to-day, though the names can still be recognized and in some cases are still in use. With few exceptions the tribes occupy the same ground as they did in his time. The careful studies of the ' Direction des Affaires indigènes ' of the French Protectorate Government have led to the conclusion that the limits of the original Rif were as follows : On the West it bordered with the Ghomara and extended Eastward as far as the Wad Nekor, which flows into the Mediterranean in Alhucemas Bay. The Rif, thus limited, contains the following tribes—Metiwa el-Behar, Beni Seddat, Beni Khannus, Tarzut, Beni Bu Nesar, Beni Bu Frah, Beni Gmil, Targuist, Beni Seteft, Beni Mezduwi, Beni Amart, Bukkoya and Beni Uriaghel. Although historically this limitation is correct, a large district to the East, part of what is known as Garet, has by process of time come to be included in the Rif, and should to-day be considered as forming a portion of that country. It consists of the region lying between the Wad Nekor and the Wad Kert, a distance along the coast of about 25 miles. The tribes inhabiting the country between the two rivers are Temsamen, Beni Said, Beni Ulichek, Beni Tuzin, Tafersit and Gzennaya. In language, customs and appearance there is nothing to separate them from the tribes mentioned in El-Bakri's designation of the Rif. But there is still another large district of Garet, lying again to the Eastward and extending as far as the mouth of the Muluya River, which to all intents and purposes to-day forms a part of the Rif. The tribes to be added to the lists already given are six more in number—Beni Sicar, Beni bu Ifru, Settut, Metalsa, Ulad bu Yahi and

Kebdana.  To the South the Rif to-day can be described as extending over all the Thamazirth-speaking tribes as far as the Wergha valley.

It is with the Rif as thus defined, extending from the Muluya to the Eastern borders of Ghomara, and from the Mediterranean to the mountains that lie along the North bank of the Wergha—a total length of 120 miles, with an average width of 45 miles—that the French and Spaniards have had to deal in the recent war.

The Rif is a country of high mountains, though in this respect none of the peaks reach the altitude of those of the Atlas farther South.  Probably the loftiest elevation is little over 7,000 feet above the sea level.  The main chain of these mountains forms a crescent extending East and West, the two points reaching the coast in Ghomara, continuing toward Tetuan and Ceuta and near Melilla. Jutting Northward from the central part of this range are spurs which at several spots reach the sea, ending in bluff cliffs.  The mountains are partially forested but otherwise barren.  Their steepness, their exposure and the barrenness of the rocky surfaces render them, except on their lower slopes, unsuitable for cultivation.  The valleys on the contrary are very fertile and are of considerable agricultural value.  Orchards of fruit trees and vines abound.  Toward the sea certain of the valleys widen, forming little plains of rich alluvial soil, renowned for their crops.  It may be that the contrast between the inhospitable rocky hills and these oases of cultivation has given rise to an exaggerated reputation of the latter, as much for charm and beauty as from agricultural wealth, but the Rifi, and even the few-and-far-between European travellers who have visited them, are loud in their praises.  There is certainly no region in Morocco better watered than are the valleys of the Western part of the Rif, though Eastward the rainfall is much less and the country more arid. The shores of the Bay of Alhucemas and the little plain which extends from the sea to the hills, watered by the Wad Nekor and the Wad Guis, are an example of the Rif at its best, and the native cultivates this rich district with ability and untiring labour. While the Arab is a determined destroyer of trees, the Rifi plants. He is by nature a gardener, and the majority of the orchards and gardens of Fez and even Tangier are tended by men of his race. As a labourer he is renowned, and a great number of these hard-working and industrious tribes migrate every year into Algeria, as well as into the agricultural districts of Morocco, to seek work in harvesting. Were it not for this source of supply, Western Algeria would suffer from a dearth of workmen. The Rif is quite incapable of supporting the population it contains, and its inhabitants are largely dependent upon the earnings of members of their families, who migrate annually for a period of time. Many, either driven to do so by the poverty of their land, or to escape from the blood-feuds which render the life of the Rifi so insecure, settle in other parts of the country. But so persistent is the type that they assimilate ill with the other tribesmen, and their families remain Rifis in appearance and in language even after long spells of exile extending over several generations.

With regard to climate, the different parts of the Rif vary largely. In the Western districts the rainfall is larger than in the Eastern. Whereas at Tetuan 665 millimetres of rain fall in the year, Melilla receives only 465 millimetres. Further East again, near the mouth of the

Wad Muluya, the yearly rainfall is only 340 millimetres, while 20 miles South of Melilla, in the interior of the Rif, it is as low as 315 millimetres. MM. Celerier et Charton, in an interesting study of the Rif climate, divide the country into four climatic divisions of (1) Oceanic type, (2) Mountain type, (3) Mediterranean type and (4) Semi-arid type. The first covers the Rif and Jibala country which is exposed to and influenced by the Atlantic Ocean. The climate is described as much resembling that of Portugal. A rather prolonged period of rain with a fall of from 600–800 millimetres and a dry summer. The temperature is mild, the humidity of the air considerable.

The second category—mountain type—is confined to the high ranges, where snow falls heavily in winter and where the vegetation is scarce.

The third—Mediterranean type—refers to the Northern slopes of the mountains which face the sea along the Rif coast. Here the influence of the Atlantic is found to be much diminished and the dry season is more prolonged. The rainfall is less.

The fourth—Semi-arid type—corresponds with the regions that fall under the influence of the Sahara, where the desert winds are felt. The annual rainfall descends to about 300 millimetres with consequent aridity.

The botany of the Rif has yet to be studied, and beyond the principal varieties of trees and shrubs little is known. On the mountain tops of Ghomara and in the Rif the cedar flourishes. At a less altitude are found the cork-oak and evergreen oaks, the Aleppo pine, the thuya and juniper, the lentiscus and the myrtle. In the valleys, along the river-beds, the willow, the poplar and the tamarisk grow. It appears from photographs taken

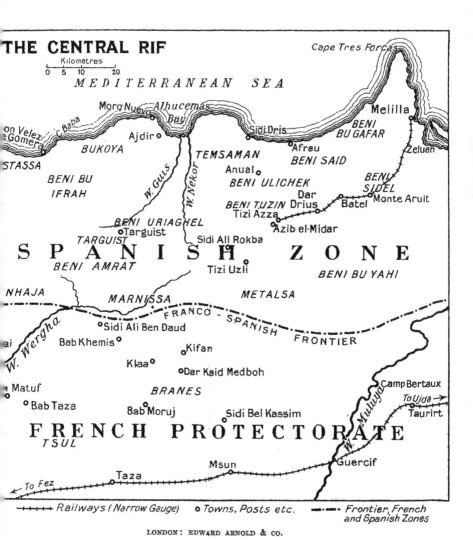

# THE CENTRAL RIF

Kilometres
0  5  10    20

*MEDITERRANEAN SEA*

Cape Tres Forcas

on Velez
Gomera

C. Baba

STASSA

Morg Nuevo   Alhucemas
Bau

Ajdir

BUKOYA

*BENI BU IFRAH*

W. Guis

W. Nekor

TARGUIST

*BENI URIAGHEL*
Targuist

*BENI AMRAT*

Sidi Ali Rokba

Tizi Uzli

*TEMSAMAN*

Anual

*BENI ULICHEK*

*BENI TUZIN*   Dar
Tizi Azza   Drius

Azib el-Midar

Sidi Dris

Afrau

*BENI SAID*

Melilla

*BENI BU GAFAR*

Zeluan

*BENI SIDEL*

Batel   Monte Aruit

# SPANISH ZONE

*BENI BU YAHI*

NHAJA

*MARNISSA*

*METALSA*

W. Wergha

FRANCO - SPANISH FRONTIER

ai

Sidi Ali Ben Daud

Bab Khemis

Klaa

Kifan

Dar Kaid Medboh

Matuf

Bab Taza

*BRANES*

Bab Moruj

Sidi Bel Kassim

W. Muluya

Camp Bertaux

To Ujda →

Taurirt

# FRENCH PROTECTORATE

*TSUL*

Msun

Guercif

To Fez

Taza

┼┼┼┼→ *Railways (Narrow Gauge)*    o *Towns, Posts etc.*    ▬ ∙ ▬ ∙ ▬ *Frontier, French
and Spanish Zones*

LONDON: EDWARD ARNOLD & CO.

from the air that the cedar forest which commences on the Ghomara mountains to the South of the Wad Lau extends throughout that tribe as far East as Targuist in the Central Rif.

It is remarkable that many of the shrubs and plants, particularly the *Cistus ladanifolius* and varieties of heath, which flourish in these districts of the Spanish zone, are not found in the neighbouring French Protectorate. But as a general rule it can be stated that the vegetation of the whole region North of the arc of Rifian mountains is analogous to that of the Mediterranean shore of Spain. The explanation is not only the similarity of climate but also the fact that in comparatively recent times Andalusia and the Rif were connected. The Jibala mountains, influenced by the Atlantic and the Mediterranean slopes toward the North coast, have another aspect. The palmeto (*Chamœrops humilis*) abounds, interspersed with thyme, cistus of several varieties, and lavender. The higher hills are often covered with wild olives, lentiscus, and here and there with juniper and oaks.

The most noticeable feature of the rivers of the Rif is the speed of their currents. They maintain as a rule right down to the sea the impulsion they have received by their precipitate descent from the mountains. The melting snow and the action of sea-cloud abundantly supply these streams, and the valleys of the Rif are well watered. Often they are torrents rushing through deep ravines. The same characteristics mark the rivers that flow Southward to the Wergha and eventually to the Sebu. The whole of this part of North Africa, as also Southern Spain, bears evidences of vast geological changes. The country seems to have taken its present formation at the end of the Tertiary period, previous to which the outlet of the Mediterranean into the Atlantic had been, first through Andalusia, following the present valley of the Guadalquivir and later to the South of the Rifian mountains, where now lies the ' Couloir de Taza,' with its plain extending to the Algerian frontier.   The Rif and the Iberian chain of Southern Spain were one until a great subsidence tore them apart and opened a new and deep channel which is nowadays known as the Straits of Gibraltar.   It is almost a shock to read in the work of an authority that ' Geologically this rift was only a small accident.'   It seems at all events to have had some importance, and may perhaps have altered the history of the world.   One is perhaps permitted to wonder whether, if suddenly the Straits of Gibraltar were filled up again, and Spain and Morocco joined, the ' accident ' would again be described as a ' small ' one.

# CHAPTER III

## SPAIN IN THE RIF

It was during the first two years of this century that definite proposals for the splitting up of Morocco into French and Spanish spheres of influence were secretly put forward at Madrid by the French Government. Although on that occasion the Spanish Government hesitated to entertain the proposition, which they thought would meet with great opposition elsewhere in Europe, there is no doubt that the idea was viewed favourably. It was only, however, when Monsieur Delcassé, the French Foreign Minister, was able to give assurances that he had obtained the goodwill and consent of the British Government that the Spaniards agreed.

The Spanish Government and army looked with distinct favour upon this proposed outlet for Spanish energies, though there was no doubt that public opinion was somewhat reluctant to embark upon any new colonial adventures. The Church was favourable to an extension of Spanish influence amongst the 'infidel Moors.' The priests were ready enough to recall that Isabella la Catolica had left in her Testament an exhortation to pursue the spread of the True Faith in Africa. To King Ferdinand, her husband, and to herself had been due the conquest of Granada and the principal acts of the overthrow of Islam in Spain, and it had been

the Queen's one desire and prayer that the continuation
of her crusade should not be abandoned.   Times have
changed since then, and even Catholic Spain has wisely
refrained from dragging into Africa in the train of her
armies a Faith that has, to the Moors, always been connected with persecution and cruelty.   In all their dealings in Morocco the Spaniards have shown an admirable
respect for the religion of the people ; a policy that is
much more likely to lead to results both practical
and spiritual than would have any too loyal and too
rigid a compliance with the Testament of the Catholic
Queen.

But it was naturally in the eyes of the army that
Morocco loomed the largest.   The return of the Spanish
garrisons of Cuba and the Philippines, after the conquest
of those islands by America, had not only been a deep
humiliation to those who had suffered defeat, but had
also brought to light a shocking system of inefficiency
and corruption.   The loss of these colonies had taken
away the last chances of active service abroad and thus
deprived the army of any opportunity of restoring the
loss of prestige which the troops had suffered in that
war.   It seemed that all adventure outside Spain was
at an end, and at an end, too, the opportunities for
promotion and wealth which such adventure offered.
The officers of the army could look forward to no more
attractive career in the future than a dreary existence in
Spanish garrison towns.   There is no doubt that, while
the loss of the colonies was in some quarters considered
as a relief from an expensive incubus which had brought
no profit and little honour, the fact that practically all
Spain's oversea possessions had gone could not fail to
stir up in the hearts of many Spaniards who were proud

Photo. Service des Beaux Arts.

FEZ.

of the past history of their country, a deep and bitter
feeling of resentment and disappointment. It was the
breaking of the last link that bound the Mother-country
to those great days of conquest and adventure. Little
by little in the past the people of Central and South
America had freed themselves from the Spanish yoke
and had determined to control their own destinies.
State after state had taken the road to Independence.
The race, the language, the faith remained, but the rope
that held them bound to the Spanish plough, so hard to
pull, was severed. A new spirit, in a manner as Spanish
as that of Spain but born in clearer atmosphere and in
new surroundings, demanded a degree of liberty which
the old country with its overwhelming traditions, its
retrograde policy, its intervention of a too Conservative
Church in every branch of life had so signally failed to
provide. And now Cuba and the Philippines had gone
too, and almost everything that Spain possessed outside
Europe had been lost. To the Spaniard it was a period
of bitter humiliation, for he knew that it was from the
incompetence of his Government that colony after
colony had fallen away.

It might have been wiser for Spain to have refused
from the very beginning the invitation to engage in
adventure in Africa. There are many Spaniards who
thought so then and think so to-day. But the temptation was great. It was a little the temptation of the
gambler, to win back so much nearer home some compensation for what had been lost elsewhere. It had been
a common argument in Spain that the colonies had gone
because they were so far away. Morocco, on the contrary, was in sight of Spain ; only a few miles separated
their shores. From Algeciras to Ceuta was an hour's

passage; from Malaga to Melilla a night at sea. In
these circumstances the task would be easy.

There was, too, another argument which was largely
used by those who favoured the intervention of Spain
in North Africa. It was discovered and cried from the
housetops that the opposite Moroccan coast, unless occupied, was a perpetual menace and danger to the ports of
Southern Spain. It was pointed out that in the hands
of any other Power such facilities as this coast offered in
bays and anchorages could be used as bases for attacks
upon the ports; and more, if ever its permanent occupation by any other Power than Spain should come
about, the Peninsula would be at its mercy. It became
in a short time an article of belief that the Spanish occupation of the North Coast of Africa was essential in the
interests of Spanish security. There were others who
expected to see in this new burden that Spain was undertaking an undoubted and irretrievable weakness. It
meant the splitting of her army into two, the division of
her none too powerful fleet and, in case of war, a position
as disadvantageous as it was vulnerable; for nothing
could be easier for any Power possessed of ships than to
cut all communication between the Peninsula and Africa.
When it is taken into consideration that the Spanish
army in Morocco is dependent for everything, in places
even for water, upon these communications and is in an
enemy country—for no matter how good actual relations
may be, a foreign population in any Islamic country, if
the Power to which that population belongs is at war,
must be so considered—the danger to which Spain rendered herself liable cannot be denied. Once her communications were cut, how long could the Spanish
army in Africa hold out? If Spain were defeated

elsewhere, what would be the fate of the Spaniards in Morocco ?

It is a problem that also affects France, but to a lesser extent. Still, it may be asked—what would happen in North Africa were France defeated in Europe and her communications cut ? In one respect her position would be vastly superior to that of Spain, for the possessions of France in North Africa are self-supporting in as far as supplies are concerned, and her army would not be forced to capitulate or to dissolve from want of food. With that exception, perhaps, the problem is almost the same. The temptation to rid itself of a foreign dominating population in such circumstances would be almost more than any self-respecting Islamic people could resist. However excellent the rule instituted, however profitable the presence of the occupying Power, the foreigner is always an invader and an ' infidel.'

There was one reason which could justifiably have influenced Spain to accept the offer of participation in Morocco. The Spaniards had confidence in their race. However effete their Government may have been at that period, however corrupt municipal life, however inefficient the control, the individual Spaniard had not failed. Often hardly able to sustain life in his own country, where justice, education and assistance were refused him, he emigrates abroad with little baggage or capital beyond his patience and his capacity for work. Away from Spain he succeeds. A skilful and untiring cultivator of the soil, thrifty and law-abiding, he has rendered the greatest service to Western Algeria and elsewhere. He settles on the land, identifies himself with his new country, and seldom returns to Spain. In Algeria in the second generation these Spanish colonists become French subjects. There is little amiss with the Spanish race, except that their Government for many years has rendered it very difficult for the people to eke out even a bare livelihood in the country districts of their own land. It is only when they come in contact with the liberty of foreign administration that they have their chance. This chance they take and keep. They find abroad facilities for the education of their children, medical assistance, co-operation and opportunity, which have been so signally lacking in Spain.

But the race, in spite of these drawbacks at home, has maintained its virility. There is no reason why, should Spanish administration be reformed and the abuses be stamped out, as it would seem they are being stamped out under the present régime, the Spaniard should not remain in his own country and bestow upon its cultivation and its improvement the effort he now makes, and so successfully, elsewhere. There is much to learn and much to forget. The reform must come from above. That it will come some day is certain. That the present effort, admirable though it has been, and is, will be entirely successful is doubtful. The opposition and the 'acquired rights' of corruption are perhaps too deeply embedded to be swept away by a change in the administration. It may mean more drastic measures, but one thing is certain: the Spaniard of the people will one day demand his rights. To-day he has to seek them elsewhere, but a time is coming when he will claim them in his own country, for himself and for those for whom he lives and toils. Between his Government and his Church he has experienced little happiness, little hope and little charity. One day he will demand and take what has been so long withheld.

By the Franco-Spanish Arrangements of 1904 Spain undertook the responsibility of a sphere of influence in Morocco for better or for worse. Few Spaniards realized then the whirlpools, the rocks and the shallows that lay ahead. Had it been foreseen how stormy the voyage was to prove, not many probably would have urged so adventurous an undertaking.

It has often been said that for colonization or intervention in a foreign country to be successful it must be popular at home. It might be added that it must either promise distinct national advantages or else the political designs that underlie the policy must be clothed and concealed in the immaculate raiment of philanthropic intention. If both can be arranged for, so much the better. But in the case of Spain it was difficult to urge either. That does not mean that she was left without a slogan. For the Army there was glory and promotion; for the Church the carrying out of Isabella la Catolica's Testament; for the investor the rumour of mines; for the politician a multitude of advantages, and for the Administration a multitude of opportunities—and after all the public was indifferent. There is no doubt that some forms of government, and especially bad government, are greatly facilitated by the indifference of the people. Decades of Spanish Governments have waxed fat on public indifference. In Spain there was, too, at that moment, the reaction already referred to after the loss of the Colonies. Would it not be possible to wipe out the humiliation of the past by inscribing a new page, and a glorious one, in the history of the country? Was it not a chance of proving to Europe, the spectator of the disasters, that Spain could rise again?

No one can deny that she went to Africa ill-prepared.

She had failed, after the American War, to clear up the mess at home and to bring to justice the perpetrators of the crimes that had so quickly led to her defeat. She went into Morocco with the evil traditions of her colonial policy unrejected, and continued to commit in Africa the faults that had led to her downfall elsewhere. The stories of the empty Government stores in Cuba and the Philippines and all the scandals of the administration at that period were to be repeated after the disaster of Anual in 1921. The lesson that Spain should have learnt in Cuba and in the Pacific had been neglected. She had to pay the price in Africa. As long as her action there was restricted to the maintenance of sufficient breathing space round the ancient Presidios of Ceuta and Melilla there was little opposition in Spain, but in 1909 the opening of iron mines in the vicinity of the latter place, and consequent difficulties with the natives, necessitated a military expedition on a considerable scale. It was not at first successful, and in a battle fought in sight of the town the Spanish troops suffered a costly defeat. There was an instant outcry against these unprofitable adventures which, it was claimed, were only undertaken in the interests of the proprietors of the mines in question and other profiteers. Even when the campaign was brought to a tolerably successful termination, public opinion continued disturbed. The people had begun to realize the cost in life and money of the task that Spain had undertaken in Africa. It was realized even then that rather than decrease as time went on, the burden would become more heavy and still more costly.

The anxiety that the 1909 campaign awoke was both natural and justified. It had been made evident that the Rifi was a foe who was not to be despised. He fought stubbornly and with complete skill. He harassed and attacked from every side, yet scarcely ever exposed himself to view. He was courageous, but wasted neither life nor ammunition. He needed no transport, no commissariat ; he possessed no hospital equipment nor even medicines. He fought, as primitive man fought, with no impedimenta, but with the great advantage of the modern rifle. He was here to-day and gone to-morrow. Whence he came or where he went it was most difficult to discover. As a rule he was present wherever an advantage could be taken, whether it was due to the nature of the country or to the passing of a convoy. Untrained except to shoot, but rich in the instinct of guerrilla campaigning, the Rifi enemy in 1909 gave a foretaste of the capacity and courage they were to show during long years of subsequent warfare.

It was no wonder that already at that date public opinion in Spain was not enamoured of the African War. It was realized that the fast changing Governments, overthrown by one another after short but bitter tussles in which every kind of intrigue and reprehensible political strategy were exerted, had no fixed policy—if they had any policy at all—regarding Morocco. The people knew, too, that a profound ignorance of the question existed in the various Departments that were charged with Spain's interests in Africa. They were aware that money was being wasted and was being misapplied. They suspected—and how truly—that the Rif was destined to become a vast military cemetery.

It was this short but costly campaign of 1909—costly both in life and money, for it was accompanied by severe losses and necessitated the presence in Melilla of a Spanish army of 20,000 men—that had opened the door of the Rif to the Spaniards. After centuries of imprisonment, for it can be described as nought else, within the fortifications of the town, they had at last been able to obtain a measure of breathing space outside the walls. Three years later the Franco-Spanish Treaty of 1912 confirmed their right to occupy, in the name and in the interests of the Sultan, the territory which fell to Spain's share in the division of the Moroccan spoils. The frontiers of the French Protectorate and the Spanish sphere of influence, outlined in the 1904 Agreement, were now delimited on paper, for the possibility of any delimitation *in situ* was out of the question owing to the inaccessibility of the regions through which the frontier line passed and to the hostility of the population. To the Spaniards, as to the French, the signing of this 1912 Agreement was of considerable importance, for it legalized the already recognized position of both Governments in Morocco, and put their future in that country on a basis of reality.

The Spaniards were, however, in no hurry, and during the following two years they made few efforts to enter upon their new responsibilities. From 1914 to 1918 the war in Europe facilitated their task, for the Spanish zone was sedulously exploited by the Germans as a base of propaganda, and of action, against the French in Morocco. This enemy programme, although in the end it met with no permanent success, was sufficiently well organized to cause much anxiety in the neighbouring French Protectorate, and to necessitate a long series of precautionary measures against attacks prepared in the security of the Spanish zone. Thus occupied, and they were well paid for the services they rendered, the Rifis remained largely indifferent to the Spanish advance into their territory. Their time was more profitably employed under the direction of the Germans.

Some mention must be made of these German intrigues which, if they are best forgotten in an endeavour to rid the world of some of its bitter recollections of the war, played so considerable a part in the subsequent history of the Rif that they are indispensable in any account of the events of that period.

Soon after the outbreak of the war in 1914, German agents, instructed by the German Embassy at Madrid, installed themselves at Melilla and elsewhere in the Spanish zone, which, conforming with the neutrality of the Spanish Government, did not close its doors to the subjects of the Central Powers, although the Sultan, Sovereign of all Morocco, was an ally of France. Important sums of money were introduced into the Rif and expended amongst the tribes as subsidies and for the local purchase of arms, of which, together with ammunition, large quantities were also introduced by contraband trade. But perhaps the most formidable weapon of the Germans was the propaganda which, from the shelter of the neutral Spanish zone, they carried on with impunity and unceasing effort. By word of mouth, and in literature, they kept a stream of incentive to revolt and rebellion flowing amongst the tribes of the French Protectorate. For this purpose they recruited a large number of influential natives. It was no difficult task. An anti-French campaign appealed to a people who had already seen part of their country occupied by the French, and expected later on to witness the rest of it

pass into their possession. It seemed an occasion not
to be missed to drive the foreigner out of their country.
The position of these German agents was largely facilitated by the presence in Spanish Morocco of quite a
number of German mining engineers and prospectors
who, with that concentration and industry which is so
remarkable a feature of the German character, had
acquired not only the language but also the esteem and
goodwill of the tribesmen. Their whole weight, and it
was no light one, was brought to bear.

Amongst the natives, the Germans had little difficulty
in winning over persons of position. Perhaps the most
important were Abdel Malek el-Meheddin and the Abdel
Krim family, father and two sons, one of the latter of
whom is now famous, Si Mohammed—or Mohand, as the
Rifis call him.

Some record of Abdel Malek's strange life may be of
interest. He was the grandson of the famous Abdel
Kader who resisted the French so long at the time of
their conquest of Algeria, and who subsequently won
the approbation of the civilized world by the courageous
manner in which he saved the lives of so many Christians
during the Massacre of Damascus in 1860. After being
educated in Syria, Abdel Malek and his brothers were
eventually allowed to return to Algeria, where they
entered the French Army. Abdel Malek himself was
appointed to the chief command of the Shereefian police
force in Tangier, which had come into existence under
the terms of the Act of Algeciras. It was a position of
no particular influence, but gave its holder a certain
precedence amongst the dignitaries of Tangier. The
failing of all the Meheddin family has been pride, and
Abdel Malek felt that this appointment was not suffi-

ciently important for a man of his Shereefian birth and
the reputation of his ancestors. He became discontented
and nursed a secret hatred against the French, whom he
believed to be purposely thwarting his ambitions. On
the outbreak of war in 1914 the Representatives of the
enemy Powers were expelled from Tangier.

Later on Abdel Malek communicated to me the
reasons for his subsequent actions. The secret preparation for the hurried expulsion from Tangier of the
enemy Ministers in August, 1914, necessitated the
intervention of the police, and Abdel Malek, as chief
of that force, was naturally informed. He secretly
telephoned to the German Chargé d'Affaires to warn
him and thus gave him time to destroy certain
incriminating documents. From Abdel Malek's frank
communications I gather that he himself was incrimin-
ated by these documents, as he had become in fact a
German agent. No trace of those papers seems to have
been discovered during the subsequent search of the
German Legation by the French authorities, and evidently they were burned ; but Abdel Malek was haunted
by the idea that his telephone message to the German
Legation had been tapped and that his life was in
danger. Whether his secret warning to the Germans
was ever known, I am unaware. At this moment,
Abdel Malek's eldest son, still a boy, committed suicide,
and his father was in despair. It is said that the knowledge of his father's treachery had caused him to take
his life. Abdel Malek disappeared, crossed into the
Spanish zone, and declared a Holy War on the French.
His extradition as a French deserter was demanded, but
was refused by the Spanish authorities. Offers were
made to the tribes to tempt them to hand him over to

the French, but failed.  Abdel Malek was well provided with German gold and bought immunity from capture. He passed into the Rif, became an acknowledged German agent, and from within the Spanish zone in the region North-east of Fez waged war on the French.  In 1917 he was a serious menace.

Towards the end of the war his influence diminished, though he still caused the French considerable anxiety and losses from time to time.  As soon as the campaign was over his adventures began afresh.  He had quarrelled with Abdel Krim, the Rifi leader, and was forced to pass an existence of some danger and hardship in the remoter districts of the Spanish zone.  From time to time he made proposals to the Spanish authorities to be put in command of native troops.  The Spaniards accepted his offer, and in May, 1925, Abdel Malek was in Tetuan enlisting native soldiers.  It was not, perhaps, unnatural that the French Protectorate authorities drew the attention of the Spanish Government to the fact that Abdel Malek was a deserter who had preached Holy War and carried on an active campaign against the French.  This French protest brought an immediate reply from the Spanish Directory to the effect that Abdel Malek would in no circumstances be employed by the Spanish authorities, and an official communiqué in this sense was immediately published by the entire Madrid Press.  Notwithstanding this, Abdel Malek left Tetuan for Melilla a few days later with tribal contingents to take command of a large native force of the Spanish Army in the Rif. The dreariness and discomfort of this life amid barren and desolate mountains, the uncongeniality of his surroundings, and, doubtless, some regrets about the past, rendered Abdel Malek very unhappy.  I received a long communication from him, in which he gave the whole story of his actions from the secret telephone message to the German Legation to his unhappy plight in the desolation of the Rif. He acknowledged having fought during the war against the French, whom he then regarded as his bitterest enemies, but since the Armistice had been signed he stated that he had ceased all action against France. He was weary of this life of adventure, and desired to be allowed to finish his days in Egypt or elsewhere in the East. In this communication he informed me, among many other details, of the instructions he had received from the Spanish authorities on taking over the command of their native forces. These instructions could not have been more correct or more honourable. Abdel Malek was strictly forbidden to do any harm either by word or deed to French interests in the neighbouring zone. Abdel Malek's communication ended with the expression of his desire to receive the pardon of France and of the Sultan of Morocco, and to be allowed to end his days in a foreign country. On July the 31st, 1925, I brought the matter to the knowledge of Maréchal Lyautey, who expressed his readiness to obtain the pardon of France and the Sultan for Abdel Malek if he would leave Morocco and never return. I was authorized to convey this message to Abdel Malek's family at Tetuan and to acquaint him with the fact that in return for his complete abandonment of Morocco the French Protectorate Government would grant him an allowance. Before I was able to return to Tetuan Abdel Malek had been killed in battle. His family were, however, informed that his pardon had been promised previous to his death and it was a great comfort to them. He never knew it himself, though on the morning of his death he had said to his son that he was sure that his prayer for pardon would be answered. He died two or three days too soon.

Besides the persons of importance, the Germans had in their employ a large number of natives engaged in contraband. The fact that the Spaniards had as yet scarcely begun the occupation of their zone on the Mediterranean coast gave the Germans complete freedom of action. Even in Melilla itself no great difficulties were put in the way of the import of arms, though instructions from Madrid, issued in a genuine spirit of neutrality, had from time to time to receive some semblance of being obeyed. But the Germans had money at their disposal and used it freely, and contraband on the shores of the Mediterranean has never been considered a crime.

These German activities, and the means and occupation they gave to the natives, detracted the attention of the Rifis from their danger—the systematic if slow occupation of their country by the Spaniards. It is not easy to grasp how it was that, while the tribesmen were so easily persuaded to go and fight against the French, they refrained from taking action against the Spaniards. Money no doubt largely influenced them, and it seems also that promises were made to the chief men of the tribes that they would share in the wealth of their highly mineralized country if they would open it to German and Spanish industry. In any case no serious attempt was made to stay the advancing Spaniards until they suffered the devastating defeat of July, 1921.

The situation in the Spanish zone at that moment was the following: The High Commissioner, General Berenguer, was at that moment completing his campaign against Raisuli and his Jibala tribes, and on the point of success. Advancing from Tetuan, the Spanish columns had surrounded Tazrut, Raisuli's stronghold. General Silvestre, who was in command of the Melilla district, took advantage of his Chief's arduous and responsible occupations to push forward as fast as possible—far faster than was compatible with security —in the direction of Alhucemas, the famous bay in which the little island of that name is situated. It was the High Commissioner's intention, after ridding Spain of the encumbrance of Raisuli's presence amongst the Jibala, to turn eastward along the Mediterranean coast, and thus approach Alhucemas from that quarter at the moment when Silvestre and the Melilla army would be within striking distance of it on the West. But Silvestre, supported it was rumoured by influential personages in Spain, was determined that the credit and success of this expedition should be his and his alone. His aim was Ajdir, the collection of villages that forms the capital of the Beni Uriaghel tribe of the Rif, situated near the excellent beach of the neighbouring bay. For years this bay had been a goal of Spanish ambition as a base for expeditions into the heart of the Rif. There was little resistance to the earlier part of his advance from the valley of the Wad Kert. The tribes received presents in money—and were not disarmed. Having installed posts to the West of the Kert valley, General Silvestre turned northward and reached the sea at Sidi Dris. Here again posts were constructed, but they were hastily extemporized, insufficiently held and badly supplied, and in every detail of this part of the campaign there seems to have been a totally unwarranted disregard

F

of danger and an absence of the most elementary precaution.

It was at this period that the family of Abdel Krim
came into public view. There were three important
members of the family—Abdel Krim el-Khatabi, the
father, and his two sons, Mohammed—or Mohand as the
Rifis call that name,—and Mahammed. The distinction between the two names, both common in Morocco,
Mohammed and Mahammed, is so slight that to the
European ear it is almost inappreciable. Both names
are written alike in the Arabic character with the
exception that the former has the accent ' damma '
above the initial letter *m* and the latter the accent
' fatha.' These accents give the pronunciation *mo* and
*ma* respectively.

The elder Abdel Krim, father of the well-known Rifi
leader and his brother, appears to have been a man of
intelligence. In any case he procured for his two sons
a far better and more modern education than probably
ever fell to the lot of Rifi boys before. He was himself
in close touch with certain mining groups, particularly
that of the Mannesmann Brothers, and he seems to have
realized the possible value of the minerals of the Rif.
He did not, however, confine his relations with the Germans to prospective minerals, for he was also actively
engaged in the introduction of arms into the Rif. In
this his two sons assisted him. The elder, Mohand, who
was destined to play a little later on so important a part
in Moroccan history, was at that period employed in the
service of the Spanish Government at Melilla, where in
addition to his duties in the Bureau of Native Affairs
he also edited the Arabic columns of the local newspaper
*l Telegrama del Rif.* He was a proficient Arabic

THE ISLAND OF ALHUCEMAS.

scholar, though the Rifi dialect of Thamazirth was his native tongue, and he also spoke, read and wrote Spanish. Meanwhile his younger brother Mahammed, who became later on the Rifian Commander-in-Chief and Minister of War, had been sent to be educated in Madrid, where he spent three years training to be a mining engineer.

Mohand's (Mohammed) employment at Melilla brought him into constant contact with the tribesmen of the Rif, and this, added to the prestige which he naturally enjoyed as the son of the Kaid of Beni Uriaghel, and his influence and popularity in Spanish official circles, rendered him in the eyes of his fellow-Rifis a personage of no little importance. It was also considered greatly to his credit that he was a master of the Arabic language and possessed a profound knowledge on Islamic religious and legal questions.

After the victory of the Allied Powers and the termination of the war, the Spanish authorities found themselves obliged to make some show of expressing their disapproval of the natives who had taken so active a part in furthering German schemes in the Spanish zone. No doubt the elder of the three Abdel Krims was amongst them. The aid he had received from the Germans was withdrawn, and the Spaniards, who had refrained from interfering with his acts in the past, now showed a certain disapproval of the undisguised assistance he had always tendered to his former friends. It may have been for this reason that Abdel Krim suddenly realized the fact—it had been apparent long enough already—that the Spaniards were progressing too fast and too far into the Rif. His relations, which had been very friendly with them from the end of the war in 1918, began to cool in the summer of 1920. While the Spanish authorities were cementing their amicable relations with the tribes of the Kert valley, Abdel Krim the elder, with a body of his Beni Uriaghel tribesmen, joined an irregular force of Rifis which had collected for the purpose of resisting any further advance of the Spaniards into their country.

Meanwhile an incident had occurred at Melilla which may explain the change in the attitude of Abdel Krim. His son Mohand had been imprisoned by the Spaniards. Various reasons have been given for this action. It was officially said he had been found talking sedition to the tribesmen, but the family of Abdel Krim have always insisted that he was imprisoned as the result of a private and none too edifying quarrel with a Spanish official. He escaped in the spring of 1920 and joined his father. His brother had already arrived from Madrid. All three were with the Rifi contingent preparing to resist the Spanish advance, when the elder Abdel Krim died and his elder son Mohand was chosen Kaid of the Beni Uriaghel in his stead.

The Spaniards were busily engaged in consolidating their positions. The important tribelands of Beni Said had already been occupied and terms had been made with the local chiefs, but the population had not been disarmed. This country was now in the rear of the Spanish lines, between the main body of the army and its base at Melilla. From the Beni Said country an advance had been made into Temsaman, Beni Ulichek and, further South, to Tafersit. Everything was now ready for a further move forward.

The Spaniards had at this juncture in Morocco over 63,000 troops, of whom some 12,000 were natives. Of this total 24,000 were in the Melilla district—20,000 Spaniards and 4,000 natives. The Spanish Government had repeatedly given assurances that this army was provided with all the necessaries of warfare. This was certainly not the case, and the soldiers were, from want of training, quite incapable of utilizing much of what they possessed. The organization was defective in every particular. There was little or no discipline amongst the officers and no efficiency amongst the men. The only good word that can be said for the Spanish army in Africa at that period was that the soldiers bore the treatment they received with an admirable patience, a patience that was under the circumstances exaggerated.

The revelations which followed the disaster were as tragic as the disaster itself. Not only were the troops wanting in every respect, but none of the precautions which ought to have been observed were taken. The lines of communication with the base were long and almost unguarded. There was a light railway as far as Batel, but from there onwards nothing but the roughest of roads, and those few and far between. The Posts along the Kert valley and in the rear had no direct intercommunication, and were inadequately manned and ill-supplied. The Spaniards themselves realized, too late, that their whole position in Africa had been sacrificed to incompetence and corruption. The sufferings of the Spanish soldiers in Morocco were recognized too late, though attention had been called over and over again to their miserable plight. Ill-fed, ill-clothed, ill-treated, the youth of Spain, courageous and patient, had been systematically deprived of almost everything to which they had a right. In good health their life was made miserable ; in sickness they were neglected. The field hospitals and medical attendance were beneath contempt. The wounded often lay for days before they were attended, and fever wrought havoc amongst the troops. I write from experience. I saw myself over and over again the pitiable plight of the Spanish soldier in Morocco. *The Times* unceasingly called attention to it, to be met with denial and abuse from Madrid and from the Spanish Embassy in London. Even in Spain voices were raised, but the vested interests of the civil and military authorities were too strong and nothing was done. The Spanish soldiers in Morocco previous to the introduction of the Directorate in September, 1923, were the victims of every kind of incompetence and corruption. Even after the terrible disaster of July, 1921, there was but little change in their treatment.

In May, General Silvestre advanced and occupied Abaran, a point overlooking the valley of the Wad Agermus. It was here that the first incident occurred. A Rifi contingent, aided by disaffection amongst the native ' Police ' force in the service of the Spaniards, attacked the Post. The Police mutinied and massacred their Spanish officers. Even then the warning was not taken and the tragedy of May the 30th at Abaran was considered as an isolated incident. The Post was left abandoned and the native Police passed over to the enemy. A few officers, it appeared afterwards, had written from the front pointing out the totally inadequate precautions that had been taken in the rear, but these letters had no effect.

On July the 18th, 1921, the military Post of Igerriben was furiously and unexpectedly attacked by Rifi tribesmen. Under great difficulties the Post was evacuated, to be immediately occupied by the enemy, who seized both arms and ammunition. General Silvestre hurried to the front and reached the fortified Post of Anual. But he arrived too late. He ordered the evacuation, and, harassed and shot down from every side, the garrison retired. Silvestre and his staff, remaining to the end, were killed or committed suicide.

With the fall of Anual began the great disaster. From tribal village to tribal village the Rifis passed on the news of victory. From Post to Post the Spaniards learned of their defeat. From every mountain the natives poured down, and those who had no arms had only to pick them up from the ground. The whole Spanish army, in a state of panic, fled, and over the heated, almost waterless tracks of the Rif, began a retreat perhaps unparalleled in its horrors. Artillery, transport, entire camps, stores of arms and ammunition, were abandoned and the Spanish soldiers, young, mostly untrained, underfed and ill-clothed—in every way unsuited for warfare—fled to seek a place of safety. A few reached a temporary haven at Bentiel, a camp 9 miles in the rear ; but the panic spread, the Spaniards themselves destroyed the camp and once more fled Eastward. General Navarro collected what was left of the army, and, attacked on all sides by increasing numbers of the enemy, began a retreat towards Melilla. With their numbers sadly diminished, 3,000 survivors reached Monte Arruit, on the Melilla railway, 30 miles from that town. But the troops were exhausted ; they could go no farther. They dug themselves in as best they could amongst the houses of the little Spanish settlement. Meanwhile the revolt had spread in every direction. Such peasants and colonists as had time abandoned their houses and fled to Melilla.  Zeluan, a town 12 miles from, and Nador, a suburb of, Melilla, were besieged.  Melilla itself was left defenceless, and the Spanish Minister of War afterwards acknowledged that there had existed nothing in the way of defence to prevent the massacre of its fifty thousand inhabitants by the tribesmen.  By July the 22nd the Rif was lost to Spain.  The garrisons of Nador, Zeluan and Monte Arruit were to hold out a little longer before they surrendered—and were treacherously massacred.  In three days the Spanish army on the front—19,000 men with 130 guns, all their transport, arms, ammunition and stores—was lost.  Their camps and fortified Posts were all burnt, and 5,000 square kilometres of country abandoned.  Twelve years' work and sacrifice were wiped out—and the Rifis were bombarding the town of Melilla with artillery captured from the Spaniards !

At first the attitude of the Spanish people in this great disaster was admirable.  Not one section of the public seems to have wavered.  Spain must not abandon her task ; her honour was at stake.  Day by day the true extent of the catastrophe became gradually known, though the censorship was very strict ; but it was not until a couple of months later, when a new Spanish army was re-occupying the abandoned territory, that the real horrors were realized.  Nador, Zeluan and Monte Arruit had fallen—after periods of brave resistance.  Relief had been promised daily, but never arrived.  Hope had died, there was nothing left but surrender—and annihilation.  When the advancing Spanish troops reached Monte Arruit they found the corpses of 2,600 Spanish soldiers—and a cemetery in which the garrison had buried its dead during the courageous defence of the place. General Navarro, part of his staff and a few others were carried away prisoners—the rest had been massacred.

It still remains a mystery why no attempt was made to relieve these garrisons. Nador was only 6 miles from Melilla ; Zeluan 12—and yet no effort was ever made to save them. It is said that the reason—it was so stated officially in Madrid—was that the reinforcements sent from Spain were in a state of complete unfitness and complete disorganization. Few of the soldiers—mostly raw recruits—had ever fired a shot. They were so weak and underfed that they were incapable of marching.

The failure to relieve Nador, Zeluan, and Monte Arruit must stand to Spain's discredit. Her dead—her thousands of dead, for it is now officially acknowledged that at least 16,000 Spanish soldiers were killed—were the victims of incompetence and disorganization, and —I am only quoting the speeches of Spanish deputies and officers in the Cortes a month or two later—of corruption. The first airmen who flew over the deserted country reported that the roads were ' strewn with corpses '—the corpses of the youth of Spain, shot down, knived, tortured, mutilated, dying of thirst, in their tragic effort to reach a place of safety. A few hundred succeeded in crossing into French Protectorate territory and were saved—a few hundred more were taken prisoners.

The state of affairs at Melilla, the base of the new campaign, became desperate. Not only were troops being hurried from Spain, but such refugees from the Rif as had managed to fly in time, had crowded into the town. The enemy approached up to the hurriedly erected wire defences on the very outskirts, and Spanish ' territory ' in the Rif became limited to little outside the actual streets. Even water for drinking purposes had to be brought across the Mediterranean from Malaga, and supplies ran out.

On August the 8th—a fortnight after the disaster— the Spanish Ministry resigned, and a new Government was formed under Señor Maura. Spain's *amour propre* was deeply injured. Her army in the field of nearly 19,000 men had been wiped out by about 2,000 to 3,000 tribesmen, dependent for their arms upon contraband trade, and without a machine to make a rifle or a cartridge. It is no wonder that Spain was humiliated. To counteract the bad effect, a system of organized propaganda was set on foot. For a couple of years or more before the disaster Spain had been boasting all over Europe of what she had accomplished in Morocco, and the Spanish Ambassador in London had deeply interested rather too credulous an audience at a meeting of the Royal Geographical Society as to his country's achievements. Every attempt was now made to conceal from the British public the real character of the disaster, which was described as nothing more than ' an incident of colonial warfare.' The efforts to disseminate in London the idea that the Spanish zone was pacified, occupied, and prosperous had been largely successful, until these events of July brought the whole construction to the ground like a house built of cards.

It took Spain nearly a year and a half to reoccupy what she lost in 1921. The fighting was at times severe, and at the battle of Tizza the Spaniards suffered between 1,000 and 2,000 casualties. It was in October, 1921, that the new advance began. Seventy thousand fresh troops had been brought from Spain, and improvements had been introduced into every branch of the service. It is true that from time to time the invading army met with checks, and that the fortified island 'Presidio' of Alhucemas was almost perpetually bombarded from the mainland with the Spanish guns captured by the Rifis. The country was found devastated; everything destructible had been destroyed. Everywhere were ruins and unburied corpses. Before Zeluan and Monte Arruit could be occupied whole days were spent in getting rid of the dead and purifying the wells.

As time went on there came a change over the feeling in Spain. The great enthusiasm for revenge which succeeded the disaster was dying down. There were rumours of fresh scandals at Melilla, and there were the vast costs of the entire refurnishing of the army and the sending to the front of another contingent of the youth of Spain. The public had learned that when, after the disaster, the military stores of Melilla had been opened in order to furnish the troops with supplies, nothing had been found in them. They were empty. There were accusations that the trade in contraband arms and ammunition had been extensive and unchecked; that many officers who should have been at the front were on leave—and other rumours too. The dissatisfaction quickly spread to the Cortes at Madrid, and a long and fierce debate took place as to the responsibilities for Spain's humiliation. Although there was a quite evident desire on the part of the Government to escape the interpellations, there were sufficient upright deputies and soldiers who insisted on telling, and hearing, the truth.

The parliamentary debate opened on October the 20th, 1921. Señor Maura, the Prime Minister, spoke first. His speech, though imbued with a certain frankness, entirely failed to satisfy his hearers. He acknowledged the appalling results of the disaster and asserted that the Government would search out those responsible for its happening; but his speech contained the expression of no definite policy for the future. It was followed by a long series of criticisms and attacks from deputies representing many parties and many policies. Señor Luzaga referred in vehement terms to the organization and morality of the army. He began by calling attention to the well-known jealousies that so largely impeded its proper functioning, and to the corruption that existed on every side. He himself had just returned from a visit of inspection to Melilla, where, he said, ' officers whose pay was 600 pesetas a month have managed to spend 12,000. The captains in charge of their men '— for in Morocco each captain directly catered for his men —' grow rich, but the soldiers starve. There is nothing in our administration but fraud and immorality.' To this speech the Minister of War, Señor Cierva, replied, but failed to impress the Cortes. The Marqués de Viesca followed. ' The only colonel,' he explained, ' who was at his post was Colonel A——'—he mentioned the name—' and it would have been better if he had been anywhere else on account of his surrender to the enemy.' He stated that officers who had been absent from their posts remained hid in Melilla, to give the impression that they were prisoners, and with the intention of turning up some day with a tale of having escaped. Señor Martinez-Campos, who had just returned from active service, stated what he had seen. The military

hospitals, he said, were worse than prisons, the treatment
of the wounded and sick deplorable. The priests
attached to the army frequented the cafés and failed in
their duties. In discussing the state of affairs he remarked : ' If Switzerland were Spain's neighbour her
army could easily invade us, such is the state of our
troops. If we continue like this, we shall soon find that
we have no Morocco, no army, and no Spain.'

Speaker followed speaker, with long lists of scandals
and accusations, to which the Minister of War replied
with energy if not with conviction. Señor Indalecio
Prieto, in an impassioned address, exclaimed : ' From
the steps of the throne our thousands of Spanish dead
are crying for justice, in a country that is desolation.'
The theme never changed—the corruption—which every
speaker asserted permeated the whole administration—
the immorality of the officers in their treatment of
Moorish women—and the suffering of the troops, whether
in sickness or in health. The Minister of War from time
to time rose to describe the accusations as exaggerated,
but he admitted much. He could do little more than
promise that the guilty should be brought to justice and
assure the deputies that everything possible was being
done to remedy the lamentable state of affairs. In
November, in reply to a bitter onslaught of Señor Ortega
y Gasset, the Minister of War replied : ' Our troops had
no preparation. Material was lacking. Our soldiers
were incapable of fighting.' On November the 10th,
Señor Maura, the Prime Minister, delivered a remarkable
speech. It gave a summary of affairs that was indeed
depressing. ' Everywhere,' he stated sadly, ' there is
the same misgovernment and the same laxity.' A few
days later Count Romanones, the Liberal leader, replied

with biting cynicism.  He stated : ' It was impossible
to relieve Monte Arruit, but a glance over the Annuario
Militar will show you that there were at that moment in
Spain 871 generals, 20,600 officers, and that the cost of
the upkeep of our army in the budget of 1921–22 is
1,172,000,000 pesetas (£46,000,000).'

The first result of these debates was that General
Berenguer, the Spanish High Commissioner in Morocco,
offered his resignation.  It was refused.  He returned
to Morocco, only to resign some eight months later.
Meanwhile, General Picasso had been charged, as President of a Commission of Inquiry, to proceed to Melilla
and take evidence as to the responsibility for the disaster.
General Picasso's mission was of long duration.  His
report was handed to a special Parliamentary Council.
The Council in turn reported to the Minister of War, who
nominated a court martial and eventually General
Berenguer himself and many others were convicted and
punished.

It was not until October, 1923, that General Picasso's
Report on Anual appeared, together with that of the
War Council.  They were immediately communicated
to the Parliamentary Commission of the Senate and to
the Chamber of Deputies.

These Reports disclosed a distressing situation, not
only at the time of the disaster itself but also previous
to the event.  Nor was that all, for there was an un-
accountable disappearance of official documents from
Melilla which might have thrown much original light
upon the circumstances that led to the catastrophe.

General Picasso's Report began with a description of
the situation existing in the spring of 1921.  It stated

that the 130 Posts scattered over the Melilla district served no military purpose. Every element that might have rendered them useful was wanting. Neither the garrisons, the armament nor the supplies were sufficient. Their defences were inadequate and there were no means of storing water, which had always to be brought from a distance under an almost daily fire from the enemy. The means of access to these Posts were badly placed, the roads often passing through ravines and gorges. The commissariat was defective, the Staff idle. It merely served to transmit orders. The officers in command exercised little or no authority, as they only left Melilla for the front at the moment of operations. They were constantly on leave. The soldiers received no instruction and orders were not obeyed. Discipline was bad and corruption of every kind was tacitly permitted. The Report continues with bitter strictures on the conduct of the officers, whom it accuses of failing altogether to raise the *moral* of their men.

The story of the disaster itself has already been outlined, but General Picasso's Report adds the details. It describes the Post of Abaran, the first to fall. It was the most advanced of all the Spanish positions and therefore the most likely to be attacked. It consisted of an enclosure 70 yards long by 13 yards wide. The parapet was constructed of damaged sand-bags and was only one metre in height. No defence was possible. The garrison and stores were entirely insufficient. Even the loss of this Post in which the native troops mutinied failed to warn the high authorities of the approaching danger. They were surprised and aggrieved at the act of treachery, and that was all. Even the High Commissioner himself telegraphed to Madrid a few days

later that ' the situation offered no cause for alarm or
anxiety.'

The next incident was Igerriben—it was the natural
consequence of what had preceded—and after Igerriben
came Anual. It was only from General Picasso's
Report, published more than two years after the disaster,
that the Spanish public learned that the garrison of
Anual had consisted of no less than 5,000 men. There
were in the stores a reserve of 200,000 cartridges and
600 shells. The Report describes the choice of the site
of this position as unfortunate. The enemy could
almost reach the wire entanglements without being
seen. The account of the evacuation adds little to
what was already known—that failing any method in
its direction it became a panic. In twenty-four hours
all the advanced-line Posts were lost or abandoned.
At Sidi Dris on the coast and at Afrau there was some
resistance, but apparently nowhere else. Important
positions were abandoned on the mere rumour of
disaster reaching their garrisons. On July the 22nd
General Navarro, who on the death of General Silvestre,
had taken command, telegraphed to the High Commissioner asking for authority to evacuate every position
on the grounds that, so low was the *moral* of his troops,
he dared not undertake any operation. The following
day he retired all his forces on Batel and Monte Arruit in
spite of orders to hold the line Dar Kebdani—Kandusi—
Dar Drius and Sok Tletza. There was complete confusion on every side.

The Report describes the retreat from Dar Drius to
Batel, Tistutin and Monte Arruit. At the beginning
there was a little order ; later it became a panic. A
battery of artillery was lost a very short distance from

Monte Arruit, and in an hour or two its guns were being employed against the Spaniards and were bombarding the position they had taken up. The second line of defence had fallen. In places the Posts surrendered without a shot being fired. The Report, in giving the details of this phase of the disaster, consists of one long accusation against individual commanders and officers. Here and there acts of heroism were reported, but they were few and far between. At the wells of Tistutin a corporal and six men held out from July the 28th till August the 5th, and eventually succeeded in fighting their way into the French zone.

They were not the only Spanish troops that reached that haven of security. The Report of General Picasso contains the following document : ' The Spanish Consul at Ujda, in his confidential despatch dated October the 12th, states that, in order that the Government of His Majesty (The King of Spain) should be kept fully informed on the events which had occurred in our (the Spanish) Protectorate, he had interrogated persons at Taurirt and Ujda, as well as the (Spanish) troops arriving from the Sok of the Tletza. His impressions are that at the moment the position was attacked there was a sufficiency of munitions. Every man had the proper number of cartridges, namely 150 each, and most had also in their pockets a reserve of from one to three packets of 50 cartridges. The commissariat department was less well supplied, but at the moment of the evacuation there was still a sufficient provision for four or five days. The value of what was abandoned under this heading is estimated at 550,000 pesetas (about £20,000). The Consul is not aware whether the garrison was in communication with the Headquarters

G

at Melilla and had received orders, but what appears
to have taken place was this. On learning what had
occurred in the rest of the district the Lieutenant-Colonel
who commanded the column summoned a council of
the officers. They recommended the evacuation of
the camp and a retreat into the French zone. During
that retreat it appears that no deployment was
made for the protection by echelons of the retiring
columns. The force which at its start numbered 1,200
men found itself reduced to 400 on a march of only
22 kilometres (13 miles). No attempt was made to
collect the wounded or the stragglers. The Consul
adds a detail which he had been able to verify : all
the wounds were on the left side which shows that the
column was attacked on the flank and that no counter-
attack was made, for there were no wounded with
woundsȚon their right side. Most of the wounds had
been received in the back. When they reached within
range of the first French Post the pursuit ceased. Our
(the Spanish) troops took refuge in the French Post of
Hassi-Uenzga and from thence proceeded to Camp-
Bertaux and to Taurirt. They were well received
everywhere. At Taurirt the lieutenant-colonel (Spanish)
gave orders for the conduct of the column which he
still commanded and immediately afterwards left by
automobile for Taza, where it is said General Aubert
(the French General commanding at Taza) submitted
him to a long interrogatory. The (Spanish) troops were
housed in barracks at Taurirt, the officers being accom-
modated in a pavilion. The attention of every one was
struck by the following facts : first, that the (Spanish)
officers did not visit their men in their huts : secondly,
that they passed their time in the cafés and every

evening danced with women of light morality. Certain members of the (Spanish) colony complained to the Consul of the bad manners of some of the officers and also of their excessive demands for money, as in the case of an officer of the Commissariat A—— S——, who deserved so severe a reprimand from the Consul that the Ministry (at Madrid) asked for the details of the case. The Consul praises Captain Francisco Alonso, who, before quitting the (Spanish) zone, strove on several occasions to turn back and twice tried to commit suicide.'

\*      \*      \*      \*      \*

The Report gives the evidence of the Colonel commanding the Regiment of San-Fernando. After a long dissertation on the inefficiency which he found existing on taking over the command, he added :

' The armament was in a very bad state, for the rifles of the regiment were the oldest of the Spanish army. I am told that some of them date from the Cuban war (1897). Hundreds were in bad condition. The mitrailleuses were in the same state as the rifles and for the same reasons ; their numbers showed that they were the oldest in the army. They choked very frequently at practice and in spite of many demands it was impossible to get them changed.'

\*      \*      \*      \*      \*

The ' Reporter ' of the Supreme Council of War and the Navy demanded the trial of a long list of officers, from lieutenants to the High Commissioner himself.

# CHAPTER IV

## SPANIARDS AND JIBALA

The Spanish campaign in Morocco was not confined to the Rif. Farther West, extending from the Straits of Gibraltar Southward as far as the French Protectorate frontier and even beyond, between the confines of the Rif on the East and the Atlantic coast, is the country known as the Jibala (Arabic : Jibli, a mountaineer ; plural, Jibála, mountaineers). At the extreme north-eastern corner of this region, on the Straits of Gibraltar, lies Ceuta, which has been since 1580 a Spanish possession and is recognized as Spanish territory. These districts—with the exception of the Southern Jibala tribes, which lie in the French Protectorate—are included in the Spanish zone of Morocco into which, by the terms of the Treaty of 1912, Spain undertook to introduce law and order. Until 1926 the Rif and the Jibala were entirely separated, the Spaniards never having succeeded—they had never even attempted it—in opening communication by land ; the result was that Spain was engaged in two entirely separate campaigns in Morocco, against tribes speaking a different language though of common origin. The sea route was the only means by which troops could be conveyed from one sector of the war to the other. In each sector, except when fine weather permitted of landing in open roadsteads, there was only one port—

THE
JIBALA TRIBES
OF THE
SPANISH ZONE.

SPAIN

Gibraltar

Tarifa

STRAITS OF GIBRALTAR

Kilometres

0  5  10          20

= Roads

Ceuta

Tangier

Alcazar
Soreir

ANJERA

TANGIER

C. Negro

FAHS

EL-HAUZ

ZONE

WAD RAS

Ergaia

Tetuan

Rio Martin

BENI MSAUR

Dar Ben
Karich

B. MADAN
B. HOZMAR

JIBEL HABIB

BENI
SAID

Arzeila

BENI IDIR

Wad Lau

GHARBIYA

SPANISH          ZONE

BENI AROS

Sok el-Arba

BENI HASSAN

Tazrut

Jibel Mulai
Abdesalam

BENI
LAIT

BENI GORFET

GHOMARA

Laraiche

SUMATA

Sheshuan

KHLOT

BENI ISSEF

AKHMAS

AHLSERIF

BENI SICAR

Alcazar

ERHUNA

GHEZAUA

FRENCH    PROTECTORATE

BENI MESTARA

Wazzan

LONDON: EDWARD ARNOLD & CO.

Ceuta in the West and Melilla in the East. Laraiche on the Atlantic coast is inaccessible with westerly winds. These two harbours were the principal bases of the Spanish army. Ceuta is connected by a broad-gauge railway with Tetuan about 20 miles to the south; while from Melilla a narrow-gauge military line ran Westward as far as Batel, a distance of 30 miles.

Between these two seats of war lay a mountainous district of unexplored and unknown country, inhabited by the Jibala, the Ghomara, and farther East the tribes of the Western Rif. It seems strange that while travellers have penetrated to almost every point of Central Africa this large and important region of Morocco has remained absolutely closed to all outside knowledge and discovery, for, like the Rifis, the Jibala tribesmen have guarded not only their independence but also their seclusion. From Tangier itself mountain ranges are visible which have never yet been reached by any European, except perhaps some deserter of the Foreign Legion, or a criminal escaped from the penal settlement at Ceuta, who may have penetrated there in an attempt to find a hiding-place in the recesses of those inhospitable valleys. Even when Sheshuan, the flourishing little mountain town of the Akhmas tribe, was occupied by the Spanish troops in 1920, the writer was the only living European who had ever been there— de Foucauld and Mr. William Summers, the only others who are known to have penetrated thus far, having died before that date. When in May, 1926, Abdel Krim surrendered, the nearest points of the two Spanish fronts in Northern Morocco were over 80 miles apart, and all the intervening district, with the exception of the triangle of Tetuan, Sheshuan, Wad Lau, which had been previously occupied in 1920 and abandoned in 1924, was totally unexplored. The sole knowledge of these regions was based on information collected from the natives and on a few photographs of the less remote portions taken from the air. It is curious to realize in 1926 that from on board the great liners, as they leave Gibraltar for the East, the peaceful traveller can see in fine weather the mountain ranges South of Tetuan which remain one of the few regions of Africa that have never been visited. More is known of the jungle-covered slopes of Ruwenzori than of the cedar forests of Ghomara.

Yet the Jibala tribesmen who inhabit these mountains are no savages, but members of an organized society, boasting an ancient civilization and closely allied in mentality, and probably in race, with Europe. Adhering to the religious tenets as well as to the social injunctions of Islam, they obey the recognized Koranic law which is only discarded in cases where their tribal traditions and system of hereditary democracy is too firmly embedded to be neglected. Courageous, indifferent to suffering, devoted to their families and their children, religious in practice yet with no very deep sentiment of religion, this white race of Arabicized Berbers presents a most interesting study. In many respects they differ from the Rifis, whose morality is superior but who lack the humour and gaiety of the Jibala. Excitable and easily led, they will readily adopt a new cause or a new leader, to abandon both with disconcerting facility should the fancy take them to do so. Their principal characteristic, in the opinion of other natives and in their own, is their inconsequence of thought and action. They are confirmed optimists in spite of constant disillusion. The Millennium is always on the point of arriving, but never comes. They have accepted a multitude of religious and temporal leaders and almost always found that they were leaning upon reeds of the weakest fibre. They have often turned against, and frequently slain, with the same enthusiastic zeal in which they accepted them, the chiefs who had failed to carry out their promises to regenerate the world or to lead them to victory. They have been the victims of a hundred impostors, many of whom became in turn their own victims. From time to time they ran up against a strong man, and adopted his cause. Such were Raisuli and Abdel Krim ; but their enthusiasm generally ended in regrets, for they found that the hands they filled with money scourged them with whips in return.

Improvident, caring little for to-day and not worrying at all about to-morrow—while the day after is much too far removed even to think about—they live their lives in the cold and rain and snow of their high mountains or in the warmer valleys below, cultivating such soil as is capable of cultivation and earning a precarious livelihood by supplying the towns with charcoal and fresh or dried fruits. Speaking Arabic with a strong local accent, for their original tongue was Thamazirth, or Shelha, and laughed at for their ingenuousness and inconsequence, the Jibli has always been the butt of the other Moors. He realizes this full well himself and his humour is sufficient to make fun of it. There is no one who will recount stories against himself with more gusto and with more enjoyment than the tribesman of the Jibala. I call to mind two of these tales, told me in the heart of their country. A Jibli visiting the plains bought a sheep, determined to start and to own a flock, for in his mountain district there were only goats. Already in his mind he saw the slopes of his mountains white with the fleeces of snowy lambs. On his return home, to celebrate his new and rare acquisition, he gave a feast to all his friends. After the repast of cooked meats he led them out to see the sheep. It was only then that he realized that he had killed it and cooked it as the *pièce de resistance* of the entertainment.

The second story treats of the same spirit of inconsequence. A local chief of the Beni Mestara tribe had been confirmed in his office by the Sultan and given the title of Kaid. He and his tribesmen being mountaineers never rode horses, but he was told that his new dignity necessitated the purchase of a steed. He bought one and appeared at the first official ceremony riding it barebacked. He was at once informed that he must add a saddle—one of those cumbersome rich expensive saddles in which the heart of the Arab rider delights. He had no money and was terribly worried as to what to do. Suddenly an inspiration came to him. He took his horse to the market and sold it and, with the money thus acquired, he bought a saddle. The next day there was an official ceremony. At dawn he staggered to the stable borne down by the weight of the magnificent saddle—but found no horse. It was only then that he realized his solution of the problem was not faultless.

Like the Rifis the Jibala have defended their country against all invasion. Once or twice a Sultan has passed through their mountains—the last time was Mulai Hassan's visit in 1890—and now and again the Moorish army has been sent to repress some local in-

surrection or to put down some too flagrant act of
pillage, but the lesson if ever learned was soon forgotten.
Forgetful of yesterday, taking no thought for to-morrow,
the Jibala returned to their independence and their
tribal feuds.

While the Rif possesses no towns, the Jibala can lay
claim to three—Tetuan, Sheshuan and Wazzan—for all
of these lie in their country, the first two in the Spanish
sphere, the third in the French Protectorate.

Tetuan, now the capital of the Spanish zone, is
well known, not only on account of its political importance but also because it is one of the most delightful
and most accessible of the cities of Morocco. Situated
less than 50 miles from Tangier, it can be reached by
motor in from two to three hours.

Although Tetuan was designated as the capital of
the Spanish zone, it was not the first of the towns to
be occupied, for, a year before the signing of the 1912
Treaty with France, which supplemented the original
1904 Agreement, the Spaniards had landed in Laraiche
and marched inland to El-Kasr el-Kebir, more commonly
known as Alcazar. This was in 1911.

It was on this occasion that the Spaniards first came
into contact with Raisuli, who was destined to play so
important and so sinister a part in the succeeding
years. Even at this moment when he held out a helping hand to the Spaniards and staged for them the
supposed attack upon Alcazar, which brought about
the hurried arrival of troops from Laraiche, he was
merely raising the curtain on the opening scenes of a
drama in which he reserved for himself the leading
part. But he was not the only claimant for the rôle
of the hero. Colonel Silvestre, who commanded the

Spanish expeditionary force from Laraiche, afterwards
so well known as General Silvestre, was a rival who
knew how to insist, and it was only a few days later
that the long struggle between Raisuli and Silvestre
began. The first interview had been cordial. Silvestre
made, and Raisuli accepted, presents. It was a way
Raisuli had and was thoroughly characteristic of his
whole attitude to life. The actual reason of the ensuing
quarrel was that Silvestre was not satisfied with the
occupation of Alcazar alone. He desired to continue
his march Northward at once and take possession of
Arzeila, a little walled town lying about half way
between Laraiche and Tangier on the Atlantic coast.
He even hinted that he intended to force his way right
through to Tetuan across the intervening tribelands of
the Jibala. He found his intentions and his desires
stubbornly resisted. Raisuli had no wish to see the
Spaniards at Arzeila, where he owned property and
which he considered as his headquarters.

The presence of Spanish troops at Laraiche and Alcazar
was a matter almost of indifference to him, for neither
of those places had ever fallen either legally in his
jurisdiction or even under his usurped authority. But
Arzeila was a different question altogether. Raisuli's
systematic obstruction forced Silvestre to abandon for
a time any movement Northward and, impatient by
nature, he chafed under the position of inferiority in
which he found himself. To remove the ex-brigand
from his path, he realized was, at that juncture at all
events, impossible. There seemed to be only one other
course to pursue, to try and win him over. Raisuli's
ambition and cupidity rendered this no easy task.
To Silvestre's discreet inquiries as to his price Raisuli

MULAI AHMED ER-RAISULI, 1924.

let it be known that nothing less than the post of
Khalifa, the Representative of the Sultan in the Spanish
zone, with almost independent powers, would satisfy
him. He felt himself worthy of this honour, the second
highest position in Morocco, for the Sultan alone took
precedence over the Khalifa.

He was a Shereef, a descendant of the Prophet, of
particularly ancient and holy lineage. The tomb of
his ancestor, Mulai Abdesalam ben Mashish, in the
Beni Aros, was a place of constant and reverent pilgrimage and the holiest spot in Morocco North of Fez.
His education was sufficient. As a boy and youth he
had studied theology and law in Tetuan and was in a
way a scholar. By nature courageous and a lover of
adventure, he had left the paths of learning for those
of a more exciting profession. Collecting a band of
youths of similar temperament and age, whose acts
like his were not by any means in accordance with the
tenets of theological education, he had taken to a life
of adventure and dissipation. He made the former
support the expenses of the latter, and their nights of
revelry in Tetuan or in the open country were paid for
by the lifting of cattle and the extortion of money under
threats. Cattle-stealing in Morocco was only looked
upon askance by the victims and sometimes by the
authorities. It was the recognized profession of many
men and it had its rules and etiquette. A man's cattle
stolen by night from his yard or farm, or even driven
off when grazing by day, would be offered him back
within probably twenty-four hours of the theft in return
for the payment of a sum of money considerably below
the value of the stolen beasts. It was better to pay this
ransom than to lose the cattle, and nearly always the

affair was arranged to the entire satisfaction of the thieves and to the very much less entire satisfaction of the victim. The actual raiders did not appear upon the scene; the transactions were carried out by a mutual friend, generally a Moor of influence and position, who got a commission from both sides.

So notorious did the young Raisuli's depredations become and so constant the complaints, emanating often from the Representatives of the European Powers at Tangier whose subjects at times suffered loss, that his arrest was ordered by the Sultan. He was captured by treachery and imprisoned at Mogador. He escaped, but was almost immediately recaught and chained to the prison wall. On the accession of Mulai Abdel Aziz to the throne in 1894 Raisuli was released. He returned to the district of Tangier to find that all his property had been confiscated and that nothing was left. In revenge he took to the hills, where collecting his old band about him, and finding new recruits without difficulty, he adopted once more his life of adventure. But he had changed. The gay, pleasure-loving Raisuli of the earlier days had become cruel and morose. The recollection of the bitter sufferings of his imprisonment at Mogador, his injured health, the scars that the chains had left on his wrists and ankles were ever present to remind him of the past, and his hand was turned against every man's. Hatred and a deep determination to revenge himself for the treatment that had been meted out to him took complete possession of his mind. His every act was marked by cruelty. A Shereef who had married his sister decided to take a second wife. The law permitted it, and it was a recognized custom. The first wife appealed to her brother. On the night of the wedding Raisuli and his band arrived and, forcing their way into the house, cut the throat of the young bride as she sat decked out in her wedding garments awaiting the entrance of her husband. Her mother, who was with her, shared the same fate. On another occasion a local Sheikh, against whom Raisuli had a grudge, had been kidnapped by a rival. Raisuli bought him for 1,500 dollars, and decapitated him upon his own doorstep.

As his acts of pillage and extortion increased, often committed in the name of justice but always for his own benefit, the Sultan and the Maghzen became seriously alarmed. In 1906 an army was sent from Fez to restore order and to capture if possible the disturber of peace. Zinat, the village where he resided, situated about 14 miles from Tangier, was burned by the troops and Raisuli's position was critical. The same evening his men captured the writer of these lines while riding in the neighbourhood and handed him over to Raisuli, who had about 2,000 Jibala tribesmen with him. I knew him well, but my acquaintance with him did not prevent his retaining me. I was kept a captive at Zinat and afterwards in the Anjera for three weeks, until Raisuli had obtained the terms he had demanded —the release of the Jibala prisoners in Moorish gaols, the withdrawal of the Sultan's army and other privileges. No ransom was demanded. A few acts of kindness and a little hospitality that I had shown to the Jibala tribesmen in the past had not been unappreciated and I reaped the reward. Tempting as money would have been to these people, they deliberately refused to entertain it. They were fully aware that the Moorish Government could have been made to pay a large sum to obtain my release, but they refrained from asking a ransom, and, when it was offered, indignantly refused it. The Moors have often been accused of a want of the sense of gratitude. Their conduct on this occasion is a proof that they have a very keen appreciation of this virtue and practised it in circumstances that made their forbearance only the more admirable.

The following year Raisuli, again threatened by the Sultan, captured Mr. Perdicaris, an American resident in Tangier, and his stepson Mr. Varley. They were kept seven weeks in captivity and a ransom of £14,000 was demanded and paid. Raisuli extorted from the Sultan, as well as this sum of money, his own appointment as Governor of the tribes round Tangier, and the Pasha of the town was dismissed at his demand. There were other terms too which Mulai Abdel Aziz was forced to accept.

Raisuli rode rough-shod over every treaty. He kept, however, the caravan roads open, and law and order were respected ; but his constant acts of cruelty and his disregard of the privileged position of Europeans led to a general outcry against him and his works. Still another army was sent from Fez and Zinat was once more burnt, but Raisuli had found time to escape to the mountains. It was then that he received a visit from Kaid Maclean, who had been sent by the Sultan to make terms of peace with the turbulent Shereef. When Kaid Maclean rose to leave he found that he was a prisoner. He remained Raisuli's captive for seven months, and it was only on the payment of a ransom of £20,000 and on the granting by the Sultan of a number of privileges that he was released.

In 1908 civil war broke out in Morocco. The Sultan

Abdel Aziz, after an attempt to maintain himself upon the throne, was beaten in battle by the forces of Mulai Hafid and in the autumn he abdicated in favour of his brother. Raisuli, who had supported Mulai Hafid's cause from the moment it appeared to be in the ascendant, proceeded to Fez and made terms with the new Sultan. He was appointed Pasha of Arzeila and Kaid of the Northern Jibala tribes, including the Anjera. In return he restored to a grateful and at that moment impecunious sovereign the £20,000 he had received as the ransom of Kaid Maclean, which had been paid by Mulai Hafid's predecessor on the throne, Mulai Abdel Aziz. Raisuli well knew that the appointments he had received from the new Sultan were worth far more than this sum of money. He returned to the North and took up his position, a stronger and greater man than ever. He was still Kaid of this region when, in 1911, the Spaniards occupied Laraiche and Alcazar, and Colonel Silvestre found himself face to face with the famous Shereef.

It was not to be wondered at that the situation was difficult. It was rendered more difficult still by the characters of the two adversaries, the impatient hot temper of the Spanish Colonel and the deep cunning and arrogance of his rival, whose obstruction he had to overcome. Ambitious, brooking no interference, taking no advice and asking none, Raisuli was a formidable obstacle in the way of Spain's progress in Morocco. His plans were never disclosed even to his intimate associates; of friends he had perhaps none, for he trusted no one. He demanded and obtained obedience from all who served him, but every one about m lived in perpetual fear. He beat and imprisoned and killed at will, giving no reason and being asked none.

The duel between these two men was a duel to the death. Raisuli, cynical and witty, seemed to take, and no doubt did take, an infinite delight in thwarting every wish of Colonel Silvestre, who could ill restrain his indignation and his rage at the continued obstruction and the unmeasured arrogance of the man who seemed to block his every road to success. It became still more apparent than ever that he must be bought. Colonel Silvestre requested the Spanish Government to appoint Raisuli Khalifa of the Spanish zone. Madrid refused. It was clearly impossible. Whatever may have been his position by birth, Raisuli's career stood in the way of such an appointment. With deep mortification he learned that the one post he would consent to fill was out of his reach—at least for the present. A high Spanish decoration ill compensated him for this disappointment. He was now residing at Arzeila, where he had built himself a palace on the sea wall, against the lower walls of which the waves broke in ceaseless music. Now and again I visited him at this period and he wrote me from time to time, bitter scornful letters describing the plight of the Spaniards and scoffing at their want of organization. 'You will find Alcazar changed,' he wrote in one of his letters, 'for the Spanish soldiers who were starving have eaten all the frogs and water-tortoises of the river and the marshes.' His resentment was deep and undisguised. He regretted having facilitated the disembarkation of the Spanish troops at Laraiche and their march on Alcazar.

The air was charged with electricity. The storm

broke one day when a small Spanish column met a
group of Raisuli's soldiery. There was an unfortunate
encounter and blood was shed. Indignant, threatening
and thirsty for revenge, Raisuli came to Tangier in
order to communicate direct with the Spanish Government through the Spanish Minister at that place. He
was suffering much pain, the results of the ill-health
that he owed to his long imprisonment at Mogador.
I saw him at times during those spells of distress. He
was lying on his back on a low mattress with his feet
suspended in scarves, hung from nails in the wall, that
raised his swollen legs and ankles a few inches above the
rest of his body. It was the only position in which he
could obtain relief. His brother acted as his deputy
at Arzeila during his absence, for in spite of reiterated protestations of friendship from Madrid Raisuli
refused to return. His attitude caused very considerable anxiety in Spain and Colonel Silvestre was hastily
summoned to the Capital to confer with the Government.
Immediately he had left Morocco, Raisuli paid a visit
to the Jibala tribes, the members of which had been
summoned to meet him at the tomb of Mulai Abdeselam
in Beni Aros. Returning a few days later to Tangier,
he learned that his palace at Arzeila had been seized
by the Spaniards and that the members of his family
were being held as hostages.

It was at this critical moment that the Spanish
Government decided to occupy Tetuan, the capital of
the Spanish zone. Advancing from Ceuta the Spaniards
entered the town in July, 1913. Not a shot was fired,
and possibly, had their arrival been followed by the
introduction of a policy of sympathy and collaboration,
no shot might ever have been fired at all. But the

Spanish troops were thirsting for glory and discipline
was lax. There was too great an exhibition of the
spirit of conquest. Morocco must give of its best, and
amongst its best were its women. Immoral the Moors
may often be, but there are laws and traditions which
hold good, and are seldom broken, and the greater part
of them refer to their womankind. The behaviour of
certain Spaniards in this respect set ablaze a flame of
resentment and indignation. Within a few weeks of
their occupation of the Capital, Spain's relations with
the people of the town and with all the surrounding
tribes were severely strained.

A cousin of the reigning Sultan was appointed to the
position that Raisuli had coveted, Khalifa of the Spanish
zone. The astute Shereef himself, still at Tangier,
showed no visible signs of discomfiture. He expressed
his desire to live quietly in his villa there, and, by
negotiation with Madrid through the Spanish Legation
in Tangier, he obtained the release of the members of
his family who had been held at Arzeila as hostages.
This accomplished, he left suddenly for the neighbourhood of Tetuan. Already angered by the behaviour
of the Spanish officers, and by the looting propensities
of the soldiery, the tribesmen were only waiting a word
of command. Raisuli gave it and war broke out on
every side. The Spaniards suffered heavy losses in
the outskirts of Tetuan itself.

Wherever there were Spanish soldiers there was
fighting, at Alcazar, at Arzeila and at the scattered
posts and along the roads. The first act of the Madrid
Government was to recall General Alfau and to appoint
General Marina in his place. The situation necessitated
the sending of reinforcements from Spain and by the

early autumn of 1913 there were over 40,000 Spanish troops in the field. There followed one of those periods of cross-purposes which have so often marked Spanish policy in North Africa. While the new High Commissioner was doing all in his power to bring about a reconciliation with Raisuli, General Silvestre at Laraiche was leaving no stone unturned to increase the mutual distrust which already existed. The result was that little headway was made and the situation remained highly unsatisfactory.

Such was the state of affairs when war broke out in Europe in August, 1914. It must not be forgotten that while this Western sector was causing so much anxiety to the Spaniards they were also engaged in a campaign on the Melilla front of the Rif. It was true that there had been a lull in the hostilities in that sector and that an advance had been made into the Beni Said tribelands which had met with comparatively little resistance. Since 1909 the Spaniards had progressed Eastward from Melilla, and at the moment of the outbreak of the Great War had reached the valley of the Wad Kert. Political negotiations had been successfully employed in that region and everything pointed to a period of peaceful penetration. The Rifi Chiefs seemed to view the Spanish progress with diminished antagonism, not a little owing to the intervention of the agents of important German mining companies, who were increasing their interests both political and industrial with the undisguised approbation and support of the Spanish authorities. A number of natives were in their employ, or in their pay, amongst them Abdel Krim, the Kaid of Beni Uriaghel the father of Mohammed ben Abdel Krim who was to play so important a part in the history of the succeeding years. On the whole this period of the campaign in the Eastern sector caused no great anxiety to Spain, and during the duration of the war no serious misadventure was suffered in the Rif. But the seeds of the coming crop of misfortune were being sown. Rifles and ammunition were being imported in large quantities into the country by the Germans, for the purpose of arming the tribes against the French farther South. That these arms were employed for that purpose is well known, but they eventually served to scatter death amongst the Spaniards themselves, when after the Armistice the Rifis turned against the invaders of their country and in 1921 annihilated the Spanish army.

During the Great War Raisuli entered into intimate relations with the Germans, though to the best of my belief he never rendered them any very signal service. He certainly never carried out the programme which they constantly put before him, to abandon his campaign against the Spaniards and to attack the French in the Protectorate. He took their money readily enough and promised much, and that was about all. Once when the situation in France was very critical he received a visit from German agents sent by the German Embassy at Madrid. They told him that Paris had been taken and the war won. After they had left, Kaid Zellal of the Beni Msuar tribe, who had been present at the interview, asked Raisuli if he believed it. The wily Shereef replied : ' I shall believe that the Germans have won the war when my English friends acknowledge that they have lost it.' There is no doubt Raisuli made use of German propaganda to lessen the prestige of France in Morocco, and to further his own ends and the interests of his personal ambition. That the Germans held out a tempting bait to him is certain, but it was easy to promise in those days, and I doubt if Raisuli counted upon the possibilities of the situation which they foretold ever coming about—a free and independent Morocco, with Mulai Hafid Sultan of the South and Raisuli Viceroy of the North! I have never found any evidence whatever of his having done anything for the Germans which was not done solely in his own interests. That he would have been content to see them drive the French out of Morocco is possibly a fact, but that he ever expected that it would come about was quite another matter. Their proposals may have tempted his ambition and aroused his cupidity, but they were offering what certainly at that moment was not theirs to give.

Raisuli was now living at Tazrut in the Beni Aros, near the holy tomb of his ancestor Mulai Abdesalam ben Mashish, whence, situated as it was in the centre of the Northern Jibala tribes, he was able to keep his finger on the pulse of the mountaineers, and to make it beat to his own music.

In the spring of 1915 occurred an incident which had no little bearing on Raisuli's subsequent behaviour. The struggle between the Spanish military party in Morocco and the Madrid Government continued as usual and Raisuli was more than ever the bone of contention. While the army, with General Silvestre at its head—for he had been promoted—was bent upon an expedition to attack Raisuli in his lair, the Madrid Government was using every possible means and all its influence to gain his goodwill and his assistance. This latter policy was being ardently pursued by the Spanish Legation in Tangier, which was in direct communication with Tazrut, much to the annoyance and indignation of General Silvestre. Having an important and confidential letter to send to Raisuli, the Marquis de Villasinda, the Spanish Minister at Tangier entrusted it to the hands of an influential native of the Tangier zone, Ali Akalai, who was a friend, and the agent at Tangier, of Raisuli. Akalai with the letter set out on horseback accompanied by a servant who was also mounted. About 14 miles from Tangier, shortly after passing a Spanish military camp on the Akba el-Hamra, Ali Akalai and his man were attacked and killed. Their bodies were found floating on a neighbouring stream, and showed every sign of violent death. It was not long before the truth leaked out. Ali Akalai had been murdered at the instigation of Raisuli's enemies, and a Spanish officer and native soldiers in Spanish employ were implicated. The object had been to obtain possession of the despatch from Madrid which was being conveyed to the Shereef at Tazrut. The charge was brought home and a great scandal ensued, which ended in the recall of both General Marina, the High Commissioner, and of General Silvestre.

General Jordana, who was at that time in command of the Spanish forces at Melilla, was appointed to replace General Marina as High Commissioner with instructions from the Spanish Government to continue the negotiations with Raisuli, which had been broken off by the unfortunate incident. Raisuli's wrath at the murder of his friend, and at the circumstances in which it had taken place, was without bounds. He turned all his powers of vituperation loose on the Spaniards and swore revenge, but he used the incident, as he did every cir-

cumstance of his life, for his own advantage. For a
time he refused to receive any communication from the
Spanish Government or from the High Commissioner
in Tetuan. He alternately raged and sulked until he
felt that the ground was sufficiently prepared to permit
of the reopening of negotiations on a new and more
advantageous basis.

One of the difficult points to which a solution had
to be found was that of the relations between the
Khalifa and Raisuli. The Khalifa, who represented his
cousin the Sultan in Tetuan and in all the Spanish zone,
was a Shereef, and a Prince of the royal Blood, and bore
the title of Imperial Highness. Tradition and policy
demanded that Raisuli should proceed to Tetuan, to
swear allegiance to his royal master, but he steadily
refused to do anything of the sort. The Khalifate was
the one post he had desired to fill himself and he was
certainly not going to make obeisance to a rival, whom
he looked down upon as a mere 'Spanish puppet.'
That the High Commissioner was very anxious to obtain
the recognition of the Khalifa by Raisuli was only
natural for the Sultan's Representative had not met
with much success. The Moors considered him as
merely a part of the Spanish show—a Shereef who had
certainly not risen in general native estimation by having
placed himself body and soul under the control of a
foreign and Christian Government. The paraphernalia
of royalty with which the Spaniards surrounded him—
the led horses, the crimson parasol, the spear-bearers
and his many titles—were looked upon with amused
indifference, for by tradition none but the Sultan had
a right to use them. To have obtained some outward
and visible sign of Raisuli's allegiance to their figure-

head would have been of distinct political value, but Raisuli refused to budge. It was part of the Spanish scheme to put forward the Khalifa upon every occasion, just as the French in the Protectorate were doing all in their power to increase the prestige of the Sultan. Raisuli was adamant and the Spanish authorities had to abandon all idea of his visiting Tetuan. To the day when he died a prisoner in the Rif, he had never returned there. The only compromise that he would accept was that he should recognize the legal existence of the Khalifa in the Spanish zone as the Representative of the Sultan. Further than that he would not go.

Slowly after long and difficult negotiations terms were arrived at between the Spanish Government and Raisuli. Enriched in money, more than semi-independent, with a little army of his own paid by the Spaniards but under his sole control, in possession of quantities of arms and ammunition which had been sent him from Tetuan, Raisuli was now to all intents and purposes ' monarch of all he surveyed.' Astute and far-seeing, he emerged from this difficult period of negotiation more powerful and more independent than he had ever been—and undoubtedly more dangerous. He kept in touch, through all kinds of channels, with the Germans, the French and the English, prepared to take advantages of whatever might be the results of the war in Europe.

It took a year to negotiate this pact with Raisuli, and it was not concluded until May, 1916, when the Spanish High Commissioner and he met for the first time at the Fondak of Ain Jedida on the Tangier-Tetuan road. The conversation was long and none too satisfactory, and the High Commissioner made no secret of

the fact that Raisuli's obstruction and arrogance severely
tried his patience.  The results of the meeting were not
sensational, for the pact was little more than an agreement to continue the *status quo* while waiting for the
termination of the war in Europe.  Both the High
Commissioner and Raisuli realized, each from his own
point of view, how much depended upon the results of
the European struggle.

The whole attitude of the Spaniards in Morocco
toward the Allies has been much discussed and much
criticized, but the position of Spain was by no means
an easy one.  Neutral in Europe she necessarily carried
her policy of neutrality into her Morocco zone.  Yet
all Morocco was under the sovereignty of the Sultan,
and the Sultan was not only an Ally but also a belligerent.
The situation from the very beginning was anomalous.
As the war proceeded it became highly complicated,
and threatened more than once to become critical.
That the Germans took gross advantage of Spain's
neutrality no one can deny, but there is every reason
to believe that the Madrid Government was innocent
of all participation in and guilty knowledge of these
actions.  That certain Spanish officials and authorities,
from sympathy with the German cause, or from other
reasons, facilitated the movements of submarines,
allowed the introduction of arms into Morocco and their
exportation from the Spanish ports, and even joined in
active German propaganda, is not to be doubted and
was difficult to prevent.  The Spanish zone became a
base for attack upon the French Protectorate, but the
position of the Spaniards themselves in the Rif was at
times far too precarious for them to venture to attempt
to control the tribes, who, egged on by skilful German

propaganda and paid in German gold, were only too
ready to carry their raids into the territory of a neighbouring and friendly State. But the action of certain
officials in Africa must not be allowed to blacken the
reputation of the country to which they belonged.
The King and the Government in extremely difficult
circumstances maintained throughout an admirable
spirit of neutrality and the former rendered, in his
great work in favour of the prisoners of war, most
valuable services to humanity. He had at least this
distinction, that he was one of the few great figures
of Europe who was not engaged in furthering destruction and in exterminating his fellow-men by every
process of barbarity and horror. Whatever may have
been the justification—if there was any—for the war,
King Alfonso at least was guilty of no participation
in its origin or in its perpetration. He has also this
immense satisfaction, that he was not a party to the
treaty of peace that followed.

Raisuli was considered by the Allies as one of the
principal German agents in Morocco, but the Germans,
it appears, had little confidence in him at any time, and
believed him to be under British influence. Now that
time has put all the events of that period into a more
reasonable perspective, it can be said that Raisuli was
indifferent to any interests except his own, and that
any proclivities he may have shown at one time or
another for either side owed their origin to self-interest.
The only countries, I believe, for which he had any
special regard were England and America, for in his
dealings with both, in his affairs of brigandage, he had
met with complete success and indisputable profit, and
his appreciation of foreign Governments was limited to

STREET IN TETUAN.

Phot. Alberto.

the personal advantages that he had been able to reap in his relations with them. In the cases of America and England he was the richer by the ransoms they had paid, or had made the Sultan pay, for the release of their captive-subjects, and he recognized that both had strictly carried out the terms to which they had agreed. He was grateful for their generosity and appreciative of their honourable dealings. So cordially did he regard those two Powers that there is little doubt that had he reverted to brigandage, he would again have shown a preference for victims of British or American nationality.

At the end of the Great War the Spanish Government fell, and the High Commissioner in Morocco, General Jordana, died under tragic circumstances. General Berenguer, who had already been Minister of War in Madrid, was appointed his successor early in 1919.

With the arrival of General Berenguer an entirely new policy was adopted in Morocco. It was time, for Spanish prestige had suffered by the long period of hesitations and confusion. Immediately after his arrival the new High Commissioner let Raisuli know that he had been much surprised not to have found him awaiting him on his arrival at Tetuan, and he requested the Shereef to come and visit him there. Raisuli, who was never in a hurry, left this communication unanswered for several weeks—though he was living within a long day's ride of Tetuan. When the reply came it was in the form of a lengthy despatch of advice and warning as to how General Berenguer should shape his policy. He pointed out the road the High Commissioner should follow, intimating that any contrary procedure would meet with his disapproval. Having launched this

literary bomb, Raisuli followed it up by instigating a
series of aggressive incidents in the neighbourhood of
Tetuan itself. This action was sufficient to confirm
General Berenguer's already formed opinion that force
was the only means of bringing Raisuli and the tribes
to reason. He determined at once upon a programme
of active opposition to the Shereef and the overthrow
of his influence and power—an entire reversal of the
policy that Madrid had adopted during the period of
the war. With an energy that was as unusual as it
was admirable, General Berenguer reorganized the
forces under his command and carried war into the enemy
country. In a few weeks Alcazar Soreir, on the Anjera
coast of the Straits of Gibraltar, had been occupied,
as well as the hills of Beni Hozmar facing Tetuan, and
a column was clearing the Tetuan-Tangier road in the
direction of the Fondak.

A series of operations in the Wad Ras tribelands
ensued, within 20 miles of Tangier. Every attempt was
made by the Spanish authorities to conceal the results,
but the truth leaked out. In three days' fighting—
July the 11th to 13th—the Spaniards lost about 300
killed and probably 1,000 wounded. A small column
of 170 Spanish soldiers were ambushed by Raisuli's
men in a ravine. The incident discloses the cunning
of the Shereef. The column in question was proceeding
along a valley when a Spanish officer and some Spanish
soldiers appeared on the hill above. The cfficer shouted
directions to the column to turn sharply into a narrow
valley and ascend the course of the stream. They
had, he said, missed the track. Obeying these instructions, the commander of the little force entered a ravine
where a few minutes later they were fiercely attacked

by Jibala tribesmen, masked and using gas grenades. The whole column was annihilated; there was not a single survivor except one or two natives who were following the column. One of these, staggering under the effects of ' gas,' reached Tangier the following day. He stated that the commandant of the column, realizing that escape was impossible and horrified at the disaster to which he had led his men, shot himself with his revolver. The soldiers, struggling in the agony of gas, were dispatched with knives, the Jibala tribesmen cutting their throats as they lay panting on the ground, so deep was the hatred of the Spaniard at that moment. The Spanish officer who had directed the column into the ravine was one of Raisuli's men in disguise.

Reinforcements were hurried to Wad Ras, and after a severe struggle the tribe submitted and their district was occupied. This success, limited though it was, warranted the promulgation of a ' Dahir '—or Edict— by the Khalifa, degrading Raisuli, confiscating his property, and declaring him an outlaw. It was the complete reversal of Spanish policy. All the struggle of the last few years, during which every effort had been made to gain his goodwill and assistance, was abandoned. Taking into consideration the ill-success of all these endeavours, this change of attitude was not to be wondered at. Raisuli, it was agreed, must bear the consequence of his obstruction. But this long period of negotiation had been fully taken advantage of by the astute ex-brigand. He had been supplied with money, arms and ammunition, and his stores at Tazrut were well stocked. He had a small army of his own, and he could count on contingents from the tribes-

men, who in spite of his extortion and his cruelty still
obeyed his every word.

General Silvestre was once more in Morocco, appointed
to the command at Ceuta by the Madrid Government,
without, it is said, any previous consultation with the
High Commissioner. The relations of Generals Berenguer and Silvestre were already strained, and friction
was inevitable and immediate. On the demand of the
former, Silvestre was removed to the command of the
Melilla front, where at all events the High Commissioner
would not be brought into constant personal contact
with him, though he remained under his orders.

To the Khalifa's edict proclaiming his outlawry
Raisuli replied by a declaration of war on the Spaniards,
in which he called upon the tribes to resist invasion
and to defend their country. The result was anarchy.
Fresh acts of brigandage, aggressions on travellers, and
attacks on the Spanish Posts followed in quick succession. At Akba el-Kola, not far from Alcazar, the whole
Spanish garrison was massacred. The Spanish Government found itself forced to undertake a new and important campaign, and General Berenguer, active,
energetic and competent, hurried on the preparations.
He was determined once and for all to rid the Spanish
zone of Raisuli. How far he was aware of the new menace
that was rising in the Eastern sector—the young
Mohammed ben Abdel Krim—it is impossible to say.

In the person of General Berenguer, Raisuli had an
enemy whose activity was endless and who had the
art of inspiring others with his own enthusiasms. His
troops met with success, and in October, 1920, Sheshuan,
the only town in the interior of the Jibala country, was
occupied. The importance of this event was evident.

Founded in 1471 by the Alami Shereefs during one of the many periods of war with Portugal, Sheshuan (the correct Arabic name is Shawan—Spanish, Xauen; French, Chechaouen) became the cradle of the dynasty of the Beni Rashid and the capital of a little independent State. It was not until 1561 that the allegiance of its population to the Sultan of Morocco was obtained, and for a century it appears to have been governed by representatives from Fez. Its remote position, its defences, and the natural strength of its site led once more to a declaration of independence, and Sheshuan remained, until the Spanish occupation in 1920, entirely outside the jurisdiction of the Moorish Sultans. Its seclusion had seldom been disturbed. Until the Spanish troops entered it, as far as is known, it had only been visited by three Europeans—the French explorer, de Foucauld, in the garb of a Moroccan Jew, in 1883; by myself, disguised as a native in 1889; and a few years later by Mr. William Summers, a missionary. Mr. Summers was discovered and his food was poisoned, from the effects of which he nearly succumbed. His health was permanently injured and he died a few years later. Of the three I alone survive.

The situation of Sheshuan is charming. It lies on a spur of the mountain of Jibel Mezjel, on a plateau rich in orchards threaded by a multitude of little streams. Straight above the houses on the one side great precipices rise to the summit of the mountain, while on the other a descent leads to the irrigated fields and fruit gardens. No town in Morocco boasts so picturesque a site, nor is the little walled town itself less attractive, with its minarets and its old feudal castle and its tiled houses, for the heavy falls of snow in winter render the flat housetops of Morocco impossible. It reminded de Foucauld of some bourg on the Rhine, but left upon me rather the impression of a small town in the mountains of Northern Italy. There is little that is Moorish in its features, and even the square minarets are more like the Campanile of Italian churches than the minarets of a mosque. The mystery that has always surrounded the little town, with its 6,000 or 7,000 inhabitants, its seclusion and its remoteness, have given it a renown perhaps beyond its deserts. To the Moor it was a symbol of sanctity and independence, a Holy Place undefiled by Christian influences and untroubled by the presence of any authority representing the Moorish Government. None the less it was the centre of pillage and lawlessness, and, sacred as it was, the people of Sheshuan were constantly the victims of extortion and blackmail on the part of the surrounding Jibala tribes. Its occupation by the Spaniards was a dagger-thrust into the heart of the Jibala confederation.

As a military expedition the advance on Sheshuan had been neither prudent nor successful. It is true the objective was reached and the political result was important, but that was all. Three Spanish columns were to have converged on the town, two operating from Tetuan and the third from Laraiche. One column alone, that which followed the direct road from Tetuan to Sheshuan, arrived at its destination. The second was held up to the West, while the third never penetrated the mountain districts that lay between Alcazar and the objective. The losses of that column were heavy, but no doubt the presence of a Spanish force on the flank facilitated the march of the troops which

were approaching Sheshuan from the North and which
eventually reached it.

The Jibala tribes counter-attacked on October the
21st, and a serious battle was fought on the outskirts
of the town, in which the Spaniards lost eleven officers
and 120 men. The rejoicings of the first days of enthusiasm in Madrid were damped by this unexpected
encounter, for the reports that had been received had
stated that little or no resistance had been met with
or was expected.

It was clear, however, that the advance had been
undertaken without the necessary precaution of protecting the lines of communication. Nearly 40 miles
separated Sheshuan from Tetuan, and for practically the
whole distance the mountains that flanked the track were
held by the enemy. To the East, high above the road
rose the peaks of Beni Said and Beni Hassan, and farther
to the South of the Akhmas, while on the West, Raisuli
at Tazrut held the key of the situation. Along its whole
length the line of communication was open to constant
attack on ground very advantageous to the attacking
forces. This was made clear in a message sent to *The
Times* at that moment, which was afterwards acknowledged as a just criticism of the actual situation. It
was pointed out that the failure of General Barrera's
column advancing from Laraiche to reach its objective
had rendered the position of the Tetuan column extremely critical, in spite of its success. Little of the
surrounding district had been occupied, and the
Spaniards could almost at any moment be cut off in
Sheshuan from their base. The submissions of the
tribes through whose country the column had advanced
could not be considered as permanent, and at any moment

I

acts of hostility might be expected. General Barrera's failure to force his way through from the West had encouraged the resistance of the tribes of that region, and only four days before the Tetuan column reached Sheshuan the Laraiche troops had been heavily attacked, losing eight officers and over sixty men. The rainy season was beginning, when all the tracks would become impracticable for wheel traffic, and the cold in the mountain districts was already severe. The troops had fought valiantly, but it could not be concealed that the occupation of Sheshuan at the beginning of winter by only one of the three converging columns was neither strategically nor politically a prudent undertaking. Not only were the rigours of the season to be feared, but that sinister individual Raisuli still hovered on the flank.

This telegram of *The Times*, reproduced in Madrid, caused a considerable stir and increased the nervous apprehension which every effort of the Government failed to stifle. A few days sufficed to confirm this criticism of the situation, and the military authorities, and the Government itself, were bitterly attacked for engaging upon an adventure without taking sufficient precautions to safeguard the lines of communication. Revelations followed—the usual distressing revelations. The troops were ill-provided, the medical service was totally inadequate, and the artillery insufficient. The Government's reply, too, was the usual one : ' We have done the best we could with the credits at our disposal. If you want better organization and better material, the Cortes must grant more money.' But the Cortes was not inclined to grant more money, for its members were not certain how much of what they already sup-

SHESHUAN.

Photo. Alberti.

plied reached its right destination. There was no guarantee that larger credits would remedy the situation, or even improve it.

For four years (1920–1924) the Spaniards maintained their position in Sheshuan, at times in peace, often with difficulty. In 1924 the situation, owing to the campaign of Mohammed ben Abdel Krim in the Rif, became so critical that the garrison was withdrawn, a strong relief column having been dispatched from Tetuan for this purpose. With immense difficulty and at the cost of many thousands of casualties Sheshuan was evacuated. Less than two years later (1926), when the energy and the ability of General Primo de Rivera had restored the prestige of Spain in Morocco, and when the Spanish Army had given brilliant examples of admirable qualities in the field, Sheshuan was reoccupied almost without a shot being fired. But much was to happen before that came about.

# CHAPTER V

## THE RELIEF OF SHESHUAN

On September the 13th, 1923, General Primo de Rivera, by a *coup d'état*, changed the order of things in Spain. The actual Government was in a state of more than usual confusion and Morocco was as usual the cause. The recent battles at Afrau and Tifarauin in the Rif had led to a renewed outcry against the military command in Africa. General Martinez Anido, who was held responsible, was recalled, and the aged General Weyler had been sent on a mission of inquiry to Melilla. The High Commissioner in Morocco was Señor Silvela, a civilian.

The Report of General Weyler brought about still another ministerial crisis at Madrid. Señor Villanueva, the Finance Minister, basing his facts on the Weyler revelations and on his own experience, published a brief survey of the Moroccan policy of the preceding years and gave the figures of what it had cost. In 1920, £6,600,000 had been spent; in 1921, £20,800,000; and from January the 1st, 1922, to March the 23rd, 1923, £16,000,000—and the sums were increasing rather than growing less. There was, he stated, no end in sight. All the war material, both in Spain and in Morocco, was in bad condition and required complete renewal. 'The scandals continue,' he wrote. 'We buy barley at double the market price,'—' The hospitals are pitiful,

116

everything is hopeless.' Under these circumstances he
concluded the only path left open to him was to resign
his seat in the Ministry. Two of his colleagues followed
suit. The Government, weakened by the resignation
of three Ministers, issued a long communiqué to the
public. It threw but very little light upon the situation, but was full of good resolutions and vague promises
and explanations. It excused the Ministry for the
ambiguity of the language, on the grounds that if they
spoke more clearly the Rifis would learn the intentions
of the Government and take advantage of this knowledge. This communiqué was but another proof that
the Government of Señor Garcia Prieto was floundering
in the mud of incapacity and inherited disorder. Still
nothing was known of the coming *coup d'état*. The
Madrid press seems to have accepted the inevitable
muddle and was in its majority inclined to support the
existing Government, probably because it was realized
that any succeeding one would be likely to be as bad
if not worse. Every one, however, was sick of the war
in the Rif, and of the inefficiency and failure that had
marked so much of its progress. The Generals were
known to be on bad terms with each other. The sentence
on General Berenguer, the late High Commissioner,
who had been held responsible for much that had
led to the defeat of Anual in July, 1921, was expected
from day to day, and the Madrid world was nervous,
irritable and restive. Morocco was going through a
period of more than usual unpopularity. It was described as not only the grave of the youth of Spain, but
also the bottomless pit down which the national wealth
was being poured. It is no wonder that the Spaniards
were weary of the whole question. Injustice and dis-

content in the promotion of officers had brought into
existence the 'Juntas' of the Army, and with the
'Juntas' came new quarrels and new jealousies and
renewed anarchy. Even the expeditionary corps in
Morocco was divided against itself on the question of
promotion by seniority or promotion by deserts. Both
points of view had their partisans, according to the
interests at stake. Since Anual, the disaster of 1921,
the position had not improved. The Army had had
little opportunity of revindicating its honour, and had
been deeply humiliated by the fact that the release of
the Spanish prisoners in the Rif had been brought
about not by victories in the field but by purchase. It
had looked on impotently while Spanish gold ransomed
its soldiers and its chiefs. Anual, Arruit, Zeluan—half
a dozen disasters remained to be wiped out, and the
Army was incapable of doing it because it lacked everything necessary to victory—from loyalty amongst the
commanding officers to boots for the men. The civil
and military authorities, between whom a complete
understanding and unity of purpose was necessary,
were openly at daggers drawn. The Government was
occupied in useless recrimination and discussion. The
Supreme Council of the Army and Navy was to meet
at once to conclude the trials of Generals Berenguer
and Cavalcanti. On October the 1st the Cortes was
to resume its sittings. Its programme was as ever the
discussion of political responsibility for the 1921 disaster
—twenty-seven months after it had occurred! There
was nothing to look forward to but recrimination for
the past and reiterated good intentions for the future—
to end where all such protestations of repentance had
always ended. The moment was ripe for a *coup d'état*.

It was even necessary if Spain was to be saved. Still nothing leaked out of the impending stroke of fate until two days before it fell. On September the 11th, a type-written copy of a manifesto reached the Prime Minister, Señor Garcia Prieto. It was a short document. It accused the Government of having countenanced anarchy in Spain and worse than anarchy in Morocco. The garrison of Barcelona, that stronghold of independent thought and liberal activity, had decided to overthrow the existing régime, and sought the aid and support of the Madrid troops. Señor Garcia Prieto seems to have been satisfied that the Madrid garrison would not respond to this appeal, on the assurance of the Captain-General of the Capital to that effect.

The following day (September the 12th) the Barcelona garrison mutinied, but the central Government, assured of the loyalty of the rest of the army, remained completely inactive. At nine o'clock that night a Cabinet Council was held which sat till dawn, its seance prolonged by the disquieting news that from time to time reached it. The King was at San Sebastian. The Prime Minister telegraphed to him, begging him to come to Madrid. The message gave a meagre account of what had occurred and was worded optimistically. The King replied that a storm prevented his immediate departure by car from San Sebastian, but he would return to the Capital by the first available train.

The date fixed for the *coup d'état* had been September the 14th, but events demanded that it should be put forward by twenty-four hours—an unusual proceeding in Spain, where delays were the order of the day. General Primo de Rivera had already announced by telegram to the Minister of War in Madrid that the garrison of

Barcelona had denounced the existing Parliamentary régime. The reply of the Cabinet was to dispatch the Minister of Public Works to the Catalan capital with instructions to dissuade Primo de Rivera from proceeding any further on an anti-Constitutional campaign. This worthy gentleman got as far as Saragossa, where he was invited to return to the Capital by the earliest train. At Barcelona, at Valencia and at Saragossa itself a state of siege was proclaimed. And yet in Madrid the Central Government seems to have remained convinced that the garrison of the Capital would refuse to countenance the action of their comrades elsewhere. A further inquiry, however, brought a reply from the Captain-General of Madrid that he still held himself responsible for the loyalty of the Madrid army to the King, *but not to the Government*. It was the death-warrant of the Civil Administration.

On September the 13th, from far and wide came the news that the government of the country had been taken over by the soldiers, but that law and order reigned everywhere. In Madrid alone the Ministers were still recognized, though powerless. They, and the people, waited the arrival of the King and the decision that he might make.

On September the 14th, King Alfonso reached the Capital, having travelled by the night train from San Sebastian. He was met at the station by the Ministry, but the usual group of General officers was absent, the Captain-General and the Military Governor alone being present. At ten o'clock Señor Garcia Prieto announced that the Government had resigned. At eleven the Captain-General waited upon the King in the Royal Palace to receive His Majesty's instructions. At a little

after midday it was announced that General Primo
de Rivera had been summoned to Madrid to form a
Government.

Without a struggle the Constitutional régime had
disappeared, and no one except the parties who had
directly benefited by it seemed to regret its disappearance or even to care.

In Morocco Spain had accomplished little ; but in
Spain the Moors had brought about a revolution and
upset the Constitution. A succession of armies from
the Peninsula had only succeeded in occupying a portion
of the Spanish zone, while a few hundred Moorish tribesmen had drained the treasury of Spain. The Rifis had
cleared the board with the loss of a few pawns and a
castle and had cried check to the King. It was indeed
time that something was done !

The first note that the President of the new Directory
of Spain, General Primo de Rivera, Marqués de Estella,
issued (September the 13th, 1923), gave a somewhat detailed description of the general situation and announced
the intention of the new Government to put an end to disorder by introducing a new policy with regard to Morocco
in accordance with the financial means at the disposal
of the Government and compatible with the honour of
Spain. The following day, referring to this subject,
General Primo de Rivera criticized the methods that
had been adopted heretofore in Morocco as ' the most
expensive, the most protracted, the most useless and
the most unworthy.' He had, he said, no intention
whatever of confusing national honour with the Morocco
question, any more than he had of showing weakness.
His object would be to keep within the means at the
disposal of the State the solution of a problem that

had become an agonizing anxiety for the country.
He proposed therefore to set about a complete reorganization of the system in existence, both in Morocco itself
and in the Departments of the Government at Madrid
that were responsible for its administration, ' where,'
as he said, ' all this confusion of order, authority, plans,
policies and systems has originated.' He took over
personally the control of the Morocco situation. In
the arena of Africa he was no debutant. He had served
in Morocco as a soldier. He had suffered for his opinions
on that vexed question. In March, 1917, he had made
a speech at Cadiz in which he had proposed the exchange
of Gibraltar for Ceuta, and the abandonment by Spain of
her African zone. The consequence of this speech had
been dismissal from his post. It was no wonder that
this sudden advent to power of a man in whose hands
the destiny of Spain lay, was regarded not only at home
but in every country in Europe and in America with
the greatest interest.

The situation in Africa had changed since the day
when, in 1917, General Primo de Rivera had counselled
withdrawal. Abandonment to-day was beset with
insuperable difficulties. To withdraw the large forces
which Spain had concentrated in her African zone would
mean the return to the Mother-land of an army deprived
of the possibilities of glory, of promotion and of honours
—an inevitable prey to discontent. Once more, as at
the moment of the loss of Spain's colonies, there would
be nothing for the Army to look ahead to but a dreary
existence of provincial garrison life on pay that was
insufficient for more than the bare necessities of existence—and an end to all ambition. To attempt to bring
the Army back to Spain under these circumstances would

SPANISH BOMBARDMENT ON THE ROAD TO SHESHUAN.

be an invitation to further trouble at home. General Primo de Rivera himself had set an example by overthrowing the Constitutional Government, an act which, however illegal, had caused no disturbance in the country's life. Could the returning Army, if Morocco was abandoned, be expected to preserve the same moderation ? Was it not more probable that in an attempt to introduce a purely military despotism the streets of the cities of Spain would run with blood ? It must not be forgotten that the Army had still failed to attain victory, that it still felt most deeply the humiliation of the defeat of Anual which no opportunity had yet been given to the soldiers to wipe out. To abandon Africa for Spain, to exchange the field of battle with all its possibilities and chances for the barracks of the provincial towns of their own country, would at any time have been hard. It was rendered still more hard because the advantageous pay for African service would be lost. But it was hardest of all in that the Army would leave Africa with its honour unretrieved, for the one success of recent years that could be claimed, the occupation of Sheshuan in 1920, was far from sufficient to wipe out Anual and the story of the Spanish prisoners in the Rif. General Primo de Rivera realized this. He knew full well that by his suppression of the Constitutional Government of Spain he had won the animosity of all classes of the professional politicians. He could not afford to add to this burden of opposition the antagonism of the Army. He must find a compromise. His first act was to examine the situation. It was not a brilliant one.

The successive Governments of Spain had left him a burden that few would have voluntarily undertaken to shoulder, and any man, no matter how patriotic his motives, might have been forgiven for turning back upon the threshold. His advent to power at this critical moment in the history of Spain was not by any means unanimously popular, and the soldiers looked with suspicion upon the dictatorship of one who was believed to be desirous of a general retirement from Morocco, even before the Army had wiped out the humiliation of its past discomfiture.

General Berenguer's activity had, it is true, brought about in 1920 the occupation of Sheshuan and the valley of the Wad Lau ; but however successful these operations appeared to be upon the map and in the Press, they were realized in many quarters from the very first to be merely rendering the Spanish position more precarious than ever. The occupation of distant points, connected with the base only by long lines of communication through hostile country, and by their nature very difficult to maintain, could only weaken the position of Spain, never strong, in the Western zone. It amounted to little more than a successful adventure necessitating a large addition to the isolated Spanish Posts that already were a weakness. General Berenguer had resigned the High Commissionership in 1922 and General Burguete was nominated in his stead. As had nearly always been the case in Spanish Morocco, the change of High Commissioner brought about also a change of policy. General Burguete, on taking over the command, had ceased all preparations for an advance and opened a political campaign the object of which was peace with the enemy. He had obtained, after long negotiations, in January, 1923, the liberation of the Spanish prisoners in the Rif, the survivors of the many who had been taken after the fall of Anual and Monte Arruit in 1921. The Spanish Government paid a sum of nearly £150,000 as a ransom. The state of these unfortunate beings was pitiable almost beyond description. In rags and broken by every kind of suffering, they presented a picture so lamentable that, when they were taken on board the ship sent to the Rif coast for the purpose of bringing them away, many of the crew were in tears. There was no cruelty, no degradation they had not suffered. General Navarro himself, who was amongst those handed over, had been kept for a time in a dungeon chained to a Spanish sergeant. In a room 3 metres square eighteen officers had been confined. Three had died of typhus. Of the 570 prisoners only 274 survived. It was no wonder that their state awoke at once the pity and the hate of Spain.

Such events, such humiliations, could not fail to exert a very considerable influence psychologically, and the effect in the Peninsula was soon felt. It took the form of a wave of indecision. No one seemed to have a remedy to propose for the amelioration of the state of affairs in Morocco or even the spirit to propose one. The Rifis were kept fully informed of the spirit of hesitation that existed from one end of Spain to the other, and they did not fail to take advantage of it. Abdel Krim redoubled his propaganda and his prestige increased. He seized this opportunity to exert his influence amongst the Jibala tribes. Freed from anxiety by the new pacific policy of General Burguete, he turned his attention to his great and only rival Raisuli, who, though ill at Tazrut, his stronghold in the Beni Aros tribe, was still a menace to the Rifi cause in the West. But a quarrel with one of his followers, almost a youth, was destined to do incalculable harm to Raisuli's cause. After a successful raid on the part of his men, Raisuli, whose avarice seemed ever to be increasing, deprived the band of what they considered their legitimate share of the plunder. None dared to protest except a certain very young tribesman of the Beni Hozmar tribe, Ahmedo Heriro by name. With a courage that was as remarkable as it was probably unwise, he told Raisuli what he thought of him, and before there was time for punishment he fled with a few followers and offered his services to Abdel Krim. They were made welcome. By an exhibition of great personal courage, by masterly leadership and by unswerving devotion, Heriro, whose origin was of the humblest, became the principal lieutenant of the Rifis in the Western zone. His one great and overpowering ambition was to have revenge on Raisuli. In the end he succeeded.

Raisuli was supporting the Spaniards, loyally if not enthusiastically, and there is no doubt that throughout all this period, when General Burguete had persuaded him to forget the animosity of his predecessor General Berenguer, Raisuli's intentions were to aid Spain and at the same time to prevent the spread of Abdel Krim's influence into country which he had learned to consider as his own.

The Spaniards were threatened on the Melilla front with a Rifi offensive, and in order to prevent the sending of troops from the Western zone to reinforce their army in that direction, Abdel Krim instructed Heriro to open a campaign of aggression against the Spanish Posts and Spanish convoys in the region of Tetuan. It was this dual threat that had brought matters to a climax and caused the *coup d'état*, but by that time General

Burguete had already been deprived of the High Commissionership on the occasion of a change of Government in Madrid, and Señor Silvela, a civilian, was at that moment the head of the Spanish Government in Morocco. General Primo de Rivera immediately replaced him by General Aizpuru.

The first few months of the Directory saw no great changes in the state of Spanish Morocco. The attention of the Government was largely occupied with home affairs, with the reorganization of the army in Morocco, and with the Conference which was being held in Paris on the vexed question of Tangier. The rainy season put an early stop to hostilities, and it was not until the following February (1924) that the Rifis began to show activity, this time on the Melilla front, near Tizi Azza and Dar el-Midar. Abdel Krim had not been idle, and during the winter months he had reorganized his forces and strengthened his relations with the Jibala tribes. In the Ghomara, too, between the Rif and Jibala, he had collected a considerable ' harka ' for the purpose of the invasion of the occupied district of the Wad Lau, and for the cutting of the Spanish communications between Sheshuan and Tetuan. This Western Rifi offensive, however, did not begin until May, when the Wad Lau Posts were suddenly attacked.

There was no doubt that General Primo de Rivera was already convinced that unless some radical change was made in the plan of campaign in Morocco the war would be protracted indefinitely. A great responsibility rested upon him. He had promised—it was, in fact, the principal reason for his *coup d'état*—to put an end to the humiliating situation existing in Africa, and already many months had passed and little or nothing

had been accomplished.    All initiative still rested in the
hands of the enemy, who had again attacked in force.
For the Spaniards, to advance farther into the Rif presented no temptation.    It would only be a continuation
of a policy of adventure and multiply the already too
numerous Posts scattered far and wide over the country.
General Primo de Rivera decided on a course which,
while it prejudiced his popularity with the Army, was
both reasonable and wise.    He made it quite clear,
without at this moment entering upon the details of his
plan, that all the troops were to be brought back to
bases nearer the coast, and the outlying Posts to be
abandoned.    It was a policy of sacrifice, but any
sacrifice was better than running the risks of a second
Anual.    It was intended, while only occupying certain
less exposed districts of the zone, which could be easily
defended behind a strong line, to leave the rest in the
jurisdiction of two chiefs, nominated by the Khalifa
of the Sultan and confirmed by the Spanish Government
—Abdel Krim in the Rif and Raisuli in the Jibala.    It
was no easy policy to carry out, for it would mean the
abandonment of certain tribes, that throughout had been
loyal to Spain, to the tender mercies of the Chiefs against
whom they had fought.    The Spanish authorities trusted
to be able to maintain friendly relations not only with
these great Chiefs themselves but also with the tribesmen.    At any rate it seemed to General Primo de
Rivera the only feasible solution of Spain's troubles in
Morocco.

Already the situation was becoming critical.    Fighting
was taking place far behind the Spanish line of advanced
Posts, and in the early days of July the sound of distant
guns was often audible in Tangier from the direction of

Tetuan, and the needless war with all the sufferings it entailed was in full blast again.

It was a tragedy for the Spaniards that, at the moment when they hoped peace might be in sight, when they were on the point of withdrawing their outlying garrisons and of abandoning their scattered Posts, Abdel Krim should have launched this new offensive. By the end of the first week in July practically all the Wad Lau Posts were besieged and an expeditionary force was attempting their relief. It needed a considerable effort to prevent the war reaching the very walls of Tetuan. So close was the fighting to the Capital of the Spanish zone that on the 29th of June twenty Spanish aeroplanes made over fifty flights and dropped more than 600 bombs on the villages of the immediate neighbourhood to the South of the town. These tribal villages consist of large agglomerations of thatched houses. The tribesmen were absent fighting, but the women and children were reported to have been in the villages and to have suffered heavily. The Moors had already begun to look upon these ' Christian methods of warfare,' as they called them, as inevitable ; but any Spanish soldier who fell into their hands at this period was lucky indeed if he escaped torture and mutilation before being put to death.

In the second week in July General Primo de Rivera arrived in Tetuan. At the moment of his leaving Madrid the *Gazette* published a Royal Decree ordering the reorganization of the administration of Spanish Morocco and concentrating all powers exercised by Spain under the existing treaties in the hands of the High Commissioner, General Aizpuru. With General Primo de Rivera's arrival in Tetuan a new period of

K

activity was initiated.  His stay there was of sufficient
duration to allow of his paying a hurried visit to Sheshuan
and the Wad Lau front, but there was an indication
of increasing hostilities, and during the whole of his visit
aeroplanes were busily engaged in bombing the hills
to the South of Tetuan.  A certain number of the Wad
Lau Posts had been relieved by the expeditionary force
that had been dispatched for that purpose, but the two
columns penetrating the Lau valley from the East and
West respectively had met with so much opposition
that they had failed to effect a junction.

July passed without any change at the front, but the
enemy pressure was surely if slowly increasing.  Early
in August reinforcements began to arrive from Spain,
and the official communiqué issued at Madrid described
the situation as being complicated ' by a general rising
of the tribes.'  On August the 13th more of the Spanish
Posts were cut off and new districts went over to the
enemy.  There were desertions, too, amongst the native
troops.  On the 17th Madrid announced still further
revolts, and the Beni Hassan and Ghomara tribes were
officially reported as attacking in a determined manner.
Posts, it was acknowledged, had been lost, and the road
between Tetuan and Sheshuan was threatened.  The
treachery of the Beni Said tribesmen rendered the
situation still more difficult, for their country lay
between Tetuan and Sheshuan and the Wad Lau front.
Nor was it the enemy alone that hampered the Spanish
movements.  Heat and thirst rendered their task at
times almost beyond human endurance, and three
columns under the command of General Serrano were
obliged for these reasons to retire to the Wad Lau base
at the mouth of the river of that name.  Nor was the

Phot. Phot.

PLAZA DE ESPAÑA, TATUAN.

Laraiche district free from trouble, and even near the Fondak of Ain Jedida on the Tangier-Tetuan road a Spanish camp was heavily attacked. Abdel Krim had turned his whole attention to the Western seat of war. The Wad Lau-Sheshuan front was only held with difficulty and no longer served any useful purpose, for the natives had risen far behind it, and by isolating and beseiging the Posts, were able to communicate with the Rif without let or hindrance. It was with great difficulty that provisions and ammunition could reach rich positions as were accessible, and the convoys were constantly attacked. On August the 24th the Wad Lau columns stormed the enemy positions on the hills overlooking the valley and drove them back, but the Spaniards suffered heavily, no less than five officers being killed with corresponding losses amongst the men. There were at this period 90,000 Spanish troops, counting native soldiers, on this Western front of the Spanish zone, and yet fighting continued almost under the walls of Tetuan.

On August the 28th the Spanish Government issued a communiqué at Madrid that did not disguise how serious the situation had become. After describing the natural difficulties of the country, the rugged mountains and the almost impenetrable brushwood, the communiqué stated that it was thirst rather than sickness or casualties that was retarding the success of the relief of the besieged posts. Heavy rains, too, had fallen, long before the usual wet season, and had alternated with spells of great heat, which had seriously affected the health of the army. With the exception of the Tetuan-Sheshuan road, little more than goat-tracks existed in the country, and generally the troops had to advance in single file. The

only means of provisioning the Wad Lau front was by
sea, but there was no shelter for the ships, and gales had
been of constant occurrence.  It was as often as not
impossible to disembark.  The troops bore these hard-
ships with courage and resignation, but it was not a
brilliant or a hopeful picture.

On September the 1st General Primo de Rivera, who
had returned to Madrid, announced that the situation
was far from satisfactory and that 6,000 more soldier
(eight battalions) were being sent to the front from
Spain.  His communiqué ended with a statement that
affairs were developing in a manner that necessitated
the greatest efforts, serenity and a firm determination
On September the 3rd a further communiqué warned
the people of Spain to be prepared for operations of a
very important character, for many more Posts were
now endangered.  The rising, it said, was now general;
it was a real war between Spain and Morocco.  On the
same day the Spanish Embassy in London announced
the fall of several positions.

But it was not only in the Tetuan-Sheshuan-Wad Lau
region that the enemy were showing great activity, for
the Tangier-Tetuan road was in their hands and the
telegraph and telephone lines were cut.  By September
Spain had 100,000 men in the Western part of her zone
of whom 60,000 were in the Tetuan district.  The
organization of such a force was putting a great strain
upon the Spanish authorities.  The newly-arrived soldiers were mostly quite insufficiently trained, and had
no idea of how to handle their rifles.  They were courageous and willing, but they had been brought straight
from their barracks in Spain into the midst of a most
difficult and trying kind of warfare.  The officers were

wanting in experience, and lacking in enthusiasm. The enemy were efficient, mobile and cruel. The hospitals were full.

Sheshuan was still accessible, but with difficulty, and the convoys suffered much. In the first days of September a number of motor lorries were destroyed by the enemy, who on the Wad Lau front had captured several Posts with their artillery and stores intact. Large quantities of arms and ammunition had fallen into their hands. On September the 1st a battle was fought within 2 miles of Tetuan and the troops of the garrison were engaged. A few miles to the West of the town the large camp of Lauzien was completely isolated and insecurity existed up to the very walls of the Capital of the Spanish zone.

On September the 5th General Primo de Rivera at Madrid announced that the situation necessitated his presence in Morocco, and that Admiral Magaz would replace him as Acting President of the Directory. He left the same night for Tetuan, accompanied by Generals Jordana, Muslera and Rodriguez. This decision, taken without any previous warning, caused no little anxiety in Spain and rendered it very evident that all was not well. It was said—and there is reason to believe that it was so—that General Primo de Rivera's sudden visit to Tetuan was as much connected with the sentiments of the Army as with the actual difficulty of the military situation. There was, as he must have been aware, a strong feeling of opposition among the officers to his plan for the evacuation of so much country before some signal victory had been obtained to wipe out the bitter recollection of the past. But General Primo de Rivera could not allow the critical situation on the front to be prolonged without running the danger of another Anual—and he realized what another Anual would mean to Spain. This second visit of the Marqués de Estella to Tetuan was paid under very different circumstances to his earlier one. Then it had been all garlands and flags and coloured lanterns. To-day many of the European women and children had already left or were leaving, and enemy bullets constantly fell inside the walls of the town. From the windows of their houses, built above the city walls, the residents could watch battles taking place within a very few miles of the gates. Sick and wounded were being brought in and sent on to Ceuta, for the Tetuan hospitals were crowded.

Events in the district was moving fast. General Riquelme, with a strong force, was reported as cut off at Sok el-Arba, about half way between Tetuan and Sheshuan, and a strong column was sent to his assistance to permit of his retiring on Dar ben Karich, near Tetuan. General Quiepo de Llano commanded this relief column. He passed the night at Dar ben Karich on September the 7th and met General Riquelme's column on the following day a few miles to the South. The united columns retired on Dar ben Karich, suffering heavy losses. By this retirement from Sok el-Arba the Tetuan-Sheshuan road was now in the hands of the enemy and communications with the latter town cut. Before retiring, General Riquelme had withdrawn the garrisons of all the Posts that were within reach, and thus the upper valley of the Wad Lau had to all intents and purposes been evacuated. The security in that region was so threatened by this retirement and by the increased enemy pressure that it was decided to withdraw all the remaining garrisons, including that of the fortified camp at the mouth of the River Lau. Continual strong East winds had forced the Spanish warships to abandon the anchorage, and the situation of the camp was precarious.

Raisuli was rendering all this time a certain aid to the Spaniards, but its value was small in face of the general attitude of the tribes. His contingents had been cut off from direct contact with the Spaniards by the invasion of armed Rifi bands.

On September the 8th General Primo de Rivera ordered the evacuation of all the remaining Posts, an operation that was immediately undertaken in preparation, it was understood, for a new offensive. Twenty-nine officers and 740 men, with six pieces of artillery, were withdrawn by sea from Mter, near the mouth of the Wad Lau.

General Primo de Rivera at this juncture again publicly declared that his policy was to retire all the outlying Spanish garrisons and concentrate his forces behind a line strong enough to withstand all enemy attacks, pending the opening of political action for an understanding with the tribesmen of the Rif and Jibala. The line that he intended to hold was now made public. It extended from the Mediterranean shore, a little to the South-East of Tetuan, along the northern slopes of the mountains facing that town to the Fondak of Ain Jedida, thence turning southward and running almost parallel to the Atlantic Ocean as far as the frontier of the Spanish-French zones to the East of Alcazar. But before this plan could be put into practice, the garrison of Sheshuan, now entirely cut off, must be relieved, and 40,000 troops were collected for this purpose in the neighbourhood of Tetuan.

The advance began on September the 23rd by a series of local movements, principally with a view to the

occupation of strategic positions near the base. General
Aizpuru de Mondejar was the nominal commander in
the field, but it was well known that General Primo
de Rivera was the originator and organizer of the
expedition, and on him the whole responsibility rested.
The advance of the troops was preceded by the distribu-
tion by aeroplane of an immense number of manifestos
to the tribes, printed in Arabic. These manifestos
stated that there was no intention on the part of the
Spaniards to abandon Morocco, and threatened the
rebellious tribes with severe chastisement. At the same
time an order to the Spanish troops was issued by General
Aizpuru. He stated that the task of the Tetuan forces
would be rendered easier by a simultaneous advance
of a Spanish army from Laraiche, but that each force
would retain its complete liberty of initiative and action.
A steady advance was to be maintained throughout
the whole operation, and no defensive action would be
fought except to protect the flanks of the columns.
'Not for one minute,' the order continued, 'must the
honour of the Spanish Army be retarded, or the deliver-
ance of the Spanish troops whom it is sent to save be
delayed.' He threatened with dire punishment those
who might forget their duty through idleness, negligence
or want of energy. He urged the Army to chastise
severely the tribes, to burn their villages and to pillage
their cattle. It had all the appearances of being the
order of a man who had little confidence in the soldiers
under his command.

The army destined to relieve Sheshuan—for it fulfilled
its mission—was divided into four columns. One,
under the command of Colonel Ovilo, was to proceed
by the main Tetuan-Sheshuan road ; while along the

mountain-tops to the East a second column, under General Castro Girona, was to make a parallel advance. To the West of the road, in touch always with Colonel Ovilo's column, was a force under General Serrano. A fourth column, commanded by General Frederico Berenguer, a brother of the former High Commissioner of Morocco, was held in reserve at the base at Dar ben Karich.

The very first day's march demonstrated that the contact between the columns was a matter of great difficulty. General Castro Girona met with serious resistance in the rugged mountain-tops near Dar Rai, and on September the 25th was forced to descend to the valley, finding further advance along the heights impossible. He joined Colonel Ovilo's column on the Sheshuan road. This of course left the left flank of the united column exposed to attack from the East, where the mountains of Beni Hassan rose directly from the road. The whole plan of advance was modified and General Castro Girona's and General Serrano's forces were sent on in advance to occupy positions along the road ahead and thus facilitate the advance of Colonel Ovilo's column with the artillery and transport. On September the 27th General Castro Girona reached Sok el-Arba—the position which General Riquelme had been obliged, so short a time before, to evacuate. Sok el-Arba is almost exactly half way between Tetuan and Sheshuan. On the 28th he occupied the surrounding heights. The enemy did not react till September the 28th, when a series of attacks were made upon the Spanish convoys between Sok el-Arba and the base at Dar ben Karich. News reached the relieving forces that Sheshuan was holding out with no great effort, but that difficulty was being experienced in provisioning the outlying Posts and block-houses.

Meanwhile in the Laraiche region no very serious attempts to reach Sheshuan from that direction seem to have been made. The concentration of the enemy on the Tetuan-Sheshuan front was, however, taken advantage of to relieve a number of Spanish Posts that were in difficulties further to the West. Raisuli was still at Tazrut, but it was proposed, owing to the Spanish withdrawal from the neighbouring region, that he should retire to Arzeila under the protection of the Spanish troops. It was considered very undesirable that he should be left exposed to the direct attack of Abdel Krim's Rifis. No matter if the aid Raisuli was actually rendering to the Spaniards was insignificant, the very fact of his prestige and that he still declared himself a friend of Spain was an asset of considerable value, and the Spanish authorities were desirous that no ill should befall him. He, however, in spite of much pressure, refused to abandon Tazrut, partly no doubt because he was very ill, partly because he refused to separate himself from the vast stores of grain and arms and ammunition that he possessed there, the transport of which to the coast was out of the question, and partly, very likely, because he had no very real confidence in the Spanish authorities. He liked to pretend, too, that his position was such that no one would venture to molest him, and that if they did, he was invincible.

As the distance between the Spanish columns advancing on Sheshuan and their base increased, the enemy pressure became more marked. General Primo de Rivera and General Jordana, visiting the troops near Dar Karich, were ambushed and nearly lost their lives.

SPANISH TROOPS ADVANCING.

*Photo, Dini.*

On September the 30th, General Serrano entered Sheshuan.  He found the town sufficiently provisioned and the garrison in tolerable spirits, but the number of sick and wounded had been, and was, a great strain on their resources.  The same day that Sheshuan was successfully relieved, the Laraiche troops fought a serious engagement in the Beni Aros, during the evacuation of a series of Posts.  Three Spanish columns were engaged and the losses were heavy.  The enemy claimed to have captured guns and a large quantity of arms and ammunition, and the important Spanish camp of Sok el-Khamis was completely isolated.  So serious was the situation of these surrounded troops that the Spanish authorities of Tetuan had to resort to the expenditure of large sums of money in order to procure their retirement.

Immediately after the Spanish troops had entered Sheshuan, the tribesmen, led by Abdel Krim's Rifis, occupied the heights above the road leading to Tetuan. There had been little resistance to the Spanish advance, but the enemy were determined to render their retirement very difficult if not impossible.  On October the 1st a convoy returning empty to Tetuan was attacked and forty motor lorries destroyed.  All along the road the troops whose duty it was to keep the communications open were being harassed.  As fast as possible, and whenever occasion allowed, the sick and wounded were evacuated under strong escort, and preparations were made for the complete abandonment of the town. The season was already advanced and rain had fallen. At any moment the road might become impracticable. In order to withdraw the few remaining garrisons of the upper Wad Lau Posts as quickly as possible recourse was made again to money. Meanwhile the troops on and near the Ghomara coast, farther East between the Jibala and the Rif, were withdrawn by sea, to be followed on November the 15th by the abandonment of all the remaining Wad Lau positions, the troops being embarked by night on warships sent for the purpose. The enemy seemed to have been quite unaware of this skilful withdrawal, and the first they learned of it was the concentrated bombardment of the abandoned camp and Posts by the Spanish warships, a precaution lest the large quantity of material left behind should fall into the possession of the enemy. To the West, too, the retirement continued, and all the outlying Posts of the Laraiche district were being one by one evacuated, an operation greatly retarded by bad weather.

General Aizpuru, the High Commissioner, whose health was said to be precarious, had resigned in the middle of October and General Primo de Rivera had himself succeeded him. He did not, however, abandon his position as President of the Spanish Directory, which he continued to hold in conjunction with his new post of High Commissioner in Morocco. Almost his first act was once more to take the public of Spain into his confidence, with a frankness and sincerity that are very typical of his character. He did not hesitate publicly to criticize the actions of his predecessors for having strewn Morocco with over four hundred Posts and block-houses, which, he said, absorbed over 20,000 men. Most of these Posts were cut off from water by the very fact that they had to be situated on high ground. Many had been captured by the enemy, together with large quantities of arms and ammunition. He intended, he said, to relieve all such Posts as were still

isolated, an operation that must be expected to cause
further losses. This once accomplished and the garrisons withdrawn, he would fortify the new base line,
rendering it impregnable, and he would then endeavour
to enter upon a period of negotiation with the tribes,
whose goodwill he hoped to win by the construction
of useful public works and by a policy of attraction.
His communiqué was not without criticism of the Army,
whose spirit left much to be desired. Every effort
was necessary, for the situation was critical, and the
winter rains were already beginning. The Spanish
garrison was still in Sheshuan and it was absolutely
essential that it should be withdrawn without delay.

On November the 3rd General Primo de Rivera issued
an order to the Army. ' It is regrettable,' it ran, ' that
the troops should give way at this moment to pessimism
which is destroying the moral of the army. In order
to remedy this disgraceful weakness I order all commanding officers, officers and soldiers to refrain from all
criticism or discussion of these questions, and that they
shall immediately put under arrest any military sub-
ordinate, or civilian, who may disobey me. They shall
pass them over to me to be tried by Court Martial.
Should their guilt be proved they will be executed. The
High Command of the Army is hereby authorized to
carry out this penalty upon the persons of any who
resist arrest, or show signs of disobedience in the field.'
The order concluded with an expression of General Primo
de Rivera's intention to act in all cases with the utmost
severity.

# CHAPTER VI

## EVACUATION OF SHESHUAN

Sheshuan was evacuated on November the 17th, 1924, by the Spanish forces which had formed its garrison and the relief column, in all about 10,000 men. It had been the intention of the Spanish Command to withdraw earlier, but very considerable difficulty had been experienced in the retirement of the garrisons of the outlying positions. Only one by one could these small Posts be relieved and the handful of men who had defended them rescued from their critical situation. At times these sorties occasioned more casualties than the number of men saved, and they could only be undertaken after careful preparation. It proved a slow and difficult operation. From the date on which General Primo de Rivera had taken over the command in Morocco 180 outlying Posts had already been suppressed. The wisdom of this policy was becoming more and more apparent, for, with the increase of Abdel Krim's influence in the Jibala, the existence of these Posts would have become a source of the gravest anxiety and of the gravest danger. Of the task he had set himself there remained now only the most difficult item, the evacuation of Sheshuan itself. From every point of view it was a serious undertaking. Sheshuan was a holy city and had always existed in an atmosphere of mystery and romance. Its occupation by the Spaniards in 1920 had been received in Spain with an exaggerated but comprehensible enthusiasm, and its capture was looked upon as opening a new era in Morocco. It could not, therefore, but be a matter of deep regret and disappointment that only four years later it had been found necessary to evacuate the town. The withdrawal of the garrisons of many small Posts all over the zone, and the suppressions of the Posts themselves, was comparatively a matter of indifference to the Spaniard at home ; but the abandonment of the only town of the Jibala, the name of which had become known throughout the Peninsula, was a blow that was much felt. General Primo de Rivera's popularity was affected not a little and his policy criticized, but he was not the man to be turned from any task which he had undertaken in the interests of his country. It was not long before it was realized that he had taken the right course and was guiding Spanish policy in Morocco in the right direction.

The garrison of Sheshuan abandoned the town on the morning of November the 17th. They destroyed nothing, merely taking away with them as much movable property as it was possible to transport, for it was the Spanish intention to return at a more propitious date and to reoccupy the place. This they successfully accomplished in August, 1926.

The first day's march was uneventful, but the enemy, who had allowed the Spanish relief column to reach Sheshuan almost without a shot being fired, was in wait for the retirement. They hailed with joy every delay in the date of departure, for they knew that if rain fell their task would be doubly easy. The night of November the 18th the Spanish forces camped at Dar Akoba. The following day the advance guard, under General

Castro Girona, reached Sok el-Arba, half way between Sheshuan and Tetuan. It was there that they learned that the rear-guard had been furiously attacked in a defile, where the road was commanded by high hills and the valley narrow. The long-expected rain had fallen and a storm swept the whole district. The country was a sea of mud, the road seriously damaged, and every stream flooded.

It was not until November the 21st that the news was published in Spain, and then only item by item was the truth allowed to appear. The retiring army had been attacked—a General and a Colonel had been killed—many officers were wounded—the casualties were heavy. Then more detailed reports appeared. General Serrano was dead; General Frederico Berenguer wounded—the casualties were over a thousand. The arrival at Sok el-Arba of the disordered troops was described as pitiable. The cold, the wet, and massacre had broken their nerves. Hundreds of stragglers, unable to keep up, had fallen into the hands of the enemy and had been brutally killed. Yet there had been acts of great courage and great endurance, and the Spanish soldier showed then, as he has shown over and over again in Morocco, an admirable demeanour in circumstances of appalling difficulty. The enemy took no prisoners—he merely killed—and the valley was strewn with dead.

From Sok el-Arba General Castro Girona, with the advance-guard, reached Ben Karich on November the 19th leaving the main body of the army cut off at Sok el-Arba. From all sides the tribes massed to attack the camp. The rain continued and every rivulet was a roaring torrent. Little by little, day by day, small bodies of troops fought their way through to Ben Karich, and it was not till December the 11th that the last of the Spanish forces left Sok el-Arba after having destroyed the camp and burnt what they could not transport. The final retirement had been carefully prepared. At dawn the Spanish airmen were bombing the hills on both flanks, while a column had been sent southward from the Anjera district to threaten the Beni Idir from the North and to cut off any enemy reinforcements that might be approaching from Wad Ras, further West. To the East, high above the road, a second column made a demonstration in the direction of Dar Rai, holding in check the Beni Said. Meanwhile the troops at Dar ben Karich advanced to meet the force retiring from Sok el-Arba.

Early in the day Sok el-Arba was abandoned and the troops set out, the rear-guard consisting of the Foreign Legion and native troops with armoured cars. The enemy's attack, in spite of all these precautions, was severe, and at times there was hand-to-hand fighting with knives, bayonets and clubs. The Spanish losses on that last day of the retirement were 450 killed and wounded. Colonel Villegas was killed. On December the 13th the retreat was over and the surviving soldiers of the Sheshuan garrison reached Ben Karich.

General Primo de Rivera issued the following order to the retiring army :

' You enter Tetuan in triumph, having carried out the most difficult operation, after having raised the sieges and assured the evacuation of outlying Posts. You have retired through a long valley, the hills on both sides of which were held by the enemy. This

L

was necessary in the interests and for the honour of
Spain. In realizing this operation, far more arduous
than any offensive, you have given an example of
sacrifice and of discipline. Bravo! Generals, commanding officers, officers and men.

'A new trail of Spanish blood marks the track of
civilization. . . . There is still work to be done, to
dominate the hearths of rebellion that have treacherously
been lit behind our lines while you have been away
fighting. The punishment will be quick but severe. . . .
As for me, I can only tell you that if with your helpful
aid I can render my country. any important service, I
shall be eternally grateful.

'Your General-in-Chief,
'MIGUEL PRIMO DE RIVERA.'

Further West in the Lukkus valley the Ahlserif tribe
continued in rebellion and the important Spanish camp
and Post of Meshra was isolated by the enemy. On
November the 16th Colonel Carrasco relieved the position
and was able to withdraw the majority of the garrison,
leaving a sufficient force to protect the Post. On November the 19th it was found possible to evacuate the sick and
wounded to Alcazar and at the same time the garrisons
of the smaller surrounding Posts were one by one withdrawn. Notwithstanding the presence of the enemy and
much bad weather this was successfully accomplished.

In his order to the army quoted above General Primo
de Rivera had mentioned rebellion behind the Spanish
lines. He referred to the Anjera tribe, who, with their
neighbours the Hauz and the Wad Ras, had at various
spots attacked the Spanish Posts and caused the suppression of not a few. There had been, too, a collision

at the Sok el-Khamis of Anjera and the Spanish soldiers
had suffered casualties. All the troops were engaged
elsewhere and General Primo de Rivera decided to postpone the punishment of these three tribes whose country
lay behind the ' Primo ' line till later. In the first week
of December the Spanish Post of Alcazar-Soreir, on the
Anjera coast of the Straits of Gibraltar, was surprised
and captured by the enemy, assisted by a number of
native workmen employed by the Spaniards. Several
officers were taken prisoners. Other Posts in the surrounding district fell or were abandoned.

By the end of the year General Primo de Rivera's task
was completed. The Spanish Army was back on its
permanent line along its whole front, from Tetuan to the
East of Alcazar. Block-houses within easy distance of one
another had been erected throughout its entire length
and its security was assured. The only spot behind this
line where there was any sign of rebellion was the Anjera.

The withdrawal of all the outlying Posts and garrisons,
including those of Sheshuan, had been costly. The
losses and casualties suffered in this autumn campaign
of 1924 were given as follows : Killed—one general, six
lieutenant-colonels, eight majors and 175 other officers.
About 600 officers were wounded and the casualties,
including missing, amongst the men reached 17,000.

On December the 31st General Primo de Rivera
surprised the public with another candid proclamation :

' I am every day more convinced that the surprise
attacks on the part of the enemy are much less due
to his competence than to our own incapacity and
negligence. Often the soldiers march in close order,
half asleep, their ears covered by the collars of their

cloaks and with their rifles unprepared. . . . It is indispensable and urgent that once again, and immediately, the commanders should summon all officers, and they in turn the non-commissioned officers and men, and warn them, showing them how to mount guard, how to carry out their duties, and how to march on the paths or tracks.

'No patrols should proceed in groups ; they should advance in open order with their flanks covered and protected, and with their arms ready to reply to the first shot fired at them. . . . It is incredible that after the long experience of this war it should be necessary to add these lessons to those unhappy experiences which this campaign has already taught us, and above all that it is needful to repeat the recommendation to train and to instruct on all occasions our soldiers, so obedient, so patient, so disciplined, so honest, but so confiding and so inexperienced. . . . From the date of the issue of this order every aggression of the enemy will be followed by an inquiry, and judges will establish whether the troop that has suffered attack has been properly instructed, has been accustomed to mounting guard ; if it has been daily inspected by the commanders, and if it was properly supported.

'I am resolved to escape the risks of these aggressions and surprises, the only danger which still exists, and I shall at once hold responsible those who have permitted their occurrence by want of preparation or of care, and I shall inscribe in their records a special mention, in one sense or another, as to how they have fulfilled their obligations.

'The Chief of the General Staff,
'IGNACIO DESPUJOL.'

ALHUCEMAS ISLAND FROM THE AJDIR PLAIN.

Photo, Díaz.

This order conveys the impression, and it was no
doubt for that reason it was issued, that in spite of long
experience neither the officers nor the men had yet
acquired a thorough knowledge of warfare in Morocco.

General Primo de Rivera now turned his attention to
the Anjera and the adjacent tribes. The tribesmen's
access to the Tangier zone was cut off as far as was
possible by placing a line of block-houses along a part of
the frontier of the two zones. This blockade, though not
entirely successful, certainly impeded the tribesmen
from obtaining supplies, though they often ventured to
pass between the Spanish Posts at night, risking death
and wounds rather than support the situation of semi-
starvation that the blockade occasioned them. A large
number of women almost nightly attempted to get
through, taking local produce to the Tangier market and
bringing back, if successful, supplies from there. Many
were shot in the endeavour. In time the Spaniards set
every kind of trap for them, and not a few were killed
and wounded by mines that were fired by wires laid across
the tracks. Yet these women of the Jibala never, until
the blockade was finally removed, hesitated to attempt
to get through. Often they were forced to bring their
young children with them on their backs, having nowhere
to leave them, and these innocent babies frequently shared
their mothers' fate. The submission of the Anjera, however, was only a question of time. They were separated from the other Jibala tribes by the strong ' Primo '
line and cut off from Tangier by the recently installed
block-houses. To support themselves became a matter
of great difficulty, to obtain arms and ammunition almost
impossible. Nevertheless, their revolt caused much
annoyance and some loss to the Spaniards and necessi-

tated the presence of 10,000 troops to guard the 20 miles of railway between Tetuan and Ceuta.

In the middle of January, 1925, General Primo de Rivera left Tetuan for Madrid, after many months of strenuous work in Morocco. He had already justified his policy, for the Spanish Army was firmly entrenched and in comparative security. The danger of the many hundreds of outlying Posts was finally removed. His task had been an ungrateful one, the liquidation of the inefficiency and the incompetence of the past and the reversal of General Berenguer's recent policy of conquest.

An amusing though dangerous incident occurred at this time on the frontier of the Tangier and Spanish zones. The frontier, although delimitated, had never been marked, and Spanish aeroplanes from time to time dropped bombs well inside the Tangier zone, causing not only damage to life and property but also much indignation amongst the peaceful inhabitants of the neutral territory. A dispute having arisen on one of these occasions as to the exact spot where the bombs had fallen, a Commission of the French and Spanish officers commanding the international military police of the Tangier zone and of officers from the Spanish zone met to examine the question and visited the spot. When nearing the scene of the incident, but well within the frontier of the Tangier zone, the Commission of Inquiry was heavily bombed by a Spanish aeroplane, and it was only by precipitate flight and hiding amongst the rocks that they escaped without injury. It was a somewhat convincing reply to the Spanish denials that their bombs ever fell in Tangier's neutral territory.

It was close to the frontier of the two zones, and at

a distance of not more than 10 or 12 miles from the town of Tangier, that on January the 22nd, 5,000 Spanish troops engaged the Anjera tribesmen.  The Spaniards advanced in force and installed a further succession of block-houses from the shore of the Straits of Gibraltar, along the frontier of the Spanish and Tangier zones, to join up 10 miles south with the ' Primo ' line near Ergaia.  This practically completed the blockade and rendered life in the Anjera far more difficult than it had been before.  There was scarcely a night that one or other of the block-houses was not engaged in firing on little bands of Jibala attempting to pass through the lines.  This battle of January the 22nd was entirely successful.  The troops were aided by the gunfire of Spanish warships in the Straits.

The withdrawal of the Spanish troops from practically all the Jibala districts left Raisuli at the mercy of the Rifis.  He had refused, when invited to do so, to retire with the Spanish forces back to the coast and insisted on remaining on at his stronghold at Tazrut in the Beni Aros.  He was already a very sick man.  Dropsy had swollen his legs and rendered his whole appearance unsightly.  He was immensely fat from the effects of this distressing malady.  But he was still the strong man of the Jibala, half reverenced, wholly feared, unforgiving and avaricious.  His religious prestige still stood him in good stead.  He was a Shereef, a descendant of the Prophet, and the Saint whose tomb near Tazrut is the most reverenced in North Morocco, Mulai Abdesalam ben Mashish, was his direct ancestor.  But no one who saw him as he was in these later days could have recognized the slight, sad-faced, handsome youth that I had known over thirty years before.  Firm in the belief of his own

invincibility, refusing to be separated from his fortune
and his vast stores of grain, of rifles and of ammunition,
he insisted on remaining on at Tazrut, always mocking
at the Rifis and their army.   But the departure of the
Spanish troops left the two strong men face to face—
Abdel Krim, capable, energetic and enduring, who had
already proved himself a successful leader of men, now
at the height of his popularity, and Raisuli, sick but deep
in cunning, with his arrogance and his unending belief
in his own luck.   And between the two stood Ahmedo
Heriro, sworn to revenge himself upon his former Chief
—Raisuli—and serving, for this end, his new master the
Rifi leader.   Heriro could never forget or forgive Raisuli's
slight and his injustice.   At his request Abdel Krim sent
him Rifi contingents to give backbone to his Jibala levies.
Collecting his tribesmen, fiercely urging them to fight,
Heriro attacked Tazrut.   The stronghold was captured
and Raisuli taken prisoner.   Long before any details of
the event were known, the news had spread from peak
to peak and from valley to valley.   Raisuli had fallen
—he was a prisoner of Abdel Krim !   The effect was
profound.   The tribes which had up to then remained
faithful to him went over in a body to the Rifi cause.
The Sheikh of Jibel Habib, a firm adherent of Raisuli's,
was taken prisoner by a handful of Rifis.   Kaid Ayashi
Zellal, of the Beni Msaur, fled to security behind the
Spanish lines with his family and as much of his property
as he could transport and as large a number of his flocks
and herds as he could drive away.   The Anjera, on
the point of submission, once more returned to open
revolt.

It was on Sunday, January the 25th, that Abdel
Krim's Rifi contingents and such Jibala tribesmen as

were faithful to the Rifi cause began the encircling movement of Raisuli's stronghold. On Monday they attacked. The fighting was very heavy and there were many casualties on both sides. Raisuli's men fought well against heavy odds all that day, but towards evening they were driven back on Tazrut and the Rifis closed in. On Tuesday Tazrut was taken.

Raisuli, who, sick as he was, had defended his residence up to the last, was carried through his dwelling into the adjoining mausoleum of his ancestors, where he took sanctuary. All firing then ceased. Three leaders of the Rifi party—Ahmedo Heriro, who till a few months ago had been one of Raisuli's most steadfast adherents, a secretary of Abdel Krim, by name Bu Lahya, and a certain Shawni—entered the precincts of the tomb. Raisuli, who was unable to stand or walk owing to dropsy in his legs, lay on the floor. He surrendered, stating that if his life was spared he would obey Abdel Krim's orders, whatever they might be. Seeing Ahmedo Heriro, who had led the attack against him, he chided him for his disloyalty, to be told in turn that it was Raisuli's own injustice to him that had driven him into the ranks of the Rifis.

One incident had to be explained. In the attack upon Tazrut there had been an act of treachery. Heriro had sent Raisuli a letter two days previously demanding that he should declare himself a true Moslem by joining Abdel Krim's campaign against the Spaniards, or die as an infidel and an ally of the Christian enemy. This letter Heriro had entrusted to the Kaid of Beni Lait, who had once suffered imprisonment at Raisuli's hands. In revenge the Kaid secreted the missive, declaring that he had delivered it, but that Raisuli had vouchsafed no reply. Questioned on this point by Heriro, Raisuli denied ever having received the letter, and the Kaid of Beni Lait confessed to having suppressed it. He was that night tried for having caused an unnecessary loss of life amongst Moslems engaged in Holy War. He was found guilty and shot.

After many mutual recriminations Raisuli finally reasserted to Heriro his readiness to use all his influence and all his fortune in the interests of Abdel Krim. He ordered his young son, a boy of about sixteen years of age, and his nephew, Mulai Ali, both of whom had been slightly wounded during the fighting, to proceed to Sheshuan and there surrender themselves to Abdel Krim's brother, who commanded the Rifi forces in that region. The young men bore an autograph letter from Raisuli stating that only his severe illness prevented his coming in person, and he begged the Rifi chief to come to Tazrut to discuss the terms of the surrender. A strong guard was placed round the village, where nothing was touched, nor was any member of Raisuli's family molested. His principal followers were also prisoners of the Rifis.

Wednesday broke unpropitiously, for the Spaniards at Tetuan, under the impression that Raisuli was still holding out, sent aeroplanes to bomb the Rifi contingents in the immediate neighbourhood of Tazrut. Abdel Krim's commanders at once visited Raisuli and told him to communicate immediately with Tetuan to demand that the bombing should cease and not be repeated. The Rifis suffered some losses, but Raisuli's message apparently reached Tetuan, for no further bombing took place.

A few days later orders came from Abdel Krim that Raisuli should be sent to the Rif. He was very ill, and great difficulties had to be overcome before a means of transporting him could be improvised. A strong open litter was built of rough wood, and on this, borne by a number of tribesmen, for he was very heavy, Raisuli was placed. One or two of his own slaves were permitted to attend him on this last journey. As he passed, borne shoulder high through the silent crowd, he raised himself on his elbow and cried out:

'Laugh at the fall of Raisuli! Rejoice at his humiliation! But the day is coming when you will gladly give all you possess to have him back again. It will be too late then. It is too late now. I go forth to die.'

The winter was spent by the Spanish troops in strengthening the ' Primo ' line, the definite instalment of which was now completed.

Early in March General Primo de Rivera returned to Tetuan, after less than two months' absence. He was convinced that some action in Morocco was necessary to satisfy the army in Africa and public opinion in Spain. The retirement had had a disturbing effect upon the spirits of the Spanish people, who seemed as convinced as ever that all was not well in Morocco. General Primo de Rivera's thoughts were already centred on a Spanish disembarkation on the shores of the Bay of Alhucemas and a thrust at Ajdir, in the very heart of the Rif country and the headquarters of Abdel Krim. The winter had prevented any advance upon any front, and the calm was scarcely broken, and General Primo de Rivera had ample time before hostilities could break out again to mature his plans. A certain number of the Spanish troops had been sent back to the Peninsula, but there were still 100,000 men on active service in the

Spanish zone.   General Primo de Rivera was the more
hopeful for the success of an eventual disembarkation
from the fact that on January the 30th the Spaniards
had retaken Alcazar Soreir on the coast of the Straits
of Gibraltar, after a successful landing of troops.   The
preparations had been carefully organized and the
operation was a distinct success.   Twenty Spanish warships, transports and torpedo boats were employed.   The
shore was bombarded at dawn and 6,000 men were
disembarked in fifteen large armoured lighters.   The
Spanish losses were very slight.   By midday the
operation was completed and Alcazar Soreir was once
more in the occupation of Spain.

The spring of 1925 was broken by no incident beyond
some small attacks of no importance along the ' Primo '
line, but Abdel Krim had become the undisputed chief of
the Jibala tribes and completely taken Raisuli's place.
From time to time there were rumours of peace overtures
and various attempts were made to open negotiations,
but never with success.

Early in April Raisuli died in the Rif.   He had been
carried from Tazrut to Sheshuan, and thence to the sea
on the Ghomara coast, whence he was taken to the Rif
near Alhucemas on board one of Abdel Krim's motor-
launches.   Already near death the journey was more
than the state of his health could bear.   He was always
in pain, his body swollen and his legs covered with sores.
He was hideous to look upon.   The dropsy had made
rapid strides.   He refused to eat or drink except what
was absolutely necessary to sustain life, and he spent his
time in moody silence, and when spoken to merely asked
to be left alone.   It was a terrible end for a man of his
position and pride, to die like a dog, as he described it,

the prisoner of a Rifi.  He seems to have been well
treated and to have been deprived of nothing—but his
fall was too great, his humiliation too deep.  Death
when it came must indeed have been a release to this
hard, cruel man who had treated so many others far
worse than he himself was being treated.

All through the summer of 1925 the question of peace
was again to the fore, and the terms which France and
Spain decided to offer to Abdel Krim were decided upon
at the Franco-Spanish Conference which opened at Madrid
on June the 17th.  Negotiations of a rather desultory
character were meanwhile going on both at Rabat and
Tetuan, and continued into the autumn.  Whether they
would eventually have been successful it is impossible
to say, but every chance of peace—at least of peace on
the generous terms that France and Spain had offered—
was dissipated by an event of vital importance in the
history of Morocco.  On September the 8th the Spaniards
disembarked in force on the westerly point of Alhucemas
Bay.

# CHAPTER VII

## DISEMBARKATION IN THE RIF

There is no doubt that a strong party in Spain itself was opposed to General Primo de Rivera's programme of a disembarkation at or near Alhucemas. The objections that were put forward were largely based upon the experiences of Gallipoli and the great difficulties that had been encountered there. It was true, it was admitted, that Abdel Krim's troops could not be compared to the Turks, but it was equally true that the British forces had been more experienced and more adequately supplied than the Spaniards could hope to be. In any case Gallipoli had served to show how extremely difficult was a disembarkation of troops on an enemy shore. Those, however, who were in favour of the project, and those who were responsible for it, made a careful study of what had occurred at the Dardanelles and profited no little from the experiences of that operation. The landing of troops on the Rif coast had so often been discussed, so often proposed and so often abandoned, that almost up to the day of its achievement there was a general belief that it would never be attempted. It was not until it became known that the Spanish Government was purchasing a large quantity of material, some of which had actually served at Gallipoli, that incredulity ceased and it was realized that the Government's intention was serious. The last doubts were dispersed when the con-

*Photo. Piaz.*

THE DISEMBARKATION AT MORO NUEVO.

centration of troops and material began at Ceuta, Tetuan and Melilla. Yet even then the idea awoke little or no enthusiasm except amongst the troops who were to take part in the great adventure. It probably needed all General Primo de Rivera's well-known courage and tenacity to carry his programme through. The King, it is said, was from the first in favour of this operation. Both King Alfonso and the President of the Directory realized fully how great the responsibility was and how disastrous any failure would be. They must have been aware that the army was not yet so thoroughly reorganized that everything could be expected to move without a hitch, and an operation of such magnitude and difficulty must have given them very serious moments of thought. There must be nothing haphazard, no failure from want of preparation, no confusion in execution. With that grit and efficiency which are so largely the characteristics of General Primo de Rivera, he entered into every detail and took upon himself the entire responsibility. For a time the French military authorities looked a little askance upon so formidable an undertaking, and it was only when the Spanish plans had been examined at Paris that the French War Office gave its unhesitating approval. It was realized that, even if success could not be absolutely guaranteed, everything possible had been done to ensure it.

For some time before the date which had been decided upon for the disembarkation—the early days of September—preparations were being seriously made. Two columns were organized—one in the Tetuan district, under the command of General Saro; the second at Melilla, under General Fernandez Perez. The usual practice was to be adopted of using as shock troops the

Spanish Legion and the native infantry, and for this purpose a special training in the attacking of entrenched positions, in the use of hand-grenades and in embarking and disembarking was instituted. What can almost be described as full-dress rehearsals took place at two points on the coast. That of the Tetuan column proved entirely satisfactory, but manœuvres with the Melilla column, and an experimental disembarkation, gave much food for thought, and certain modifications were found necessary. General Primo de Rivera would take no risks over and above those which could not possibly be avoided. The French put their fleet at the disposal of the Spanish Government, though it was mutually agreed that no French sailors were to be disembarked. With the exception of the exact date and the spot, or spots, at which the disembarkation was to take place everything was known beforehand. It was naturally quite impossible to keep so important a movement secret.

On September the 1st General Primo de Rivera presided at a council of the commanding officers at Tetuan. Six days later, before embarking on the Spanish warship *Alfonso XIII*, he issued a proclamation to the army in which he called attention to the necessity for the coming action. Attempts to come to terms with the Rif had failed. Everything, he said, had been carefully prepared. He expressed his confidence in the army and trusted that he enjoyed their confidence in return. He called upon the Legion and the native troops to realize the justice of Spain's cause and the necessity of ridding the country of the rebel chief. He pointed out that the dangers and difficulties were many. ' We can be proud,' the proclamation concluded, ' of being of a superior race, of coming of a strong people and of belonging to an organized and well-governed nation.   Your Commander-in-Chief hopes soon to congratulate you on your triumph.'

At the same time General Primo de Rivera issued an ultimatum to the tribes.   The Spanish Army, it ran, had decided that Abdel Krim must be punished and the Rif invaded by the troops of France and Spain.   Many of the Rifi chiefs would fight on Spain's side, men who had recognize, the crimes of Abdel Krim.   The ultimatum gave three days for surrender, and stated that it was only by submission that the tribes could escape the severest punishment.   Pardon would be granted to all who came to the Advance Posts and surrendered.   Should they refuse to do so, they would pay the price and they would shed tears of blood.   Meanwhile any ill treatment of the French or Spanish prisoners would be met with reprisals. The decision of peace and war, it concluded, rested with the Rifis.   This proclamation was widely distributed by aeroplane.

There was no doubt that Abdel Krim was kept informed of the Spanish plans of disembarkation, but he certainly knew nothing of the exact spot at which it would be attempted.   Everything, however, pointed to Alhucemas Bay, where the beach was suitable and there was some protection from the prevailing winds.   It was, too, the nearest spot to Ajdir, his 'capital,' and the Spaniards already possessed the island Presidio just off the shore.   The rest of the Rif coast, with one or two exceptions, was quite unsuitable for any operation of the kind.   Even where landing was possible, no particular advantage could be gained by disembarkation on a barren coast with no vulnerable point within reach.   Alhucemas had always been the Spanish objective and could scarcely fail to be so on this occasion.   Abdel Krim accordingly made

M

every preparation for the defence of that part of the coast. At the same time, realizing that the Spanish preparations were well advanced, he attempted to cause a postponement, or even the abandonment of the expedition by a diversion in the Tetuan district. Although he was not successful to that extent, he eventually upset the details of General Primo de Rivera's programme by causing the hurried despatch to the Western zone of three battalions of troops destined to disembark with the Melilla column to the East of Alhucemas Bay. It was not improbable that the absence of these soldiers necessitated the eventual abandonment of that part of the operation. In any case it never took place.

It was during the first few days of September that Abdel Krim's diversion in the Tetuan district manifested itself. Ahmedo Heriro, with a large number of Jibala tribesmen, each detachment commanded by Rifis sent by Abdel Krim for that purpose, penetrated between the Posts of Gorgues, Ben Karich and Kudia Taher, a few miles South and South-West of Tetuan, and took up a strong position in the rugged summits of the mountain. Kudia Taher was completely isolated. The Jibala tribesmen had brought with them nine guns and skilful gunners, who for a time were supposed to be Europeans, so ably did they handle their artillery. The first shot fired struck the muzzle of one of the Kudia Taher cannon. But the Rifis were not content with attacking the Post alone; they threatened the important position of Ben Karich and kept up a desultory fire on its fortifications. But it was upon Kudia Taher that they turned their principal attention. They realized that the capture of this Post would break the 'Primo' line and allow them to bring their artillery to the heights that overlooked

Tetuan, whence a bombardment of the town was not only feasible but easy. A sustained bombardment of the capital of the Spanish zone, the residence of both the Sultan's Khalifa and the Spanish High Commissioner, would, Abdel Krim realized, cause consternation in Spain and increase enormously his prestige amongst the tribes. It was, therefore, all-important that Kudia Taher should be taken.

This sudden change in the situation at Tetuan jeopardized the expedition to Alhucemas, on the point of setting out, and for a time there was some intention to postpone it; but it was realized that a check at this moment, and the moral victory for Abdel Krim that a check would entail, would be highly disadvantageous. The critical hour of the Rif had arrived. The Spaniards must go on—or fail, and failure meant—it was impossible to say what failure might mean. General Primo de Rivera realized this. The thrust he was about to make at the heart of the Rif must not be retarded. He started on September the 6th with the expedition, not without some little hesitation. So fierce, however, became the struggle to the South of Tetuan that in a few days he returned, bringing back with him two battalions of the Spanish Legion and a battalion of the (native) Melilla regiment which had not yet been disembarked at Alhucemas. Meanwhile the situation of Kudia Taher had become critical. The Rifis concentrated the fire of their guns upon its parapets, which crumbled away faster than they could be repaired. The tents of the little camp took fire and were burnt. Amongst the first men of the garrison to be killed were an artillery officer and nine of his men. Only one gun remained in use, and the water tanks were destroyed. The plight of the garrison seemed hopeless.  Every attempt to relieve them failed.  The ground was boulder-strewn and all access to the Post was over rocky country where the relieving force was exposed to the fire of an invisible enemy.  On September the 5th the Rifis made a general attack and the small Post of Nator was captured.  At Kudia Taher the same day the commanding officer was killed.  The Spanish airmen rendered great services, and it was only by dropping ice and provisions into the Post that it was able to hold out.  Several of the pilots were wounded.  Again on the nights of September the 6th and 7th the Post was fiercely attacked, and at Tetuan all hope of saving its brave little garrison was abandoned.

The enemy were now more securely entrenched than ever and even Ben Karich was seriously threatened.  On September the 8th two columns were prepared for the purpose of the relief, and on the 10th the three battalions of troops that had been sent back from the Alhucemas expedition reached Tetuan.  On the 11th the three columns started.  The centre was formed by the two battalions of the Legion and the battalion of the Melilla regiment which had just arrived.  In spite of having been nearly a week on board the transports, the men were in excellent condition and proud of the difficult task that had been allotted them.  The fighting on the 12th, as the troops ascended the steep mountains that rise to the immediate South of Tetuan, was severe, and even the little villages, perched high up amongst the rocks, had to be taken at the point of the bayonet.  The garrison of Kudia Taher was now reduced to twenty-five men and three wounded officers, and it seemed impossible that it could hold out.  Fighting every yard of the way the column spent the night at Dar Gazi, a little over a mile from the besieged Post. The following morning Kudia Taher was relieved after ten days of almost incessant fighting. The enemy suffered severely as the column advanced, over 150 dead being left at the spot where they made their last stand. The little garrison of Kudia Taher had lost twenty-two killed and ten wounded.

The following day the survivors entered Tetuan and were received with the highest honours. The relief column marched past General Primo de Rivera, the men of the Legion bearing on their bayonets trophies of war, which led to a severe reprimand from the Commander-in-Chief. It was the reprisals perpetrated by men of the Legion on enemy prisoners on this occasion that led General Primo de Rivera to order once and for all the cessation of such acts of barbarity. In so doing he removed, it is to be hoped for ever, the principal cause of an absence of British sympathy with Spanish action in Morocco.

On September the 5th, eight days before the relief of Kudia Taher, the Tetuan column, under the command of General Saro, had embarked at Ceuta, and the following day the plan of the expedition was made known to the commanding officers. It was on Cebadilla beach that the disembarkation was to take place, a spot on the West shore of the rocky promontory that forms the Western point of Alhucemas Bay. The Melilla column was to land a little farther to the East, should the local situation prove satisfactory. All other naval demonstrations, at Wad Lau, at Sidi Dris or elsewhere, were to be merely diversions, to call off the attention of the enemy. The ultimate object was Ajdir, Abdel Krim's capital, situated a few miles inland from the shore of Alhucemas Bay.

The warships and transports anchored on September the 5th off Rio Martin, the open roadstead which serves as the port of Tetuan, and proceeded the next day southward along the coast to the mouth of the Wad Lau. The expedition counted nearly 100 vessels of all sorts and conditions. The coast was heavily bombarded and a feint of landing was made, the men even being put into the lighters, but under the cover of night the expedition turned eastward and proceeded toward Alhucemas. It was the sudden departure of these ships that set abroad amongst the natives the story of an attempted landing at the mouth of the Wad Lau and of a Spanish defeat. The Jibala even claimed to have sunk some of the Spanish vessels.

The disembarkation at Cebadilla was to have taken place on the morning of September the 7th, but the strong currents on the coast had retarded the progress of the fleet which transported the Tetuan column, whose landing was to be the first item of the programme ; and at dawn, when the ships ought to have been in front of Cebadilla, they were many miles to the westward, opposite Badis on the Ghomara coast. The transports, on board of which was the Melilla column, on the contrary found themselves too far to the westward, in exactly the position in which the other section of the expedition should have been. This entirely upset the plans of General Primo de Rivera and a surprise was no longer possible. It was not till nearly midday that the fleet with the Tetuan column reached Moro Nuevo and Cebadilla. The disembarkation was postponed and instead a heavy bombardment of the whole shore of the Bay of Alhucemas was undertaken by the warships. The following morning, under the protection of gunfire, the landing was begun. The beach

*Photo. Worth.*

NATIVE TROOPS IN ACTION NEAR TAÏUAN.

of Cebadilla slopes gradually into the sea, and the water was found to be too shallow to permit of the lighters reaching the shore. The soldiers, nothing daunted, waded to the land up to their chests in water. The surrounding heights were occupied with little resistance and a Moorish battery of three guns was captured.

The delay in the disembarkation, and the withdrawal of the three battalions which were required for service in the Tetuan district, had rendered necessary an entire change of plans for the second (Melilla) column, under General Fernandez Perez. It had been the original intention for these troops to be disembarked on the East side of Alhucemas Bay, as soon as General Saro's column had gained a secure footing in the West. But the reduction of the number of General Perez's force rendered this operation unwise, and it was decided that the Melilla troops should remain on board ship in the offing and reinforce General Saro's disembarked forces as soon as an advance should have given more breathing space round Cebadilla. It was not till September the 11th that this second disembarkation took place, the men having passed six days on board the transports. On the 16th the last men were put ashore. Until September the 14th fine weather had facilitated the operation. The sea had been calm, for the strong East wind, so persistent on that exposed coast, had failed to blow. Everything had been favourable, but it was too much to hope that such good fortune would be permanent. On September the 14th the ' Levante ' rose and the disembarkation was much hindered, with consequent disagreeable results, the most important being the extreme difficulty of landing water for the troops, of whom there were now about 20,000 ashore. With the exception of one or two quite inade-

quate wells no water was available in the occupied area.
It had all to be brought from Ceuta or from Malaga.

The enemy had shown but little resistance to the landing, and on the day of the disembarkation the Spaniards
only suffered about fifty casualties.   There is no doubt
that the spot chosen, just outside Alhucemas Bay to
the West, came as a surprise to the Rifis, who had expected the landing to be made inside the Bay and had
taken every precaution accordingly and had concentrated
nearly all their artillery in that locality.   During the
bombardment of the coast on September the 7th and
the succeeding days, more than one shell struck the
Spanish and French warships, though the small calibre
of the Rifi guns rendered these hits almost without effect.
It would seem that the Rifis, not suspecting a landing at
Cebadilla, had left that district with little means for its
protection, though the hills above the beach were found
to be trenched and fortified.   The three guns captured
almost immediately after the landing took place were
probably all that at that moment commanded the beach.
But the enemy was not slow in repairing this mistake,
and his bombardment of the Spanish camp increased
almost from hour to hour.   During the day the Rifi
guns were generally silent, in order that the positions of
their artillery should not be located by the Spanish airmen ; but no sooner did darkness fall than the bombardment began, the shells falling fast into the occupied area.
By day the much reduced gunfire was chiefly concentrated on such vessels as approached the coast, one or
two of which were hit.   On the nights of September the
11th and 12th the Rifis made determined attacks upon
the Spanish lines, but were successfully driven off.

Although optimistic reports were circulated in Spain

there were many who realized that the position was precarious and that some immediate effort was necessary to increase the occupied area. Wind and sea were now unfavourable and the landing of stores and water was difficult. The Spanish forces were aptly described as clinging like flies to the rocks of a waterless promontory under the constant fire of the enemy.

On September the 20th the mules and horses were at length landed, the bad weather and the scarcity of fresh water ashore having prevented this from being done earlier. Everything was now ready for an advance, and the same day General Primo de Rivera returned from Tetuan.

On September the 22nd the first move was made. Only native regiments were employed. The object was to ascertain the position of the enemy's artillery. In spite of a bombardment of the enemy's trenches by the Spanish guns and bombing from the air, the advancing troops were met, within a thousand yards of the Spanish lines, by a sustained rifle-fire from the Rifis hidden amongst the rocks and entrenched on the hillside. The troops suffered heavily, and it being clear that no frontal attack was possible except at a great cost, they were ordered to retire. This check caused deep disappointment in the Spanish camp, accompanied as it was by so many casualties. A wave of pessimism seems to have passed over the whole expedition, and it was judged absolutely necessary that an immediate advance in force should take place in order to restore the moral of the army. Everything forbade delay—the cramped ground, the insanitary state of the camp, the want of water and the constant menace by the enemy's guns.

On the morning of the 23rd accordingly a general

advance took place.  The objectives were : on the left
the coast of the other side of the promontory near Moro
Viejo, in the centre the enemy's position on Mount Malmusi, and to the right the hills known as the Cuernos de
Shawan.  The Spanish forces were divided into three
columns.  That on the right was to make a feint of
reaching the Cuernos de Shawan, but not to push as far,
leaving the ground open for the centre column to attack
the Rifis in the flank and rear.  The third column was
to be held in reserve until required.

From the beginning of the action the fighting was
severe, the troops having to advance as far as was possible
under cover of the boulders and rocks, so accurate and so
constant was the enemy fire.  The plan was accurately
and successfully carried out.  The Rifis resisting the
advance of the right column at the foothills of Cuernos
de Shawan were taken in the flank by the centre column
and lost heavily.  The men of the Legion had to drive
many of the enemy from the fissures and caves in which
they had taken refuge and there was much hand-to-hand
fighting.  The tribesmen in the centre abandoned their
trenches and took to the higher hills, but everywhere
the resistance was stubborn.  Mount Malmusi was
carried by assault, with but one check, when the native
troops suddenly found themselves amongst a number
of mines which exploded amongst their advancing
numbers.  For a few minutes there was panic, but the
ground they abandoned was quickly retaken by the men
of the Legion, who charged at the critical moment.  It
was the native regiment's first experience of mines, and
it cannot be wondered at they caused a little panic
amongst men totally inexperienced to that particular art
of warfare.  Little by little the retreating enemy were

driven up the steep mountain side.   Only once was there a pause when all the available Spanish guns concentrated upon the mountain-top a formidable and incessant fire. The summit of Mount Malmusi was said to resemble the crater of a volcano, for the heavy guns of the warships added their high explosive shells to the bombardment of the artillery.   Suddenly the gunfire ceased and with a rush the summit was reached and the Spanish flag unfurled.   The Spaniards found only one man alive, a Rifi, who stood there and continued to fire until he was stabbed to death by men of the Legion.   The rest were either killed or had fled at the moment of the bombardment. With this advance the Spaniards held practically the whole promontory and were in possession of two useful sheltered coves on its Eastern shore.   The Spanish casualties on September the 23rd were about seven hundred.

The effect of the landing at Alhucemas upon Abdel Krim and his Rifis must have been one of consternation. They had always believed, or at all events stated, that no Spanish landing was possible on their coast.   They knew now that Mount Malmusi in the occupation of the Spanish forces, Ajdir was as good as lost, and it seems that the evacuation of ' the capital ' and the surrounding villages began almost at once.   Abdel Krim himself explained the success of the Spaniards as due to the treachery of the Bukkoya tribe, who inhabit the neighbouring territory to the West ; but it would seem that the Rifis were taken completely by surprise and had failed to protect this little strip of the coast, on which, it must be confessed, a landing was not to be expected.

The Spaniards did not advance again until September the 30th, the interval being occupied in constructing a pier for the further disembarking of stores, in sinking wells, and in fortifying the occupied positions. A storm of wind and rain added much to the discomfort of the troops.

On the last day of September General Saro's division, in two columns, under Colonels Franco and Martin, occupied Mount Palomas in the direction of Ajdir. Other columns advancing on the left installed themselves on the hills overlooking the valley of the Wad Guis and Nekor, and the plain on which Ajdir lay. It had been intended to advance no farther, but the temptation was too great to be resisted, and without receiving any orders to that effect, the soldiers of the Legion invaded the plain below and pillaged all they could lay their hands on. The whole countryside was deserted, and the Rifis had carried off all of their possessions that were of value or removable. Ajdir was looted of the little that was left.

In November the new Khalifa of the Spanish zone was appointed—Mulai Hassan, a son of the late Khalifa Mulai el-Mehdi who had died two years previously. Meanwhile the post had remained vacant. Mulai Hassan was a boy of fourteen years of age. At the same moment, General Primo de Rivera handed over the High Commissionership of Spanish Morocco to General Sanjurjo. The situation in Morocco, greatly modified by the disembarkation on the Rif coast, allowed now of some hopes of a period of peace. It was winter and all operations would be difficult—and Ajdir had fallen. This success seemed to have finally converted General Primo de Rivera to the policy of complete military occupation of the Spanish zone, and all idea of its evacuation, of which he had been at one time the advocate, was abandoned. His efforts were now centred upon the disarmament of all the tribes in the occupied regions and an understanding with the tribes. But Abdel Krim was still at large, and as long as a solution was not arrived at as to his future, Morocco would continue to be a source of difficulty and danger. Before leaving the country in the middle of November (1925) General Primo de Rivera visited Laraiche, Alcazar and Arzeila, where he addressed the troops. Everywhere he adopted the same optimistic tone. ' In a few months,' he said, ' we shall have finished with this question of the Rif. In a few years Morocco will no longer be a source of anxiety to us.'

At Alcazar he had an interview with Monsieur Steeg, the French Resident-General, who had come from Rabat to see him. General Naulin, in command of the French troops in Morocco, accompanied Monsieur Steeg. The interview was considered as highly satisfactory on both sides and tended to cement the entente between France and Spain.

Yet even in this hour of satisfaction and victory Tetuan was to suffer a new and annoying threat. Heriro and his Jibala contingents had succeeded in transporting a gun, or possibly more than one, over the mountain-tops, through the Spanish lines, and had mounted it—or them —in a cave in one of the steep limestone precipices on the South that overlook the city from a great height. From this point of vantage from day to day a few shots were fired, destroying a little property and causing a few losses in the town. This bombardment of the capital of the Spanish zone continued over a protracted period and caused much worry to the Spaniards. The gun after being fired was evidently immediately withdrawn into the recesses of the cave, where it remained immune from

the bombs of airmen and from the shells of the Tetuan
batteries which were always in readiness to reply the
moment the little white puff of smoke was seen issuing
from the mouth of the cave.

The rest of the winter passed in comparative quiet on
all the fronts, but the French and Spanish were busy
organizing the spring campaign in which it had mutually
been agreed an end must be put to the Rifi menace.
The events which culminated in the surrender of Abdel
Krim will be related in subsequent chapters.   But the
independent operations on the French front, up to the
time when joint action by the French and Spanish
armies was inaugurated, must first be dealt with.

WOUNDED NATIVE SOLDIERS

# CHAPTER VIII

## THE FRENCH IN MOROCCO

With the death of Mulai Hassan in 1894 the last strong Sultan of Morocco passed away. His unflagging energy, his constant military progresses through his country in the pursuit of peace or of war, his excursions far afield into the barren Atlas and into the still more barren desert, had rendered him master of the greater part of his turbulent dominions. In choosing one of his younger sons, Mulai Abdel Aziz, a boy of thirteen years of age, to succeed him on his throne, he must have had some misgivings as to the future, for he must have realized that the empire which he had held together only by constant repression and by constant warfare could ill be maintained by a child. Fatalist, like all his race, he probably bestowed the throne upon his favourite son and left the rest to Providence.

Mulai Abdel Aziz for the first six years of his Sultanate lived a life of seclusion in the palace, appearing only in state on the great national feast days. It was not till the death of his Grand Vizier, Ba Ahmed, that the young Sovereign emerged from the palace to take part in the affairs of his country. The manner in which Morocco, under his feeble rule, was ruined politically and financially is well known. Gentle and timid by disposition, with much weakness and no little charm, he neglected the affairs of State and spent his time in amusements which his courtiers were only too pleased to facilitate. The country's money was wasted on playthings, innocent enough in their kind, but eminently unsuitable to a descendant of the Prophet who held his throne more by a reputation of hereditary sanctity than through any temporal ascendancy. The fanaticism of the tribesmen was aroused and Mulai Abdel Aziz's power and prestige declined. Even the more educated and rational part of the population disapproved of his European proclivities and were not slow to show their disapproval. Rebellions broke out in different parts of the country, which were either suppressed with difficulty or remained unsuppressed. Taxes became more and more difficult to collect, and at the same time the greed and the corruption of the Moorish Court increased. Little or no money found its way into the Treasury. The Moroccan sun was setting, and was setting fast.

In 1908, after a long series of indecisive battles, Mulai Abdel Aziz and his army were defeated by the forces of his brother Mulai Hafid, who had raised the standard of revolt in the South, and had had himself proclaimed Sultan in Marrakesh. Abdel Aziz fled to the coast, where he abdicated, and Hafid was proclaimed throughout the whole country. For a time it appeared that the new Sultan would be able to restore some measure of the throne's lost authority, but the state of decay into which Morocco had fallen had entered too deeply into the country's system. It was past remedy. Meeting with ill success on all sides, he became morose and discouraged. His nervous temperament drove him to excesses. His cruelty became proverbial, and Morocco sank during the last two years of his reign into a state of chaos and confusion.

The tribes rose in revolt, and in 1911 Mulai Hafid found himself and his capital besieged by rebel forces. The Berber tribesmen raided up to the very walls of Fez, and every road was insecure. In a moment of panic the Sultan asked for a French force to be sent to relieve the capital. The French had occupied Casablanca in 1907 after the massacre of some Europeans, and had already extended their sway over a number of the coastal tribes. In answer to the Sultan's appeal for help, a French column, proceeding by forced marches, reached Fez in May, 1911, and drove off the attacking tribesmen. It was the beginning of the end of the independence of Morocco, and a year later (1912) Mulai Hafid signed the treaty by which the French Protectorate came into existence. A massacre of the French officers commanding the native regiments followed, and Paris hurriedly sent General Lyautey to Fez as Resident-General. In August Mulai Hafid abdicated and a younger brother, Mulai Yussef, was proclaimed Sultan in his place. The same autumn a French column, under General Mangin, occupied Marrakesh, where a fanatical rising had taken place, and where the French residents were held as prisoners.

With the occupation of Fez and Marrakesh, the two capitals, a large extent of Western Morocco passed into French hands, but a vast work yet remained to be accomplished. Morocco was in a state of chaos. The last two Sultans had witnessed their prestige—temporal and religious—diminish almost to vanishing point. The greater part of the country was in open revolt, the tribes were raiding one another, all governmental authority had disappeared, and only a few of the great chiefs were sufficiently powerful to maintain even a semblance

N

of order amongst their tribal followers. No taxes
were being paid, and the population, except in such
districts as the French had already occupied, were
entirely out of hand, and when the tribesmen of Morocco
get out of hand the result is pandemonium. They love
fighting for itself, and for the opportunities of loot that
anarchy offers. They were well armed with modern
rifles, and in the possession of much ammunition, which
they were able to replenish, thanks to the contraband
trade. If they held their own lives cheaply, they held
those of others much cheaper—for death means very
little amongst the Berber tribesmen. In the towns
every kind of intrigue was rife, and no one trusted his
neighbour or his friend. The roads in every direction
were insecure, pillage and robbery existed everywhere,
and the French columns engaged in restoring order found
their every step in advance disputed.

Such was the state of Morocco when, in 1912, General
Lyautey, the French Resident-General, took up his
duties in Fez. His first acts were to bring about an
amelioration in the local situation. He reprieved such
of the Moorish soldiers—a number had been condemned
to death for the massacre of their French officers—as
had not already been executed. The effect of this
clemency was instantaneous. The inhabitants of Fez
realized that the new chief sought no revenge. He then
countermanded the heavy fine that had been imposed
upon the city, for he realized that the massacre of the
French officers had been due to a sudden military revolt
and that in no way was the population of the town
responsible. At the same time he let it be clearly seen
that he was the master. His orders had to be carried
out, and very quickly; but they were always orders

that were issued in a spirit of justice and that avoided all unnecessary humiliation of the people. While he took the strictest measures to ensure the security of the European population, he was equally strict in insisting that no insult or slight should be offered to the religion or the persons of the native population. He entered into direct and sympathetic relations with the chief men of the capital and asked for, and obtained, their co-operation in the restoration of order. He threw as much responsibility as was possible upon their shoulders and gave them all the military assistance they might require to maintain peace.

When, a few months later, General Lyautey returned to the coast he left a highly satisfactory state of affairs behind him in Fez. The inhabitants appreciated his qualities, and made no secret of their liking for this sympathetic strong man, who had succeeded in so short a time in bringing about a normal situation. In turn, the General realized that he was dealing with men of intelligence and understanding, and that his principal support in the very difficult task that lay before him could be found in the people themselves. He guaranteed them the full enjoyment of their religious, historical and traditional institutions without let or hindrance. He confirmed in their posts such as were to be trusted, and many who formerly were not to be trusted too far, but who, under this new régime—from fear or from higher motives—became more worthy citizens.

On his arrival at the coast General Lyautey turned his attention to the important question of the administration of the whole of Morocco, including those wild mountainous districts which had rarely or never in the past submitted even to their own Sultans. The outlook was not promising. The last Sultan had abdicated under circumstances which threatened the prestige of his successor. He had, in the eyes of his people, in signing the Treaty of the Protectorate, sold his country to the Christians. His predecessor on the throne, Mulai Abdel Aziz, had been a weak and vacillating sovereign who had wasted the revenues and emptied the treasury. The actual holder of the throne, Mulai Yussef, had accepted it at the hands of the French, and, though the necessary religious formalities had been gone through and his recognition by the Moslem authorities obtained, his prestige was necessarily none too great. The whole country was in a state of rampant anarchy. The great Berber chiefs of the Atlas were alone able to keep order amongst their tribesmen—and even their authority was limited. The rest was chaos. If the new Sultan was tacitly accepted by the people, it was owing more to indifference than to any respect for his personality. He was an unknown prince, young, of sufficient intelligence, of pleasant manner and of a thoughtful and serious disposition. The choice was a wise one, and Mulai Yussef, who is the reigning Sultan to-day, has filled his post with tact and ability.

It can be perceived that such a state of anarchy as existed in Morocco was no firm base upon which to build up a new administration—and no decision had as yet been taken as to the form or character that this new administration was to assume. The French had not been altogether successful in Algeria. At the time of its conquest and occupation in the middle of the nineteenth century, France had little experience of colonial government, especially of Islamic peoples. The introduction into Algeria of the French legal code, so entirely opposed to the Islamic law on which Moslem legislation and Moslem society are founded, was a mistake that cannot be exaggerated. It led to endless difficulties and endless dissatisfaction which succeeding modifications have only partially removed. Its results are still felt. In Tunis, with their Algerian experience to guide them, the French introduced a new system of collaboration with the already existing Government which, though it has not failed, has proved more a *modus vivendi* than a successful policy. Tunis was an improvement on Algeria, just as Morocco has been an improvement on Tunis.

It was decided to introduce into Morocco a real Protectorate in the highest sense of that word; to change as little as possible the outward and visible form of government; to retain and support the religious institutions, to respect the native customs and traditions, to govern through the Sultan and his Viziers, but at the same time to guarantee that the government should be good. With reference to the tribes, French and Moroccan forces should act together to restore order and bring the recalcitrant to heel, invariably in the name of the Sultan. The submission of the tribesmen should be a submission to the Moslem Sultan, and not to the foreign Christian Government which was aiding him; for the Sultan was their spiritual and acknowledged chief and the head of their religion. The Sovereigns of Morocco are descendants of the Prophet Mohammed, and spiritually are owed allegiance. It was the return of straying sheep to the fold rather than the bowing of the head to a stranger of another faith. No doubt the tribes realized that the force behind the throne was France, and that without this force the Sultan would be powerless to bring them to reason; but, in Morocco as elsewhere, the wind is tempered to the accommodating conscience, and the fact that the army was acting in the name of the head of their faith rendered defeat less unpalatable and sub-mission theoretically excusable.

The French quickly organized a native army. There was no lack of volunteers, for the Moor has always been a fighter. When a tribe submitted, its younger men, no longer able to oppose the invading force, joined their yesterday's enemy, and in a spirit of complete indifference set off to fight the neighbouring tribe in the interests of the very men they were doing their best to annihilate a few days before. ' Yesterday was yesterday,' they say, ' and to-day is to-day. To-morrow is God's, and who knows what it may bring ? '

The efficiency of these native troops was admirably proved during the war in France and elsewhere. The remnants of their regiments returned home to Morocco with their colours decorated and their tunics striped with ribbons—a little indifferent to it all, and ready to fight again anywhere and at any time. Natives from all over Morocco, they have drifted into the Moorish Army—for there is no conscription—have been drilled and learned discipline, and gone forth to fight their co-religionists and fellow-tribesmen without a moment's hesitation, imbued with an hereditary love of battle, regardless of the nationality or faith of the enemy or the reason or nature of the campaign.

In the organization of this army the French have adopted a practice that is in absolute contradiction to the Anglo-Saxon point of view. They have instituted mixed regiments in which French and Moorish soldiers serve without colour distinction and without discrimina tion of treatment. When out on expeditions they fight,

FRIENDLY TRIBESMEN.

*Photo. Gröllé & Kulel.*

feed, sleep together. They learn each other's language sufficiently well to converse at ease, for they are young recruits when drafted into these mixed regiments. They become fast friends. They share their duties and their amusements with no feeling of aloofness from religion or race. The colour line does not exist. The French military authorities are highly satisfied with this arrangement. Their generals in Morocco state that its success is indisputable. The presence of Frenchmen gives a certain tone to the mixed native regiments which they would otherwise lack, and the native soldier appreciates, if he gives it a serious thought at all, the fact that he is receiving equality of treatment. The attitude is natural, for all idea of differentiation on account of religion, race or colour is absent on both sides.

It may be that Morocco is a particularly favourable country in which to carry out this system, owing to the qualities of the native population. It may even be that it would be impossible outside North Africa, but in any case it is a success. It is an argument, and a strong one, in favour of the theory that the Berber population of Morocco comes of a Northern stock. Their outlook on life, their intelligence, and their mentality are closely allied to our own. In the progress of civilization they have been left a long way behind, though as late as the seventeenth century they were living a life which could well be compared with that of many parts of the continent of Europe at that epoch. Art, literature, and architecture flourished at the universities of Fez and Marrakesh up to the very end of the seventeenth century. The tribal administration of the Berbers is founded on the broadest principles of democracy, and in certain aspects borders on Socialism, especially in the common

ownership of land. While the Arab never possesses
the European mental outlook, the Berber from the mountains or the Sus has to all intents and purposes a European mind. His attitude towards women, his honourable
tribal traditions, his sense of humour, his quickness of
thought, his merry laugh, all render him an agreeable
and intelligent companion and a firm and trustworthy
friend. He will sit down and talk without hesitation
and with no shyness, and so similar is his manner of
expression, so near is his humour to our own, that it is
difficult to realize that he comes from the great snow
peaks of the Atlas, or from far beyond them, and that
in all probability he is talking to a European for the
first time in his life. His topics of conversation are
necessarily limited by his environment, but his ability
to acquire knowledge is remarkable. He accepts his
new surroundings and adopts them. It is no doubt
this facility of assimilation that renders the French
system of mixed regiments not only possible, but also
successful.

The problem of military collaboration was followed
by that of civil government. The French at once began
to study the form of administration which could most
profitably be introduced in order to carry on the new
Protectorate in its most advantageous form. They
trusted not only to their own past experience in Algeria
and in Tunis to guide them, for a Commission was also
sent to Egypt to study the methods adopted by the
English there. The situation in Egypt did not, however,
present the same features, except in so far as it dealt
with a Moslem population under European control.
When the English entered Egypt the country was already
largely Europeanized. Roads and railways existed,

and there was a large Christian population. The country in fact was already ' opened up.' In Morocco this was not so. For centuries a barrier of fanaticism and political jealousy had sternly defended the interior of the country against all European innovation. The foreign residents of Fez and Marrakesh could almost be counted on the fingers, and their position, if not actually danger-ous, was at least difficult. But there was still much to be learned from the Egyptian situation. Egypt had reached in 1912 what Morocco might expect to be about thirty years later. It was therefore possible to judge of the effects of the policy which England had introduced into Egypt in the early eighties of the last century. This policy had in the thirty years which had then elapsed borne fruit, and the Commission which the French sent to Cairo made a careful examination of this fruit. In many cases it was judged admirable ; in many it clearly demonstrated what ought to be avoided in Morocco.

Especially was this so in the movement in education which England had inaugurated. No one doubts that education is excellent, but education, unless it can find its legitimate outlets, and furthers the ultimate interests of the scholar, has its drawbacks. Such portion of the youth of Egypt as was reached by the movement became educated above the measure of opportunity which awaited them. Their intelligence, their desire for knowledge, are highly to be commended, but the result was that there came into existence an educated class which found no outlet for its talents. Lawyers, doctors and engineers almost hustled each other in the streets, and could not find the means to live in anything like the social status which their education warranted. The

French Commission was not slow to appreciate this fact, and many others, good or bad, which could be taken as measures to adopt or to avoid.

France had two assets in her favour which stood her in good stead. First, she possessed in Algeria and Tunis a Moslem army ready to hand, and of which the majority of the troops were bilingual. This army furnished not only the men but also a number of French, Algerian and Tunisian officers accustomed to command natives of North Africa, the majority of them fluent speakers of the Arabic language and not a few inured to the climatic and physical conditions of countries resembling this new field of action. She had at the same time at her disposal a whole civil Administration consisting of men who had worked out and followed the problems of Christian and foreign control of Moslem populations. It was true, Morocco presented many new problems, but the basis of the situation was very similar.

France had still that other asset which in her task in Morocco has been invaluable—the absence of the colour question. Whatever may be the advantages or disadvantages of a distinct colour line in negro countries— and even there an exaggeration in either direction is to be deplored—the real inhabitants of Morocco are not black in any sense of the word. The negroes that are seen in considerable numbers, especially in the South, are of Soudanese origin. The practice of marriage with slave women has tainted the Moorish blood in many of the towns, but the country population of the interior of Morocco is almost entirely free from this disadvantage. The country Moor is burnt by the sun and by exposure, but the tribesman of the Atlas and the Northern mountain ranges is by nature a fair-skinned, not infrequently red-haired man, often lighter in complexion than the inhabitants of Southern Europe. But not only is the Northern Berber untainted with negro blood; he is generally free of the mixture of the Arab which tends so largely to conservatism of manner and custom, and to the retarding of civilization and progress.

All these elements were taken into account by the French authorities in arriving at their decision as to the form of government that they would introduce. It was at once realized that the first duty of a Protectorate was to safeguard the interests of the people who were to be protected, that is to say, the population of the country; and General Lyautey, in 1912, made no secret that the very basis of his policy was the improvement of the welfare of the Moroccan people. To carry this out, the first and most important essential was equality between all races, religions and colours. Morocco was not a conquest. France's rights were based upon a treaty to which the Sultan and his Government were parties. France was in the country to reorganize the State, to put an end to anarchy and chaos, to improve the condition of the people. Acting on General Lyautey's wise recommendations, the French Government decided to preserve as far as was possible—that is to say, almost in its entirety—the form and practices of the old Moorish régime. The Sultan would retain his privileges. He would issue all laws and all edicts under his hand and seal. His word was final. He was not only the supreme Sovereign, but also the head of their religion, in whose name prayers were offered in the mosques as a direct descendant of the Prophet and as the Khalifa in North-West Africa. Such, with varying success, had always been the attributes of the Moorish Sultans, and such they must remain. In great pomp and majesty, Mulai Yussef rides forth from his palace on the Moslem feast-days, surrounded by an imposing and gorgeous retinue, while over his head is held the crimson and gold parasol, the emblem of his exalted rank.   Nothing is changed from the old days, every detail of tradition, every item of etiquette is as strictly adhered to as it was in the time of his ancestors.

The Sultan is assisted in his government by his Council of Ministers, who are all natives, with the exception of the Minister of Foreign Affairs, a post that is held by the French Resident-General himself.   The Grand Vizier, the Minister of Justice, the Minister of the Crown Domains, and the rest, are Moors of the old régime who to-day fill posts in the new Protectorate Government similar to those they held during the reigns of the last two independent Sultans of Morocco.   At the Moorish Court scarcely an European is to be seen, and to the native who arrives at the Capital there is little or no visible change from what he and his ancestors saw in the past. It is behind this outward and visible form of government and pageantry, in offices situated away from the palace and its Oriental surroundings, that the French Adminis-tration is working.   There all is French, except the guards and attendants.   The brain of the Protectorate, the force that makes the wheels go round, the energy, the foresight, are all concentrated in the groups of buildings which surround the Residency at Rabat.   It is there that everything is originated and thought out, to pass in its more completed form to the palace of the Sultan.   The viziers are consulted, and act as advisers; the Sultan himself plays a wise part in the native affairs of his country, though he and his ministers may be thought to be little more than a gorgeous façade between the gover-

nors and the governed, the protectors and the protected.
It is, however, an active and useful collaboration. To
the Sultan and his Court the French pay the greatest
respect. The Resident-General himself treats Mulai
Yussef with all the dignities of an independent sovereign.
The viziers are accorded full honours as Ministers of
State.

In the country districts native governors have been
retained or appointed, always in the Sultan's name.
They collect the taxes, assisted by French technical
experts for the estimation of agricultural and produce
values. In many parts French officers or civilian officials
discreetly and almost invisibly assist the governors
with their advice, and control their actions. In other
districts of the country the governors act alone, and there
is no direct control on the part of the French authorities.
The great Berber Kaids of the South can almost be
described as independent chiefs, so large are their powers
and so extended their authority.

In the towns a large measure of self-administration
has been granted in the form of municipal councils. The
' Mejlis ' of Fez is a Moslem body with only one French
member, the representative of the Government. The
Moorish members have proved to be able and competent
men, with considerable liberty of action and entire liberty
of speech. In other cities, where the population is less
accustomed to civilization than are the people of Fez,
there are mixed French and Moslem municipal councils,
with members elected or chosen. Everywhere it is
collaboration between the protectors and the protected,
a collaboration the full benefit of which is obtained by
an almost entire absence of racial feeling. It never has
existed, and while it appears to the French as totally

unnecessary and irrational, it has never struck the native
even as a remote possibility, nor would he support it in
silence.   The Moor is amenable to government, but he
would revolt at any sign of humiliation.

That such a system of close and intimate collaboration
can exist without certain difficulties is impossible.   Even
if the Moor is in his mentality not far removed from
the European, the long period of stagnation and corruption through which his country has passed has not left
him untouched.   His propensities for looting, his vague
ideas as to the morality of taking bribes, his desire to
speculate on every possible occasion, render control
necessary and arduous.   To check corruption in its
entirety is out of the question, but corruption as practised
by the natives is not in their eyes an offence.   They
view these matters on a different plane from the European
—though corruption is rife enough nowadays in Europe.
The Moor has a spoken and avowed respect for absolute
justice, but in practice it rather bores him.   It takes
away from the many 'changes and chances of this
mortal life.'   In the time of the independent Sultans,
only a very few years ago, the Moor speculated in
everything, and his head was generally at stake.   If he
won he made a fortune—generally by extortion—if he
lost, his life was in danger—and a Moorish official's days
ended as often as not in prison.   To-day this insecurity
of life and property has disappeared.   A man owns his
own existence and his own possessions, but generally
he is still desirous of adding to it the property of others
as well, procured in any manner whatever that is less
expensive than legitimate purchase.   To a very great
extent the French have stamped out this corruption,
but there is no doubt that the Moorish country officials,

and perhaps even those in the towns, find a means of adding to their incomes in a manner that cannot be exactly described as legitimate.

In principle, abstract justice is admirable, and in Morocco it may possibly come in time, but it will never win the wholehearted approval of the Moor, for it removes from his life the delightful thrill of uncertainty. As a rule he dislikes regular taxation. He would prefer to have the chance once in a way of paying nothing, even if it meant that nine times out of ten he paid more. A fixed sum is merely a dull certainty. He prefers the $x$ of algebra which may turn out to be anything—the unknown quantity which only the final result can deter mine.

It is a moot question in the control and government of Oriental peoples by European States what form of administration is most to be commended. The legitimate desire for abstract justice, which civilized races look upon as the ideal, has little fascination for the Eastern. An unbending code of law administered by a judge whose knowledge and integrity are equally distinguished appears to him almost inhuman. He prefers the rough and ready justice of a soldier to the balanced judgment of a judge. He is amenable to arbitration by his own tribal people, and will accept their verdict in a spirit that no legal judgment can instil. His outlook on justice is not our own, and it never will be. He does not demand our impartiality or our integrity; on the contrary, he rather dislikes both. But there is one thing that touches him deeply—that goes straight to his heart—and that he seldom gets. It is sympathy. Sympathy in his simple joys and sympathy rrrow—a word, an expression, a smile is enough.

The friendship which no system of the highest integrity can awaken will burst into existence at a kindly spoken word. He craves for sympathy, and how rare it is! He gets so little in his own life, from his own people. Their very traditions and faith, the long years of oppression that they have suffered, have suppressed outward emotion and crushed deep feelings. His own existence has generally been so hard a struggle that he has scarcely time to give thought to others. But deep behind the hard, stern features, hidden in the secret places of the soul, is this intense desire for sympathy. It needs but a touch, but a look, but a word to unlock the doors of the hearts of the people—and it is worth doing.

Sympathy has been the principal feature which rendered successful Maréchal Lyautey's administration of Morocco. Imbued from the first with the determination that the native should receive no humiliation and be in a position of no inferiority because of his race, his colour or his religion, the Maréchal achieved a great work.

With uninterrupted success the French Government carried on its task of reorganization. There were periods of difficulty and now and again a period of local danger. During the Great War Morocco became a 'front.' General Lyautey in August, 1914, had refused to countenance the French Government's proposition to retire the garrisons of the towns of the interior and their European population to the coast. He had despatched to France the troops, the artillery, and all the material that had been asked for, and with what remained, aided by a few regiments of 'territorials,' he held the country against all the efforts of the Germans to raise a rebellion

—and he held it successfully. Untiring, seldom enjoying a few hours' consecutive rest, Lyautey travelled from one end of the land to another—long rough journeys by car across roadless tracts of country or on horseback —in the cold and rain of winter and in the great heat of summer. Wherever there was a victory he was there to congratulate the soldiers ; wherever there was a weak spot he was there to remedy it. Imbued with a spirit of unquenchable patriotism, a man of deep emotions, he knew how to cheer the flagging spirit, how to reconcile to their lot the officers who were fretting to be sent to the French front, and how to retain the loyalty and affection of the population.

It was my privilege to accompany him on many of these journeys to the very ends of the country and to spend weeks in his company. Untiring in body and in mind he never ceased his almost superhuman effort to hold Morocco together until the war should cease. He enjoyed a prestige that was probably unique in the history of colonial enterprise. A Christian in a Moslem land, governing a Moslem people, he was nevertheless honoured and loved. I saw him as he addressed the officers and non-commissioned officers of the columns that had just occupied the frontier regions of the Beni Mgild and Zaian tribes. It was at Ain Hammam, 6,000 feet up in the Atlas, in surroundings of deep ravines and forest. They stood spellbound as he, eloquent and deeply moved, spoke to them, cheering them, consoling them, praising them. I was with him on the next day when the submitted tribesmen with their women and children came down from the higher mountains to look at ' Lyautey.' The women, decked in their best, and weighed down with their silver jewellery, offered him the traditional bowls of milk, and he walked about amongst them, gazed at wonderingly by the small children who pressed round to touch or kiss his hand. It was the magic of his name, the magic of his personality. He had the greatest gift of all the qualities of colonial administration—sympathy. That day the tribesmen of those wild hills laid down their rifles and shouldered the pick and the hoe, and made roads. From that day to this all that region has remained tranquil and loyal, and security of life and property reigns undisturbed. The result of Lyautey's policy during those years of the war was that when the Armistice was signed France was in occupation of more of Morocco than when war broke out. I often wonder if the French really know how deep is their debt to the Maréchal.

Yet France went through dangerous days in Morocco then and since, and once at least the whole fabric of Protectorate seemed threatened, when in April, 1925, the Rifis overran the frontier districts of the French Protectorate and only failed to reach Fez.

The Franco-Spanish treaty of 1912 had defined the frontier between the French and Spanish zones, but the country through which the line passed was almost entirely unknown and unexplored, and had of course never been mapped. No detailed delimitation was therefore possible until a Franco-Spanish Commission could visit the frontier region. This possibility had not yet come about. At the beginning of 1924, when the first complications between the Rifis and the French arose, neither of the two protecting Powers, France or Spain, had occupied their frontier regions in this direction, and the line remained undefined and vague, and even in dispute. The Spaniards, recovering from the disaster of July, 1921,

TRIBAL GATHERING AT TAZA.                    *Photo. Coutanson.*

A TRIBAL CONTINGENT                    *Photo. Coutanson.*

were too busily engaged elsewhere to risk penetrating
so far from their bases, and public opinion in the Peninsula was such that any fresh expedition, costly in life
and in money, might have had disastrous effects at home.
The French, on the other hand, were employed in wiping
off the map of Morocco the ' spots of dissidence ' in the
Middle Atlas and to the South of Taza, districts which
they had not yet fully occupied. Their Northern frontier
region could wait. It lay off the main roads, and
important though its pacification and occupation were,
it could well be left over till the task elsewhere was
accomplished. That an effort would have to be eventually forthcoming the French fully realized, and they
were fully prepared to make it when the auspicious
moment arrived.

Throughout the period of the Great War one of the
most strenuous necessities of the Moroccan situation
had been the keeping open of the Fez-Taza-Ujda light
railway and road, the highway of traffic and the sole
practical means of communication between Morocco and
Algeria. The Germans had employed much money
and still more ingenuity in their attempts to cut this
important line. From the security of the Spanish zone,
the frontier of which lies parallel with this road a short
distance to the North, the Rifi contingents in the pay
of the Germans had made constant raids, and Abdel
Malek Maheddin, rebel renegade, had caused much
anxiety in Fez and in Paris by his continued presence
near the frontier in command of a contingent of Rifi
and Arab tribesmen. From time to time the telegraph
wire and even the railway were cut, and I remember in
1917 seeing a long line of telegraph posts lying on the
ground felled the previous night. The danger in this

region was increased by the proximity of the 'tache de Taza'—a centre of 'dissidence' lying in the high Northern spurs of the Atlas to the South of Taza. The fear was ever present with the French military authorities that these tribesmen of the 'tache' might be successful in joining hands with the enemy contingents that came from across the Spanish frontier to the North. It required no little skill and great labour, with the scarcity of troops at the disposal of the French during the war, to prevent a disaster in that direction. It had become necessary to hold a strip of country to the North of the road and railway by the installation of Posts, which if not sufficiently numerous or strong to prevent the raids, certainly rendered them less frequent and served often to cut off the returning tribesmen. By untiring effort the communications had been kept open.

At the conclusion of the war the only country occupied by the French to the North of this road was a strip almost parallel to it, none too strongly held. Nearer Fez, however, the French had penetrated into Sheraga and a part of Hayaina, but Eastward the line of posts in Tsul and Branes were much less far afield. Once the war was over, with more troops at their disposal, the French consolidated their position in that region without, however, making any attempt to occupy the country up to the frontier. By the end of 1923 they had reached the Wergha valley and the whole district South of the river was now in their possession. But between the Wergha and the vague treaty line of the frontier there still existed a long strip of territory which was vacant. To the North of this frontier line, within the Spanish zone, the situation was similar, and an even wider strip of unoccupied country stretched between the frontier and the nearest Spanish Posts. From the Southernmost of the Spanish Posts to the Northern French Posts a ' no-man's land ' of very considerable extent therefore existed, which remained independent of France and Spain and of the Maghzen. Through it, vaguely and unde-limited, passed the frontier line. Taking advantage of these circumstances Abdel Krim extended his jurisdic-tion over the tribes that inhabited it, and by the end of 1923 his authority was undisputed, in that he collected taxes in money and in kind and called upon the tribes nearest to the Rif to supply soldiers for his war against the Spaniards.

From their camps and Posts on the Southern bank of the Wergha the French overlooked the wide fertile valley. In front of them across the river lay the rich Northern bank with its well-cultivated spread of corn-fields, perhaps the most productive of all Morocco's agricultural districts. There was every incentive to advance into that region. Not only was its material wealth tempting, but it was also desirable politically. These rich districts were the main source of Abdel Krim's supply of grain, for the Rif is unable to raise sufficient crops to be self-supporting. The corn that found its way Northward would, by the occupation of these lands, take another direction and find a ready and acceptable market 30 miles away in Fez. Nor was the French position on the South bank of the river one of guaranteed security. The Wergha is fordable at most times of the year, though subject to floods in the rainy season, and for that and other reasons, notably the possibility of an enemy approach to the French camps without discovery, an advance across the river was considered expedient. After much political preparation amongst the inhabitants of the North bank of the Wergha the French forces advanced in the spring of 1924, crossing the wide undulating stretch of ground on the other side and occupying the line of hills that ran parallel with its course. There was no resistance and the advance took place without any mishap or difficulty. Once on the hills the French fortified their new positions, occupying the summits of the range that overlooked the Wergha valley to the South and the wild rocky and wooded ravines that lay at the foot of the high range of Tarzut to the North. The whole of the region occupied fell within the Treaty frontier of the French Protectorate. The only criticism that could be offered was not as to the legality of these acts, for the French were undisputably within their rights, but whether, taking the actual strained situation into consideration, they were not rash, in that it might appear to the Rifis a challenge to battle by an encroachment on their territory. It was the first time that the excuse for a conflict was offered them, for it was the first time that the French had entered any territory over which Abdel Krim claimed authority. The Rifis could not be expected to know the treaties, and to them effective occupation was a much more justifiable claim to ownership than the contents of any document drawn up between two Powers neither of which had ever exerted any authority in the district in question. The frontier tribes disturbed by this advance sent deputations to Abdel Krim and demanded his assistance to drive back the invaders. Abdel Krim, beyond protesting at what he described as a breach of faith on the part of the French, took no measures to carry out the demands of the tribes.

It was no doubt this forward movement that brought

THE FRENCH IN MOROCCO 199

about, a year later, the war in the Rif. Not only was
it a menace to his authority, but it cut off Abdel Krim,
his army and the Rif generally from its principal granary,
for it was from the Wergha valley that their supplies
of grain were obtained. He was wise enough to realize
that until he had consolidated his position in the Spanish
zone it would be madness to attack the French. It
would seem that during the whole of 1923 and 1924 an
understanding might have been possible and war avoided,
but the opportunity was lost on both sides. In ordinary
times it is more than probable that the frontier tribes
would have accepted the French Protectorate, and
prospered under the security and the increased facilities
to trade that would have come with it. But the war in
the Rif had set abroad a spirit of unrest, a wave of
nationalism. The local tribes, although they had taken
no part in the campaign against the Spaniards, had been
witnesses of what had passed only a short distance away.
They were aware of every detail of the great disaster that
had overwhelmed the Spanish army in 1921. They had
seen the extension of Abdel Krim's influence amongst the
Jibala tribes to the West, and within the last few months
they themselves had come under his direct authority.
At his headquarters at Ajdir, where they went with their
caravans of grain, they had even seen Christian prisoners
engaged in road-making, ill-treated and despised. It is
no wonder that a spirit of fanaticism was abroad and
that they were prepared, should the occasion arise, to
throw in their lot with the leader who seemed destined
by the aid of Divine Providence to uphold the creed of
Islam and to drive the infidel invader out of the country.
Why should they hesitate when their co-religionists to
the North were already destroying the power of the

Christian ?  They appealed again to Abdel Krim—
asking for Rifi troops and arms.  He put them off
once more, pretending that there was an understanding between himself and the French; that the French
occupation was only temporary and that he had the
situation well in hand.  He guaranteed that they would
advance no farther.  With these excuses the tribes
had to be satisfied, and with the exception of one or
two small raids they preserved the peace with their
new and unwelcome neighbours throughout the re-
mainder of 1924 and during the first three months of
1925.

Meanwhile the French were not idle.  They erected
and fortified a long line of Posts and constructed roads.
They were aware that with such neighbours as Abdel
Krim and the Rifi tribes precautions were necessary.
There were no doubt many officers who desired war,
there were perhaps some who took steps to bring it
about ; but Maréchal Lyautey, who had been ill and at
the door of death, was steadfastly in favour of peace.
A conflagration in Morocco was the last thing in the
world that he desired to see.  His career was nearing its end.  He had created French Morocco.  He
cannot be accused of any spirit of militarism or imperialism.  He had no greater desire than to hand
over to his successor his great work accomplished—a
Morocco at peace.

I paid a hurried visit to the French lines in January,
1925, at the invitation of General Colombat.  The front
was reached by a metalled road, 60 miles in length,
running almost due North from Fez, through Ain Aicha
to Taunat.  Ain Aicha was the principal base camp in
the Wergha valley, a few miles behind the front line of

Posts. This road, at which squads of men were still
at work, was on the point of completion and was already
open to military motor traffic. The country passed
through was hilly and well cultivated ; the villages wore
an air of prosperity ; the population appeared contented
and friendly. Fifty miles from Fez we reached the River
Wergha which was crossed by a military bridge. The
river, which is wide and shallow, is liable to heavy floods
in winter and often in that season unfordable. On
the North bank—which the French had occupied in
the previous spring (1924)—we continued over undulating country of rich black soil, extensively cultivated and
of great agricultural value, to the line of steep hills
that ran parallel to the course of the river. These
hills rose from the rich cultivated fields in rocky, and
in places wooded, slopes. On the summits of their peaks
could be seen the French advance Posts. Our destination
was Taunat, the principal Post of that region, 2,000 feet
above the level of the sea, where there was also a Bureau
de Renseignements and a small garrison. The road
climbed steeply up from the plain to the Fort. One felt
that the French had come to stay ; everything had an
air of strength and permanency. The whole hill-top
was walled and fortified and within were excellent
quarters for the officers and men. The view was extensive and beautiful. To the North, across rocky and
wooded ravines, was the great mountain block of Tarzut,
its crest 7,000 feet above the sea level. From the
ravines below it rose in wooded and rocky slopes to great
bare precipices, crowned at the summit with snow. To
right and left of Taunat, lying along the ridges of the
hills, lay other Posts with a reserve line slightly to the
rear. A long wide road connected these Posts with one

another and with Taunat. To the South we looked
back in the direction from which we had come, across
the Wergha valley to the hills beyond, and far away
beyond to the snows of the Northern spurs of the Atlas
to the South of Taza.

It was evident that preparations had been made to
meet any Rifi advance, which those on the spot informed
me was ' inevitable.' One little thought then, when the
strength of this line of Posts was being explained, with
its artillery cross-fire from every fort, that with the exception of a few of the strongest points, the French front
was to crumble up in a few months' time before a Rifi incursion, and a number of these very Posts were destined
to be evacuated, destroyed or captured, many with their
artillery, their arms, ammunition and their little garrisons. Taunat was to hold out, hard pressed, until relief
came, and other of the Posts—after acts of great gallan-
try and immense suffering on the part of their garrisons ;
but many fell, and deeds of horrible cruelty were perpetrated upon the few officers and men who were captured
alive. Yet it seemed that nothing had been left undone
to render the line secure, and the High Command asserted
that no Rifi force could penetrate it. Yet how quickly,
when the moment arrived, was it to be broken through.
Did the enemy attack in unexpected numbers ? Had
the Rifi and tribesmen's courage and military ability
been underestimated, or was it the rising behind the
lines that was responsible for all those months of
great anxiety and intense strife ? It is difficult to say.
The French guard their secrets well. The most I
have ever heard confessed was that an error had been
committed.

It was only later that the public learned how critical

A French Post.

Photo R. Kate

had been those days of the spring and summer of 1925. Even to-day the details of what took place have never been fully published, nor the names of all the Posts that were evacuated or lost, nor the number of guns captured by the Rifis. It was not until July, 1926, when the Spaniards disarmed the tribes of the Northern Rif, that any idea was obtained by the outside world as to what the French had lost in the captured Posts. Thousands of French military rifles were surrendered to the Spaniards, and many cannon, with large quantities of ammunition and other war material. The remoteness of the scene of action, the control that the French authorities maintained over the movements and messages of the Special Correspondents, the wording of the official communiqués, all sufficed to disguise the truth, and gave rise to a spirit of optimism which the authorities themselves were far from sharing.

In the autumn of 1924 General Primo de Rivera had ordered the abandonment of all the more distant Spanish Posts in the Spanish zone, and the retirement of their garrisons to the bases on or near the coast. Sheshuan itself was evacuated, not without great loss. It was a courageous and wise policy, but there is no doubt that it led Abdel Krim, relieved of this Spanish pressure, to turn his thought Southward and to undertake the campaign against the French. It has often been stated that he would not have hesitated to enter upon this new war even if the Spaniards had pursued a different policy. It is very doubtful, for Abdel Krim was a man who never engaged himself in any adventure until he had made all his plans accordingly. Nor even under the actual circumstances does he seem to have been enthusiastic. Force of circumstances rendered it impossible to do otherwise than to resist the French threat of invasion from the South, though this danger existed largely only in his own imagination and in that of the frontier tribes.

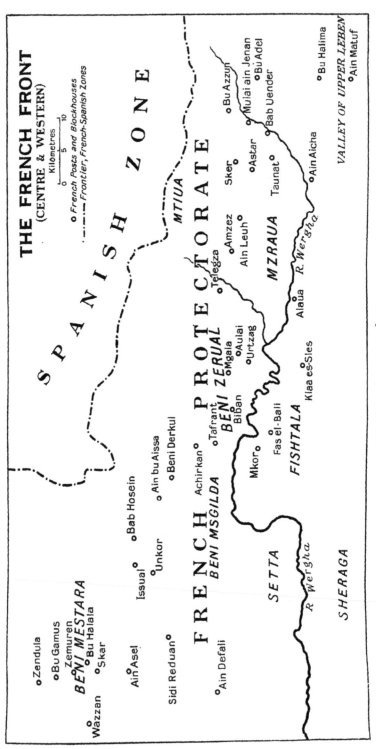

# THE FRENCH FRONT
## (CENTRE & WESTERN)

Kilometres

0   5   10

o French Posts and Blockhouses

·–·–· Frontier, French-Spanish Zones

SPANISH ZONE

FRENCH PROTECTORATE

MT'IUA

MZRAUA

BENI ZERUAL

FISHTALA

SETTA

SHERAGA

BENI MSGILDA

BENI MESTARA

Zemuren

Wazzan

o Zendula

o Bu Gamus

o Bu Halala

o Skar

Ain Asel

Sidi Reduan o

o Ain Defali

Issual o

Unkor o

o Bab Hosein

o Ain bu Aissa

o Beni Derkul

Achirkan o

Tafrant o

Mkor o

Fas el-Bali o

Biban

Mgala o

o Aulai

o Urtzag

Klaa es-Sles o

Telegza o

Ain Leuh o

Amzez o

Alaüa

Sker o

o Astar

Taunat o

Bu Azzun o

Mulai ain Jenan o

o Bu Adel

Bab Uender o

o Ain Aicha

o Bu Halima

VALLEY OF UPPER LEBEN

o Ain Matuf

R. Wergha

R. Wergha

LONDON: EDWARD ARNOLD & CO.

# CHAPTER IX

## THE FRENCH CAMPAIGN : SPRING, 1925

If Abdel Krim did not open his campaign against the French with any enthusiasm, he was at least a consenting party and must bear his full share of the blame. It was his constant argument that this war was forced upon him. To a certain extent it was. He was certainly under the impression that the menace of French invasion of the Rif was a very real one, and again, the pressure put upon him by the demands of the frontier tribes was difficult to resist. Yet he would have sacrificed much to have escaped this complication. He realized that by engaging in a war with France he jeopardized his hopes of a victory over the Spaniards. All possibility of success in that direction disappeared with the entry upon the scene of a new and formidable enemy.

Except perhaps for a certain number of ardent spirits, the French on their side were desirous of ridding the Protectorate of such vestiges of anarchy as still remained before engaging in any new adventure. The 'tache de Taza' and the Middle Atlas still required their attention, and the Protectorate Government would have preferred to be free of the anxiety that those centres of dissidence occasioned before entering upon any adventure elsewhere. This new complication necessitated the despatch of numerous reinforcements to the frontier, which the French would gladly have employed elsewhere in districts near the heart of their zone. This alone was an incentive to peace that Abdel Krim should have taken advantage of. Had he approached the French—at Rabat and not the military authorities at the front or at Fez, who could not be expected to view the situation from the same point of view as the responsible Administration of the Protectorate—there would seem to be no doubt that he might have come to an arrangement, temporary perhaps, but satisfactory to all parties, by which peace could have been maintained. Maréchal Lyautey was known to be desirous of avoiding hostilities. Any solution in the interests of peace that at the same time would have been compatible with the honour and the security of France would have been welcomed and no doubt accepted.

It was unfortunate that the Spanish withdrawal of their forces and garrisons from the interior should have coincided with this delicate situation on the French side of the frontier. Excellent and wise as was General Primo de Rivera's policy in the Spanish zone, it could not fail to affect the situation further South. It freed Abdel Krim from any fear of a Spanish offensive. Raisuli, too, was his prisoner in the Rif, and with his capture the last danger from the Jibala had disappeared. The tribes were solidly with him, and it was to them that he left the surveillance of the Spanish lines. His army and his tribal contingents were now at his full disposal. He could dispatch them to any front without hesitation. He chose the French front.

The bone of contention that brought about the opening of hostilities was the Beni Zerual tribe. The geographical situation of the Beni Zerual had already rendered it a matter of controversy between the French and the Spaniards. By the treaty of 1912 this tribe was included in the Spanish zone of influence, for the frontier line passed to the South, but in order to bring about a strategically better delimitation it had been agreed in principle that the tribes inhabiting the districts the streams of which drained into the River Wergha should fall under French Protectorate administration. The Beni Zerual was included in this category, though it formed an awkward enclave into the Spanish zone, a disadvantage the Spaniards hesitated to accept. It was difficult, however, for them to do more than protest, for their occupation of the Rif had so far not reached that district, while the French to the South were on its very limits.

But Abdel Krim was, as he was never tired of protesting, no party to any of these arrangements. He regarded with anxiety and indignation the French pretensions in a region over which he had already extended his authority, and which approached the Rif so closely. So long as the French remained on the South bank of the Wergha he had no intention of interfering with them, but this constant menace was disquieting. Nor was this all, for in order to strengthen their position in the Beni Zerual the French were already engaged in a very active political campaign in that district. Their principal and most important agent was the Shereef of the Derkawa sect, whose ' Zawia ' was situated at Amjat in the very centre of the tribe. His influence extended over all the surrounding country, and in him the French had found a staunch ally and friend.

Abdel Krim was aware that, although no actual deci-

sion had been come to, the French and Spaniards were
prepared to arrive at a compromise on the subject of
the frontier of the Beni Zerual.  It had been proposed
that the tribe should be divided, the Southern third
falling in the French Protectorate and the Northern
two-thirds in the Spanish zone.  Unsatisfactory as was
recognized to be the splitting up of tribes under different
administrations, it was considered a more reasonable
solution than the irregularity and inconveniences of
frontier that would be occasioned should the whole tribe
be considered as French, which would lead to an objec-
tionable French enclave within the Spanish sphere.  But
the Zawia of the Derkawi Shereef at Amjat would in
that case fall into the Spanish sphere, and the French
neither desired nor intended to lose the valuable influence
of this important personage.  They had in view, therefore, an eventual demand on the part of the Beni Zerual
tribesmen themselves to be included in the Protectorate,
a request that it would be difficult to refuse.  It was
for this reason that, in spite of an understanding in
principle with the Spaniards, they continued their
active political work amongst the tribesmen.  The
Derkawi Shereef was fully aware that as Abdel Krim's
authority extended, the power and wealth of the religious
institutions such as he himself controlled were bound
to diminish, if not in time to disappear.  Already the
subtle campaign of nationalism, uniting tribes that had
never in the past entertained any but hostile relations,
had done much to destroy the privileges of the Shereefian
families in the Rif, who formerly had earned an easy
and comfortable livelihood by the practice of hereditary
sanctity and as arbitrators in tribal and family feuds.
Abdel Krim's antagonism to these powerful sects was

THE FRENCH CAMPAIGN: SPRING, 1925    209

well known. He had not dared openly to break with their Chiefs, but he had found the means of lessening their prestige and influence. He would brook no rival, and he required the money that continually found its way into the pockets of these religious personages. The Derkawi Shereef knew that with the introduction of Abdel Krim's authority into the Beni Zerual, his prestige, his fortune, his position and perhaps his life, would be in danger. Powerful as is this sect all over Morocco—and it appears to be the only one that boasts any real organization—the blow would have been too near its heart not to have proved fatal, for Amjat is the ' holy of holies ' of the Derkawa. It was, therefore, very necessary for the Shereef to defend himself. Alone he could not have ventured to do so, for his attitude toward nationalism and toward Abdel Krim was severely criticized in the surrounding tribes, and even amongst his own people. Without his own reputation for sanctity and the assistance both in money and in arms that he received from the French, joined to their promises for the future, he could never have attempted to resist the popular Rifi cause.

If the French were at work, Abdel Krim himself was not idle. He connected Ajdir, his headquarters near Alhucemas Bay, with the French front by telephone, while another wire was laid to Sheshuan, with branches to Dar Rai, in the mountains near Tetuan and to the Beni Msuar not far from Tangier. At the same time, freed from hostilities with the Spaniards, except that the Jibala tribesmen were harassing their retirement, he redistributed his forces, installed military Posts and ' Mahakmas '—seats of Government—at various spots along the French front, and organized the tribes that

P

had recently joined him. From all these centres his agents carried on an active and effective propaganda. It has often been argued that if any proofs of Abdel Krim's intention to attack the French were wanting they could be found in these warlike preparations, but it must be allowed that they might equally have been due to an appreciation of his own danger from invasion. They were in fact more precautions against a French advance than preparations for an offensive.

Abdel Krim wrote to me on several occasions during this period, protesting against the hostility of the French and asserting his reluctance to be dragged into war on this front. It is not wise to believe everything that Abdel Krim wrote, for his correspondence was often intended to serve other purposes than those of giving reliable information, but he pointed out so clearly his own disadvantages in any campaign against the French that it is scarcely possible to credit him with being a willing agent. He made no secret of the fact that the Spaniards were his real enemies ; that he had no quarrel with, but many complaints against, the French. He saw no reason, he said, why war should come about between them, unless the French had ulterior motives. The Rif did not extend into French Protectorate territory, from which, by its race, its language, and its very position and nature, it was entirely separate. His desire and his intention was to drive the Spaniards out of Africa and he would leave no stone unturned to do so. He had no reason to fight the French, though they seemed to desire to pick a quarrel with him on every possible occasion. They would not let him alone, as was proved by their hostility to himself and his cause in the Beni Zerual, where they were continually plotting

A FRENCH BLOCKHOUSE, SHOWING THE TRENCH CONNECTING IT WITH THE POST.

against him.   Nor could he accept the frontier that they occupied, still less the frontier that they claimed.   He had been no party, he pointed out, to the treaty of 1912, or to any other treaty, which he looked upon as a monstrous example of unwarranted interference in the affairs of an innocent and disinterested people.   Any arrangement the French and the Spaniards might have come to on the subject of a frontier in a country which they had never visited, knew nothing about, where they had failed to exert authority, and where they had no subjects and no material or moral interests, was a preposterous act of totally unjustified and unjustifiable imperialism. The Governments of Europe were always talking about the advantages of the restoration of peace and the introduction of law and order.   He had introduced both into the country in question and was now threatened with invasion and war for having done so.   As a matter of fact, he added, he ought to have received thanks for what he had accomplished.   He did not dispute the right of the French to act South of the Wergha, but in crossing it they had broken their word, they had encroached upon his domains and were undoing all the good work he had achieved.   They seemed, in fact, intent upon reintroducing anarchy into a region he had carefully and successfully pacified.   Abdel Krim was not only a good organizer and a good fighter, he was also a plausible and proficient letter-writer.   He had learned in any case to adopt the tone which we are nowadays so accustomed to read in Europe in dispatches concerning mandates and such like—the injured refutation of misjudged motives and the unctuous protestation of unselfish intentions.

There is no doubt that both sides—the French and

the Rifis—honestly believed in the hostile intentions
of the other, and not without reason.  In the face of the
French precautions against attack the Rifis took steps
to protect their own country from invasion.  In face
of the Rifi steps the French, rendered anxious, sent more
troops to the front.  The reinforcing of the French lines
led to the dispatch of further Rifi contingents.  It was
a striking example of the fallacy of the absurd argument
that the existence and presence of armies, and readiness
to repel attack, prevents war.  It does nothing of the
kind : it only renders it inevitable.

It is difficult to distribute the blame in this case.  The
French on the front had been indiscreet.  To advance,
as they had advanced in 1924, was to invite attack.
The Rifis, whose sole experiences of European good faith
had not been very edifying, were the victims of their
own suspicion and anxiety, and to a certain extent also
the victims of their own waywardness.  They thought
themselves invincible and were deeply stirred by senti-
mental and emotional propaganda, by the appeal to their
faith, and by hopes for the success of national aspirations
of the very meaning of which they had but the faintest
glimmer.  I am convinced that even up to the end of
1924 an arrangement might have been come to for the
maintenance of peace—if those on the spot had really
desired it.  Did they ?  The preparations on both sides
continued, and in February, 1925, further French reinforcements were sent to the front.

It was on April the 13th, 1925, that the smouldering
embers burst into flame.  The ' Zawia ' of the Derkawi
Shereef at Amjat was attacked by Abdel Krim's partisans, numbering, it is said, about 1,500 men, principally
drawn from the surrounding tribes of Beni Mestara, Beni

Ahmed and Ghezawa. At the same time two other 'harkas,' one consisting largely of tribesmen from Ghomara, reached Bu Berih and Tazugert respectively. Abdel Krim seems to have made every preparation with extreme care. The contingents were well armed and well organized, and their arrival upon the scene produced the effect that he had expected and that he desired. A certain number of the frontier tribes, inspired by this show of Moslem independence, threw off their allegiance to the Sultan and to the French and rebelled. Amjat was pillaged and burned, in spite of its reputed sanctity, and the Rifis and Jibala advanced right up to the French lines. In places they passed through them. French Posts were isolated and surrounded and certain tribes behind the lines rose. Anarchy spread over the whole region. As far South as Tissa in the Hayaina, and Sheraga, rebel bands were active. On the South bank of the Wergha the large and important camp of Ain Aicha was threatened and molested. The French lines had failed to hold the Rifi's invasion and a period of grave anxiety ensued. Jibala tribesmen and the Rifis were miles behind the French Posts, and Fez was in danger. Bands of the enemy were within 20 miles of the Capital, and the attitude of the intervening tribes, and even of the population of the city itself, was uncertain.

The situation had become very serious. All available troops were hurried to the front and four battalions arrived from Algeria. There were altogether at this moment eighteen battalions of infantry, six squadrons of cavalry and twelve batteries of artillery at the front. It was totally inadequate. Four thousand Rifis were engaged and another four thousand held in reserve. The position of the French was rendered doubly difficult by the fact that they were responsible for the lives and security of the tribes in the French Protectorate. To abandon them was impossible, but unfortunately it was almost impossible to protect them. The mobility of the Rifis was exasperating. They were everywhere, egging on the tribes to rebellion and burning their villages and their crops in case of refusal. It was no wonder that many tribes wavered, and went over. Maréchal Lyautey arrived in Fez on May the 2nd and drew up with General de Chambrun, who commanded the Fez district, the plan of campaign against the Rif offensive. It was decided to divide the French forces into three groups —the Western, under General Colombat; the centre, under Colonel Freydenberg; and the Eastern, to operate to the North of Taza, under Colonel Cambay. With great celerity these details of reorganization were carried out and all three groups entered into immediate action. A column under Colonel Nogués was dispatched to relieve some of the isolated Posts, a mission which was successfully accomplished; while General Colombat's force, which had concentrated at Fez el-Bali on April the 29th, forded the Wergha, the enemy having success-fully impeded the construction of a military bridge. Meanwhile Colonel Freydenberg was holding the enemy's offensive in the upper valley of the Wad Leben, where the Rifis had penetrated far behind the French Posts. They had even reached Sok el-Arba of Tissa, less than 25 miles from Fez. Colonel Cambay was also heavily engaged in the district of Kifan to the North of Taza, where another incursion of the Rifis had taken place.

The events of those early days of the campaign created something not far removed from consternation in the circles of the Protectorate Government, and even amongst the officers of the army. It had been every one's opinion that the front was invulnerable. The numbers and the fighting qualities of the Rifis had been entirely under-estimated. It was only when they came face to face with Abdel Krim's tribesmen that the French began to understand what had led to the Spanish discomfiture in the Spanish zone. They had blamed the Spaniards for incompetence and disorganization. Yet when the French Protectorate was attacked the French Posts experienced the same fate as the Spanish Posts had suffered. Not only was this whole system of defence found to be a danger, but the individual Posts failed to withstand the Rifi onslaught in many cases, and where they did withstand it, proved highly disadvantageous to the course of the campaign, necessitating the constant despatch of columns to relieve, or to withdraw, their garrisons. The losses to convoys alone, engaged in provisioning the outlying Posts, was far in excess of the services rendered by their maintenance.

Although the road to Fez seemed for the moment at least to be closed to the Rifis, Abdel Krim did not abandon his activity. His agents were everywhere, stirring up the tribes to revolt. He redoubled his propaganda, both by letter and by word of mouth. He strengthened his tribal contingents by the addition of Rifi regulars and he supplied them with artillery and men to serve it. Taunat was closely invested, and other Posts were evacuated, or were captured. The want of fresh troops was badly felt. Those that there were fought valiantly, but their task was no easy one. They had no respite and no rest. The Rifis had already captured on this front both guns and a large quantity of arms and ammunition and hand-grenades, and encouraged by this loot they renewed their attempts to break through to Fez. On May the 9th the French Government issued a communiqué that began ' The situation is neither grave nor disquieting.' It was both—very grave and very disquieting.

The rest of Morocco held firm, a fact of which Maréchal Lyautey and the Protectorate Government had every reason to be proud. The Rifi successes of these days might easily have stirred many other tribes farther afield to revolt. It says much for the administration that the French had introduced into Morocco, and for the policy that this administration had pursued, that the campaign was localized to this Northern part of the country. There was every reason to fear that the Berbers of the ' tache de Taza ' and other regions as yet unoccupied might seize this opportunity to open hostilities. That they did not do so was an immense relief to the authorities. From time to time there were rumours of coming troubles in those regions, but on no occasion did they reach a head. In fact many of the Berber tribesmen, whose loyalty had been open to doubt, joined the French forces as volunteers and fought on their side. A high military authority in Morocco, who knew well both the situation and the Moors, told me that in a great many cases the anticipations of the officers of the Bureaux de Renseignements were at fault. The tribes behind the French lines, which had been counted upon to remain loyal, had rebelled, while such Berbers as the Beni Warain, the Ait Tsageruchen and Riata, whose immediate revolt was expected, sent contingents to fight on the side of the French.

It is not easy to follow in detail the events on the French front during the month of May. The authorities,

perhaps justifiably, concealed much of the truth. It
was evidently unwise for them at that moment to disclose the loss of Posts or even of men. It would but
have called attention to their own miscalculations as
to the enemy's strength and fighting qualities, and have
weakened confidence at home. There was a large party
in France opposed to the war, and any revelation of the
actual circumstances would, it was no doubt realized,
have a particularly bad effect at that moment. France
was not without her troubles at home—the falling franc,
the weakness of the Government, the question of Syria
and other matters—and any signs of failure and discomfiture in Morocco would be quickly seized upon and
used for political purposes. It is an unfortunate fact,
and one that all friends of France must deplore, that
during this whole period of the Rif War the vital interests
of France in North Africa risked being sacrificed in the
game of party politics. It was only owing to the untiring
energy of a few able men, themselves as desirous of peace
as was any Communist, that the ship of Government was
steered safely over a sea that was beset with rocks and
whirlpools. The position of France in Africa at that
moment was a question that should have been far above
all questions of party. A genuine desire for peace was
not only justifiable but was reasonable, and legitimate
endeavours to persuade the Government to bring it
about were equally so ; but there was more than that,
there were direct incentives, issuing from Deputies of
the French Chamber, to the Rifis to continue the struggle,
and hopes expressed for their victory and the downfall
of France in North Africa. Unfortunately these activities were not confined to France alone.

It is therefore not surprising that the accounts of the

events of these earlier days of the campaign only reached Paris in a modified form. They could only have served as oil for the flame of political jealousies and party strife. As it was, the position in which the French Government found itself was not an easy one. It was hoped by those responsible for the conduct of the campaign that the very grave situation which had arisen would be rectified before the details became known. It is always doubtful whether a policy of semi-concealment is satisfactory. It often has the contrary effect to that desired and only increases the suspicions and anxieties of those whose fears it is meant to calm. In this case it would seem that the fact that all the truth was not being published only added to the feeling of uncertainty and unrest.

From May the 1st the fighting took a serious character. The following day General Colombat advanced from Tafrant in the direction of Biban. His force met with strong resistance from a large Rifi contingent which had entrenched itself near the French Post of Aoudur. This was the first occasion on which the French troops came up against an entrenched Rifi enemy, who had dug themselves in with considerable skill and much labour. It was a detachment under Colonel Nogués that drove the Rifis out of their position and rushed the neighbouring village, which the enemy had occupied. Colonel Nogués' troops were almost immediately counterattacked, and so hot was the fighting that bayonets and knives were employed. The French force held its ground and relieved the two neighbouring Posts of Achirkan and Beni Derkul.

On May the 4th General Colombat was in front of Biban, which was considered by both sides the most important position in that direction. It was the key of

THE ATTACK ON BIBAN.

*Photo. Coutanson.*

FRENCH CAMP AT AIN AICHA.

the door that opened the road to Fez. The enemy had taken up a very strong position on the steep slopes, which they had fortified and entrenched. Surrounded by the Rifi forces, the Post of Biban, heavily invested and continually attacked, was holding out valiantly. The garrison was short of provisions and depended for water on blocks of ice dropped from aeroplanes. Nor was this the only Post that was cut off from a supply of water. Aoulai was in the same plight and heavily attacked by night and by day, the Rifis using artillery, rifles and hand-grenades.

It was clear that Biban could not be relieved without the troops under General Colombat being reinforced, and it was not until May the 13th that he was in a position to storm the Rifi trenches. The battle began at daybreak by a heavy artillery bombardment, supported by a concentrated bombing by aeroplanes, and the enemy were driven out of the valley of the Wad Anoser. These preparations concluded, the troops advanced, preceded by a barrage of artillery fire. The steep slopes on which the Rifis were entrenched were stormed and before mid-day the enemy began to give way. The fight continued without a break till three o'clock in the afternoon, when the Posts of Biban and Dar Remich were relieved. Later in the evening the Post of Mjala was reached and the garrison evacuated.

There was no rest for General Colombat's troops. On May the 15th they relieved Aoulai, where for two weeks three French officers, two non-commissioned officers and sixty Senegalese soldiers had brilliantly defended the fort. The second in command, two of his subordinates and a number of the men had been wounded. During the latter part of the siege, since the enemy had

succeeded in capturing an outlying blockhouse, the Post
had been bombarded by a Rifi gun at a range of only
400 yards.  Other Posts were reached.  In many only
the bodies of the officers and men of the garrison, often
horribly mutilated, were found.  General Colombat's
column returned via Kla es-Sless and Tafrant to its base
at Fez el-Bali, but on May the 19th they were again
called upon to relieve Biban, to the investment of which
the Rifi hordes had returned.  They provisioned the
Post, but again had to fight their way through the
enemy trenches.  The battle much resembled that which
had taken place on the first relief of Biban—an artillery
barrage covering the advance of the infantry.  Once
more, too, there was hand-to-hand fighting which lasted
for six hours.  This second successful relief of the Post
seems to have discouraged the Rifis, who for a time abandoned their investment of the position.  This gave the
garrison the much desired opportunity of reorganizing
the Post, which it was considered absolutely necessary
to hold as commanding the road to Fez.  The troops
under Colonel Féral, who had assisted in the work of
strengthening the Post, were furiously attacked on their
return march toward their base, both sides losing heavily
in a battle of more than usual stubbornness.  It was
only the arrival of General Colombat's force that terminated a combat the results of which might have been
tragic.  No sooner had Colonel Féral's troops left Biban
than it became again the object of fierce Rifi attacks.
On May the 25th, 26th, and 27th the garrison had no
rest.  The Rifis had brought up cannon with which
they bombarded, while the tribesmen tried again and
again to rush the parapets, making use of large numbers
of hand-grenades.

Perceiving that all the Posts in this region were in danger, General Colombat withdrew the garrisons of Aoudur and Achirkan and reinforced that of Beni Derkul. In spite of all resistance the Rifis advanced, and Tafrant itself was attacked at the same time as Teruel in the Beni Msgilda. To the West, Wazzan was threatened, and toward the end of May, Jibala contingents in large numbers arrived in that region from Sheshuan, in the Spanish zone. They were said to number in all about 3,000 men. General Billotte was in command at Wazzan and every precaution had been apparently taken to protect the town. Two columns were despatched to Mzufrun on the Wad Lukkus and to Terual in the Beni Msgilda respectively, while a third mobile column defended the front between those two Posts. Wazzan was not only of importance as a town of some size, but it stood on the direct line that the Jibala would have to follow should they attempt to invade in force the rich plain country of the Gharb lying to the West between the hills on which the town lay and the Atlantic Ocean. So threatening, however, became the situation, and so constant the attacks upon the neighbouring Posts, that it was considered advisable to withdraw the European civil population of the town. General Colombat's force was requisitioned to assist in the defence of this part of the country, from the valley of the Wad Lukkus to Terual.

Meanwhile the Rifis had made their principal effort in the centre of the French front, for there lay the most direct and the easiest route to Fez. In the middle of May the enemy appeared in largely increased numbers. Their first advance had been checked by Colonel Freydenberg in the valley of the Leben, but they returned

and attacked again with renewed vigour. The Post of
Taleghza fell and Amzez was bombarded by the Rifi
cannon. Taunat was once more closely invested. On
May the 20th Amzez, Ain Leuh and Taunat were fiercely
assaulted and the blockhouse of Bu Azzun was rushed.
Face to face with this renewed offensive, Colonel Freydenberg appealed for reinforcements and Colonel Cambay
was sent to his assistance. The two groups were placed
under General de Chambrun, who commanded the Fez
district. On May the 21st Colonel Freydenberg with his
column captured the fortified slopes of Ghiua. On the
left Colonel Callais with a detachment of native troops
occupied a Rifi position, while on the right Bab Uender
and Remila, on the heights of the right bank of the
Wergha, were successfully carried after a stiff fight.
Pushing on, the French troops successfully entered
Mulai Ain Jenan, and Bu Azzun, which had been abandoned, was reoccupied. Colonel Cambay's column,
advancing from the East toward Mediuna, met with
stubborn resistance and only gained the plateau after
a long day's fight. Although the success of this combined movement was evident, it did not deter the Rifs
from continuing their attempts to push Southward
toward Fez.

In these circumstances it was decided to withdraw
the garrisons of most of the outlying Posts. It was
no easy task and Colonel Freydenberg's troops were
heavily attacked. A further general retirement was
necessary and still more Posts were abandoned. The
garrisons of Mulai Ain Jenan, Bu Azzun and Bab Uender
were retired. On May the 26th Anizer and Ain Leuh
were evacuated. Sker was in difficulties, for as fast as
the Posts were abandoned the Rifis advanced. A few

days later they were back in the upper valley of the
Wad Leben, where Colonel Freydenberg hurried in order
to check this new invasion.

The Taunat district was again the scene of much
fighting. The Post of Astar was captured by the Rifis
and Sker was surrounded. Sahela fell, the garrison
fighting its way back to Taunat. Pushing forward,
the Rifis crossed the Wergha near the important camp
of Ain Aicha and reached Sidi Allel el-Haj several miles
farther South, but Taunat, hard pressed, had been relieved and Sker and Astar reoccupied. On June the 4th
the Rifis returned to the attack of Taunat. General
Billotte was now in command on this part of the front,
where Colonel Freydenberg and Colonel Callais's troops
had been concentrated. Astar and Sker, under intense
enemy pressure, had to be once again evacuated on
June the 6th. The fighting was continuous. Ain Maatof
and Mediuna were furiously attacked, and it was not
till June the 16th that the Rifi forces which had crossed
to the South bank of the Wergha were driven back
across the river.

To the East the fighting was scarcely less continuous.
Here again the Rifis had brought artillery into action
and were making every endeavour to reach and cut the
Fez-Taza-Ujda road and railway. It was said on good
authority that between 5,000 and 6,000 Jibala tribesmen were engaged in this offensive, with Rifi contingents
in reserve. Even as far East as Msun there were
skirmishes with Rifi patrols.

# CHAPTER X

## THE FRENCH CAMPAIGN : SUMMER, 1925

It was not in Morocco alone that the French were having trouble. In Paris the Communists were carrying on an active anti-war campaign. On June the 4th Monsieur Painlevé, who was both President du Conseil and Minister of War, recalled in the Chamber the origin of the war, and gave some account of what had occurred and of the losses suffered. He informed the Deputies that reinforcements and artillery had been sent to the front. He gave the losses to date at 318 killed, 1,115 wounded and 195 missing—three-fifths of these casualties being, he said, amongst the native troops. The entire medical service and sanitary department of the army was being reorganized. He praised, as he had every reason to do, the conduct of the troops.

On June the 10th Monsieur Painlevé, accompanied by Monsieur Aynac, the Under Secretary for Air, and General Jacquemot left Toulouse by aeroplane for Morocco, reaching Rabat that evening. At Fez, where they proceeded the same night, the Minister of War met General Daugan, who was in command of the whole front, and Generals Billotte and de Chambrun. The next morning he was at Ain Aicha, on the Wergha, where he conferred with Colonel Freydenberg. On June the 12th he visited Wazzan and discussed the situation with General Colombat, returning to Rabat the same evening. On the 13th he left for Paris. He had made certain declarations as to the desires and intentions of the French Government. Like nearly all his compatriots, he was convinced of the presence of European officers with Abdel Krim's forces. It was not until the Rifi leader's surrender in May, 1926, that the majority of Frenchmen were persuaded that Abdel Krim, with the exception of two or three deserters from the French Foreign Legion and a Norwegian masseur, depended entirely upon his own capacities, and those of his brother and a few native advisers, for his military measures. With those few exceptions he had no European in his employ.

On his return to Paris, Monsieur Painlevé found that the Communists had by no means abandoned their campaign in favour of peace and for withdrawal from Morocco. It was no doubt in face of this movement that Monsieur Briand, the Foreign Minister, declared in the Chamber on June the 19th that the French Government was 'passionately in favour of peace. Not a minute will be lost, from the moment that we can be certain that peace is possible, before we turn our efforts toward obtaining it.' This firm and honest declaration calmed the anxiety in France, though it was realized that the situation was still serious on the front.

On June the 20th enemy pressure was again exerted in the upper valley of the Wad Leben while the Jibala contingents near Kifan were reinforced by Rifis. The tribes of Tsul and Branes, who up till now had loyally supported the French, became the victims of Rifi reprisals and wavered. From farther South, across the

Fez-Taza-Ujda road came disquieting rumours. Taza
itself was in danger.

But it was in the centre that the situation had become
critical. Abdel Krim's brother, Si Mahammed, who
was Commander-in-Chief of all the Rifi forces, had
arrived in that neighbourhood with a considerable force
and the French Posts of Ain Maatof and Bu Halima
were surrounded. Sok el-Arba of Tissa, in the Hayaina,
was again threatened. The villages of the loyal tribesmen were being systematically burned, and a convoy
of military cars was attacked on the Tissa-Fez road.
The Rifis in this district alone were reported to number
over 2,000. On June the 27th the enemy was driven
back and the pressure relieved.

To the East, in the Taza district, the Rifis had not
only held their ground but had advanced. Their
objective was clear—to cut the Fez-Taza-Ujda road and
join forces with the ' dissident ' Berbers of the Atlas.
During three days—June the 23rd, 24th, and 25th—
the Rifi offensive was continued, only to be repulsed
with heavy loss. They counter-attacked with great
courage, but were again defeated. Everywhere along
the front the enemy were ' filtering ' through, passing
the lines in small numbers, and concentrating when
once behind them. These bands continued the harassing
of the loyal tribesmen, burnt their villages and pillaged
their farms. So numerous and so mobile were they that
it was almost impossible to rid the country of these
marauders who were doing incalculable harm in dis-
heartening the loyal tribesmen.

On June the 27th General Billotte's forces were seriously engaged at Bab Taza, in the upper Leben valley,
where the enemy again attacked in force. Bab Mizab

BURNING VILLAGES IN THE RIF.

[To face p. 288.]

was evacuated, while a number of small Posts in Tsul and Branes were invested by the enemy. To retire would leave the Fez-Taza-Ujda road and railway at the mercy of the Rifis and facilitate their contact with the Berber tribes, with probably disastrous results. A retreat would, too, most seriously affect the loyalty of other districts. A battle was fought on July the 5th, when General Billotte's forces were attacked. The French held their ground and the engagement was considered a success, but it did not prevent the precautionary measure being taken of evacuating all the European women and children from Taza. On the upper Leben, the Post of Bab Taza, which must not be confounded with the town of Taza, was lost and re-taken and the French position was subjected to fierce attacks on the nights of July the 5th, 6th, and 7th. The Rifis employed machine guns and hand-grenades. The fighting was at times desperate, but the French counterattacks were successful and for a short time the tribesmen seemed discouraged.

At the end of June the Sultan of Morocco, Mulai Yussef, arrived at Fez from Rabat. There had been a question of his coming at an earlier date, but it was felt that he was too valuable an asset in the game to be placed in a position of danger, and Fez had been seriously threatened. Nor was it considered advisable to bring him to the Capital as long as there remained any possibility that he might have to beat an ignominious retreat in a direction of safety. There had been some doubt, too, as to the loyalty of the Fezis themselves.

Fez is the soul of Morocco—an uneasy, disturbed soul, the sort of soul that can be imagined wandering in Purgatory soothing its kindred sufferers with ill and interested advice.

From the moment of its foundation in A.D. 808 by Mulai Idris, the founder of the Idrisite dynasty, Fez has played an important part in the history of the country. A seat of learning, a place of pious pilgrimage and a centre of Islamic propaganda, its fame spread far and wide outside Morocco. Its university, renowned in the Middle Ages, became the resort of Moslems from far afield. Leo Africanus, describing the city in the opening days of the sixteenth century, writes : ' A World it is to see, how large, how populous, how well fortified and walled this citie is.' There were periods, of course, as in the history of all Oriental places, when the glory of Fez temporarily departed, but always to revive. Without recognition by its people no Sultan could ascend the Moorish throne. He might seize the power in the South, but until Fez, by goodwill or by force, had accepted him his kingdom was divided.

The Fezis, astute, politically unscrupulous, and grasping, have always used this privilege for their own purposes. They have bargained their recognition of succeeding Sultans in return for diminution of taxes and for other benefits, which although promised have not always been for long performed, for the word of their Sultans has seldom proved more binding than their own loyalty. What they might have given they sold, and in selling drove the best possible bargain ; but the undercurrent of intrigue and sedition, due to avarice, jealousy, and malice, has never ceased to flow. Nothing has ever satisfied the Fezis ; nothing probably ever will satisfy them. Skilful, and in their foreign dealings honest, men of business, their main and sole endeavour

is their own enrichment.  Proud of being citizens of so
distinguished and so beautiful a capital—in their eyes
it is incomparable—they look upon the inhabitants of
the rest of Morocco as distinctly inferior beings, and
upon Europeans as dangerous barbarians.  Without
any sentiment of real religion, they are none the less
fanatics.  While the aristocratic inhabitant of Fez, in
his surroundings of luxury, turns his attention mainly
to trade, he is not idle elsewhere.  His influence per-
meates the universities and the native schools, even the
shops and the narrow streets, in an indefinable atmosphere of unrest.

Just as in the past, secretly, the Fezis carped at the
Sultan and the Maghzen, even though often serving both,
so to-day they criticize all authority.  Were they all
the salaried servants of the State, their salaries would
not suffice.  Were the doors of Paradise opened to them,
they would complain of the doorstep.  And yet when
Fez was their very own, so few years ago, they did
nothing to improve its condition.  It is the French who
have so skilfully restored the monuments and revived
the lost arts of other days.  It is the French who have
paved the little streets and brought roads right up to
the walls of the capital—the French who have cleared
away the accumulated filth of ages and restored Fez
to its ancient renown and beauty.  The Fezis complain
that the accommodation in the hospitals and schools
is insufficient.  What hospitals and what schools existed
when the French came to Fez in 1912 ?  Had they then
been offered them they would have indignantly, in their
pride of ignorance, refused them.  They complain of the
insufficient power of the electric lamps that light their
streets.  How few years ago they had to guide their

feet, stumbling on wooden pattens, through the muddy by-ways by the light of a flickering lantern!

They have shown, it is said, an aptitude for municipal administration. It is possible, for there may still exist some memory of a remote and civilized past, but what administration existed in those years previous to the introduction of the Protectorate? Little more than twenty years ago—and I was in Fez at the time—during a severe and ghastly famine the representatives of the principal families of the city formed a ring and cornered all the foodstuffs and charcoal. Using the authority of such of their numbers as were members of the Government, they posted men all round the outskirts of the city and allowed no produce to enter. It had all to be sold to their agents, and by them introduced into the town. The poor died, but the merchants and aristocrats of Fez grew wondrous rich. The caravans of camels that should have brought grain from the coast arrived laden with marble for the decoration of their costly houses. The same men in many cases still form the aristocracy of Fez and those who have died have been replaced by other members of their families, and to-day they criticize every action of the authorities, complaining of oppression and want of consideration.

There has never been a revolt or a revolution in Northern Morocco that has not been fostered in Fez. Through the students of the universities and the visiting tribesmen sedition has been spread far and wide. Every pretender to the Throne has received support of some kind or another, and it is no secret that the majority of the population of Fez secretly prayed for the success of Abdel Krim. That he was a Rifi, and therefore to them a barbarian, mattered little. They did not even consider what manner of treatment they and their property would have received at his hands, for Abdel Krim must have known them well. They merely blindly desired to overthrow the existing authority, as in the past they have desired, and sometimes succeeded, in overthrowing their own Government.

The moment was well chosen for the Sultan's visit. The Eid el-Kebir, commemorating the incident of Abraham and Isaac, which is the most important of all the Islamic feasts in Morocco, was to be celebrated on July the 2nd. Abdel Krim had announced that it would be he himself and no other who would sacrifice the sheep on this occasion. The emptiness of this vain boast could not be better demonstrated than by the presence of the Sultan and the death of the sacrificial ram at his hands. The tribes had been deeply impressed by the Rifi leader's arrogant assertion and even the people of Fez had not escaped the contagion. The whole situation had become more delicate. For forty-eight hours before the feast took place the moral atmosphere was disconcerting. A sort of stupor seized the native population and the people appeared to be in a state of ecstatic expectation. So universal, probably by sug-gestion, was this emotion that even the high Govern-ment officials were affected. It was to the intense relief of the authorities that the ceremony passed off without any untoward incident. For Abdel Krim to have been there would have necessitated a miracle, but it was a miracle the people expected. There is no doubt what-ever that, had he been able to carry out his promise, he would have been accepted as a saviour of Islam by a vast majority of the people of Fez. That they would have soon regretted their enthusiasm is equally certain.

They never proclaimed a Sultan in the past without experiencing disappointment and disillusion, owing often to the character and conduct of the Sultan, and still more often to their own innate spirit of discontent.

From Fez the Sultan addressed a letter to his people. After the usual salutations and an account of his journey from Rabat to the Capital, the letter continued:

' The principal motive that determined Our journey is the situation created by the error which has pushed certain of the mountain tribes to follow, on the path of rebellion, a disturber of the peace who has come from the Rif to light the flame of anarchy amongst the tribes that inhabit the Wergha valley.

' You are aware that the Rifi hordes have found in front of them the valiant troops who are defending the integrity of Our empire. They have found a barrier that they, the " dissidents," have in vain tried to penetrate.

' You will soon learn, if it so please God, that entire success will crown the troops' courageous efforts, by inflicting upon the invader the punishment that he deserves and by bringing back under Our benign authority the unfortunate people who have been led into rebellion.

' In awaiting the happy termination of the military operations We cannot warn you too seriously against the lies and the false news that instigators of trouble are disseminating in the villages and in the country districts. We exhort you to be calm and to continue your ordinary occupations, for it must not be lost to view that the actual events are of an essentially local

character and should have no repercussion in the rest
of the empire.

'No one can fail to recognize the benefits which
Morocco, since Our accession to the throne of Our venerated ancestors, has received from the introduction of
order and security, thanks to which the country has been
able to develop the riches with which nature has endowed
it, with the result that the task has been crowned with
its just reward of well-being.

'But this era of prosperity, by which Our country
has up to now been favoured, cannot fail to be succeeded
by periods of gloom, if anarchy is to take the place of
order and of respect of persons and of property. You
are therefore earnestly recommended to close your eyes
to all kind of incitements whether from within the
country or from without, for they can have no other
result than to deprive you of the fruits of your labour
and to bring about your ruin.

'Let those who have allowed themselves to be led
astray hasten to return to obedience, so that they may
obtain pardon and be able to return to their former lives.

'The Prophet has said " Anarchy sleeps. Cursed be
him who awakes it."

'Perfect happiness resides in peace and tranquillity.
May God guide you into the best of all ways.'

'Salaam.'

This letter was followed, on July the 4th, by the
announcement that His Majesty had decided to follow
the traditions of his ancestors and call upon certain
tribes from different parts of Morocco to supply levies.
The Sultan's appeal met with an immediate response,
and a considerable number of irregular troops arrived

from the South of the country. They consisted almost entirely of cavalry. That they could render great service on the front was naturally not the case, but they were employed in useful work amongst the tribes behind the lines where, accustomed to the native methods of warfare, they were able to scatter a number of the Rifi marauding bands, and they patrolled the regions which were threatened with enemy depredations. The political effect of the summoning of these levies was good, and the tribes of the frontier, who had been told that all Morocco was disaffected, were surprised and impressed to see the cavalry of the Southern Kaids arriving on the scene of action, as loyal and voluntary combatants on the side of the French.

Although the Sultan's visit to Fez was not without its effect, it brought about no very real amelioration in the situation. No sooner had he returned to Rabat in the early days of July than further tribes that had up till now remained loyal began to show signs of disaffection and restiveness. It was natural. The French had failed to protect them and their possessions from enemy aggressions and reprisals, and the Rifis were continually bringing fresh pressure upon them to revolt. Many, completely ruined, had been obliged to take refuge away behind the French lines. The effect was what might have been expected. After waiting for the promised protection and failing to obtain it many of them went over to the enemy. They had seen their villages burned and their crops pillaged or destroyed. Their cattle had been driven off and members of their families had been killed, and no relief was apparently forthcoming. The French had won no decisive victory. The frontier tribes of the Protectorate were still—and it was July—overrun by the enemy hordes. The front now extended from Wazzan almost to Algeria, a distance of over 200 miles. Its defence was arduous and difficult for a force of 60,000 French and native troops, a number evidently quite inadequate for such a task. The important tribes of Tsul and Branes had now definitely declared for Abdel Krim, and others followed their example.

On July the 7th General Naulin, who had much experience of colonial warfare, was appointed to the command of the army in Morocco. A decree announcing his appointment was issued by the President of the French Republic on that day. It explained the position of General Naulin *vis-à-vis* to Maréchal Lyautey. The Maréchal remained responsible for the security of Morocco and was in supreme command of all military and naval forces in that country. General Naulin was designated ' Commandant supérieur des troupes du Maroc.' He was to receive from the Resident-General (Maréchal Lyautey) instructions necessary for the direction of the operations, but was himself to be responsible for the manner in which the operations were prepared and carried out. In the limits of the war area the ' Commandant supérieur ' should be in absolute command of the district and of all the branches of the corresponding administration, including the ' Department of military Intelligence.' He should have power to appoint and to change all officers who did not hold a special commission direct from the Minister of War. His correspondence with the Ministry of War should, however, pass through the hands of the Resident-General. General Naulin was given the rank of a General commanding an Army Corps.

The publication of this decree was accompanied by a declaration from the President du Conseil, Monsieur Painlevé, which stated :

' This appointment has been made with the entire approval of Maréchal Lyautey whose political and administrative duties are heavy enough at this moment without his being charged with the weight of the military operations as well.'

The day of General Naulin's appointment was marked by another Rifi offensive, the objective of which was again Fez. On July the 12th 2,000 Rifis and Jibala attacked Kla es-Sless, but were repulsed after strenuous fighting.

It was then the turn of the Wazzan front to become active, and under the menace of large enemy forces the French outlying Posts were evacuated and the line of defence brought back to a distance varying from 3 to 7 miles from the town, for the enemy attacks to the East and centre of the line necessitated a withdrawal of troops on this front. Only a force sufficient to guarantee the security of the town of Wazzan could be spared for this sector.

The feeling in France was not unnaturally one of pessimism. The hopes expressed for a speedy amelioration of the situation had not been warranted. Reinforcements had arrived ; three months had passed since the outbreak and yet it was impossible to say that the situation was any better than it had been when hostilities had first broken out. The climate was bad and the troops were suffering from fatigue and the effects of the intense heat. The task that they were given to perform was almost beyond human endurance. No words of praise are sufficient to express the determina-

TRENCH ON THE FRENCH FRONT.

tion of the men and officers alike to overcome the great difficulties of the situation. I have seen the Morocco front on many occasions, in winter and in summer. It would break the spirit of many. The utter forlornness, the inaccessibility, the fatigue, the extremes of climate, the depressing atmosphere, the continual alarms and the continual disappointments, the cruelty of the enemy—all tended to breed a spirit of hopelessness and a sense of desolation that is unrealizable if not actually experienced. The courage, the ' moral ' of the officers and men during those months of unceasing effort was above all praise.

At least forty of the frontier Posts had now been evacuated or taken. There were many acts of heroism performed that have been reported, there were many more that will never be known, and of which the only traces were the mutilated and burnt bodies of the men who did their duty to the very last.

Every attempt was made in Morocco to give an extraordinary importance to the fêtes of July the 14th, but the spirit was one of disappointment and anxiety. Maréchal Lyautey in addressing the French and native officials and residents at Rabat, after praising the conduct of the army turned to the actual situation. ' Confidence ! ' he said. ' The hardest days are over. Up till now we have resisted with forces below the minimum of necessity, thanks to the courage and energy of all. I have passed days of the deepest anxiety. To-day our means of resistance are being constantly increased, and will continue increasing. We are sure of being able not only to resist the blow, but also to remain masters of the situation.'

On July the 15th the French Government issued a

communiqué in Paris. It was direct and to the point.
In the Wazzan district the front had been brought
back much nearer the town ; there was an insufficiency
of troops owing to the necessity to send forces farther
East. In the Centre affairs were better. To the South
of Fez el-Bali the country was clear of the enemy, but
a battalion of Algerian tirailleurs was surrounded and
cut off. Their commander was wounded. Near Bab
Taza the enemy had forged ahead, nearer to Fez than
they had ever previously been, but had been driven
back. In the district of Taza itself it had been necessary to hurry reinforcements to the spot in order to
defend the town the security of which was threatened.
Any failure on this front would almost certainly bring
about a revolt of the neighbouring Berber tribes. The
communiqué ended by explaining that the tactics of
Abdel Krim necessitated the continual movement of
troops, which prevented the following up of successes
and demanded an unceasing change in the disposition of
the forces on the front. I quote the last words of the
communiqué : ' Our security in Morocco, in the opinion
of those who are the least favourable to a continuation
of the war, is a question of effectives ; reinforcements
are indispensable.'

This was perhaps the gravest period of the Rif war.
On July the 17th the road between Ain Aicha, the
most important French camp near the front, and Fez
was cut, and the camp itself attacked, while the Zawia
of Mulai Bushta in Fishtala was destroyed. On July
the 19th there was a fresh Rifi offensive all along the
line from Kla es-Sless to the upper valley of the Leben,
but reinforcements were now arriving from France and
from the Colonies. It was time. The actual losses

had not been excessive, but the wear and tear were very great. The French Government reported that in the first three months of the campaign the troops had suffered the following casualties : killed and missing, 1,473 ; wounded, 2,775.

It was decided in Paris, in order to calm public opinion, to send Maréchal Pétain to inspect the front. At the same time the despatch of further reinforcements was announced. On July the 20th the camp of Ain Aicha, which had been completely cut off, was relieved. The following day General Naulin, succeeding General Daugan, took over the command of all the war area. On his way to Fez he had conferred with Maréchal Pétain and Maréchal Lyautey at Rabat.

Maréchal Pétain's Report was only made public on August the 9th. It gives perhaps the best summary of the situation up to the conclusion of his visit to the front near the end of July.

' The brutal fact is that we were unexpectedly attacked by the most powerful and the best armed enemy that we have ever met with in our colonial campaigns.'

' The Rif and the Jibala districts, independently of the Rifis and of the dissident tribesmen on the front, can count upon a reserve of from 30,000 to 40,000 fighters, keen, vigorous, skilled in the use of their arms, exalted by their successes in previous years, knowing thoroughly the rough country in which they fight, requiring so little that they are able to do without the convoys which so weigh down our columns, and in possession of machine guns, of cannon and an abundant supply of ammunition.'

' Under these conditions the task of our troops, scanty in number, during the early days, could only be extremely difficult and thankless.'

' The Posts of " surveillance," across the Wergha, the establishment of which has been subjected to severe criticism, carried out their object in breaking the first invasion of the attacking forces, in maintaining for a time the loyalty of the frontier tribes and have served as bases of information for the command. One can understand that public opinion was moved at times by their retirement and by the fall of some of them, but it must not be forgotten that the mission of all front-line Posts entails sacrifice.'

' Our troops, swamped by an ever increasing wave of rebellion, fighting without respite against an enemy remarkably mobile, were forced to give protection where the pressure was greatest ; to bring aid to, to provision or to escort back, the retiring garrisons of the Posts that were in danger, and to hold up the " dissident " tribes that threatened the roads to Fez and Algeria.'

' This overwhelming task they only accomplished thanks to their extraordinary qualities of tenacity and devotion, at the price of super-human privations and fatigue, and with a patriotism and in a spirit of sacrifice for which we can never be too grateful.'

' One can only render homage to the great chief (Maréchal Lyautey) who, in spite of his age and of all the weight of his trying colonial career, has been the soul of this defence and has been able to preserve from the inrush of these barbarians his work of civilization that is the admiration of the whole world.'

' Thanks to the arrival of further reinforcements, it will now be possible to replace, in order to give them a rest from their heroic labours, the units which have been victoriously resisting the enemy for three months, while the principal body of our troops will be organized

and will continue its preparations for a speedy repulse
of the enemy, in order to strengthen everywhere our
authority and to bring about a solid organization
which will guarantee us in the future against new
incursions.'

'The horizon grows brighter. The adversary in
spite of his repeated attacks has failed to attain his
political objectives (Fez and Taza) which he had boasted
he would enter as conqueror. What has not been
sufficiently pointed out is the fact that Abdel Krim has
never reached Fez, that the Taza road is still open and
that at the present moment those two towns are secure
against any enemy attack, and that the interior of
Morocco remains completely loyal.'

'The discretion which was necessary in the hour of
peril has not perhaps allowed French public opinion
to comprehend in all its gravity either the nature or
the import of the events which have been passing in
Morocco since the beginning of the Rifi aggression.
To-day when one can speak with freedom public opinion
should be kept fully informed.'

'I who have just come from seeing our officers and
soldiers at their work feel it my duty to say how pro-
foundly I appreciate the value of the effort accomplished
by our troops and I proclaim aloud my admiration.'

These were the words of a great soldier who was
speaking of what he had seen and heard on the front
and were a splendid tribute to the troops whose unfailing
courage and unceasing energy had not improbably saved
France in North Africa.   It was only right that the truth
should be known and justice rendered.   How different
was this outspoken communiqué to that issued by the

R

French Government not so long before : 'There is nothing disquieting and nothing grave in the situation'!

In the first week of August, Abdel Krim renewed his attempts to break through the Wazzan front, whence, as has already been mentioned, troops had been withdrawn for employment on the Centre and Eastern fronts. Zendula was evacuated on July the 27th. Ain bu Aissa was hard pressed and could only be provisioned by aeroplane. Pushing across the spurs of Jibel Sarsar the enemy reached the Tangier-Rabat road not far from Arbawa, burning and pillaging one or two French farms. On July the 30th the Post of Ain bu Aissa was destroyed by the bursting of an enemy shell in its magazine. Of its garrison only a wounded native sergeant and fifteen men managed to fight their way to Terual, but a smaller group of survivors was rescued in a critical position on August the 5th. So serious had the state of affairs become on the Wazzan front that Colonel Freydenberg was sent in all haste with a mobile column to relieve the situation. Armoured cars accompanied him. He arrived on the front on August the 2nd. The hill of Asjen—only a very short distance from the town of Wazzan—where the enemy had taken up a strong position, was stormed and successfully carried, a success largely due to the use of the tanks. The following day the slopes of Jibel Sarsar were cleared of the rebel contingents and the tribesmen retired on almost all parts of the line. Simultaneously a little farther East an important engagement was taking place, which resulted in the relief of Fez el-Bali and the provisioning of Tafrant.

On Jibel Amergu overlooking the plain of Mulai Bushta in Fishtala are the ruins of a Portuguese fortress,

TRANSPORT OF WOUNDED MEN.

*Phot. Coutanson.*

*Photo. Coutanson.*

**FRENCH** TANKS CROSSING THE RIVER WERGHA.

perched on a rocky peak and dating from the seventeenth century.  Its situation rendered it almost inaccessible except over exposed ground.  In this strong position the Rifis had decided to make a determined stand, as it served them as a base for their raids into the surrounding country.  The French, realizing the importance of Jibel Amergu, commenced operations for its occupation by a continuous bombardment of the ruined castle from the air.  So destructive was the effect that when on August the 7th, a direct attack by infantry began, the enemy speedily retreated.  The loss of this strong position so injured the Rifi prestige amongst the surrounding tribes that some of them immediately submitted.

On the Eastern front General Boichut, commanding the XIX Army Corps, was now in command.  The principal danger in that direction lay in the revolt of the Tsul tribe which caused a new and serious menace to the French line.  The fighting was continuous and it was only on July the 26th that a detachment under Colonel Féral, which had been cut off for three weeks, was extricated from its perilous position.  On July the 29th a band of the enemy reached the Fez-Taza railway near the station of Sidi Abdullah and tore up the line, but the following day they were in retreat.

The arrival of large reinforcements in Morocco necessitated a redistribution of command.  General Naulin remained Commander-in-Chief with General Pruneau on the West, General Marty on the Centre and General Boichut on the East fronts.  The most important event that was reported from the Western scene of operations was the co-operation of the French and Spanish forces on the frontier of the two zones, in the

valley of the Wad Lukkus, where on August the 10th
General Freydenberg—he had been promoted—met the
Spanish General Riquelme and conferred with him on
the situation. It was the first tangible result of the
accord that had recently been arrived at in Madrid for
Franco-Spanish co-operation in Morocco.

August passed in tolerable tranquillity on that and
on the Centre fronts. There was much to be done—
reorganization of the forces and the incorporation of
the newly arrived reinforcements. Regiments that had
borne the brunt of the three months' campaign were
at last sent to enjoy a well-earned period of rest elsewhere in Morocco.

On the Eastern front General Boichut advanced in
three groups on August the 19th. Two columns formed
the flanks, while the Centre consisted of ten battalions
of infantry with a strong force of artillery. Advancing
simultaneously over difficult and mountainous country
the territory of the Tsul tribe was occupied. The
operation was completely successful and little resistance
was met with. It led to the submission of Tsul and of
a large part of the neighbouring tribe of Branes. The
heat during this operation was extreme.

On August the 18th Maréchal Pétain left Paris to take
over the supreme command in Morocco. At Algeciras
he and General Primo de Rivera, President of the Spanish
Directorate, met and discussed the agreed policy of common action which had been the subject of recent negotiation. On August the 26th Maréchal Lyautey, summoned
home to report on the whole question of Morocco, left
Rabat for France.

It was only natural that the relations of these two
Marshals of France should become a matter of discussion

in the Press.  An official communiqué, published in Paris on September the 2nd, explained the intentions of the French Government.  Maréchal Pétain was solely responsible for the military operations, while the Resident-General, Maréchal Lyautey, was in charge of all the administrative and political affairs of the country. His stay in Paris was a short one, and on September the 12th he left France to return to his post.  He had undertaken to work in cordial co-operation with Maréchal Pétain.  It was what every one who knew Maréchal Lyautey's high sense of duty and patriotism expected, though his was a character that with difficulty brooked interference.

Maréchal Pétain lost no time.  After a visit to the front, no detail of which seems to have escaped his notice, he opened the new phase of the campaign by an artillery bombardment all along the Wergha valley.  It was followed by a series of successful advances in the direction of Biban, Ain bu Aissa and Amjat.  Astar and Sker, near Taunat, were retaken.  The Rifi forces retired Northward.  On September the 12th the advance was continued and fresh objectives were reached.  Part of Biban was cleared and Amjat occupied, and the French were almost back on their original front from which they had been forced to retire by the Rifi invasion.  The abandoned Posts—for over fifty had been evacuated or taken by the enemy—were once more in their hands. The whole front was pushed forward.  On September the 15th the enemy's last fortified positions on Biban fell and the whole of that mountain was occupied.  The Rifis had held it since June.  The loss of Biban was a severe blow to Abdel Krim's cause.

Farther North in the Spanish zone an event of the

highest importance had taken place. On September the 8th the Spaniards had successfully landed on the Western extremity of the Bay of Alhucemas, and occupied the surrounding heights. It was a venturesome undertaking successfully carried out, and was destined to have the greatest influence upon the subsequent history of the Rif. It is fully treated of elsewhere in a chapter dealing with the Spanish operations. There is no doubt that the landing at Alhucemas facilitated the French successes farther South, just as the French advance assisted the Spaniards in their future actions.

During October the West and Centre fronts were cleared of the enemy and preparations were made for the winter. But on the Eastern front there was much more activity and early in the month the French and Spanish troops joined hands at Sidi el-Hassen. On October the 10th combined Franco-Spanish forces, advancing from Tizi Uzli and from the Western front of the Melilla zone respectively, were at Sidi bu Rokbar and the Gznaia and Metalsa tribelands were occupied. Winter was approaching with its inevitable rainy season when every road and track would become impracticable. It was evident that the campaign was over for the year, and that the troops must now go into winter quarters. They had been fortunate indeed that the rain had delayed so long.

On October the 21st Monsieur Painlevé made a statement in the Chamber on the subject of Morocco. The cost of the campaign, he stated, to date, was 950,000,000 francs (£8,700,000). The number of troops employed was roughly 158,000. The losses from the beginning of the campaign to October the 15th had amounted to 2,176 killed (including 39 officers) and

8,297 wounded.    Of those killed 632 were Frenchmen.
The number of Frenchmen wounded was about the same
proportion.    Monsieur Painlevé explained that the
military operations were now practically over and it
only remained to exploit the success already attained.
In December the Under Secretary of War speaking in
the Chamber revised the casualty list and gave the
following figures :   Killed—140 officers ;   other ranks,
2,500, of whom 780 Frenchmen.    Wounded—259 officers,
other ranks, 7,300 (1,800 Frenchmen).    Missing—20
officers ;   other ranks, 1,200 (225 French).    Total casualties, 11,419.

It had taken eight and a half months to regain the
territory lost and the future still remained uncertain.

# CHAPTER XI

## IN SEARCH OF PEACE

Early in July, 1923, when the summer campaign had already begun, delegates of the Spanish Government and Abdel Krim's representatives met on board a steamer off the Rif coast to discuss terms of peace. No solution, however, was reached, but it is evident that both parties desired an entente, for on his return on July the 12th to Melilla the Secretary-General of the Spanish Protectorate, Señor Diego Saavedra, wrote to Abdel Krim's chief delegate, Si Mohammed Azerkan, stating that in reply to a letter he had found awaiting him, the Spanish Government was prepared to reopen negotiations. The Secretary-General's letter took to some extent the form of an ultimatum and was recognized as such by Abdel Krim.

This correspondence, of which Abdel Krim forwarded me what purported to be Arabic copies, clearly demonstrate the impasse which had been reached.

The letters follow.

*(Translation.)*

15 *July*, 1923.

Praise be to God.
From the Secretary General Don Diego Saavedra to Sid Mohammed ben Mohammed Azerkan.

$$* \quad * \quad * \quad * \quad *$$

It is necessary to establish the points on which we shall negotiate.

It must be as follows : There will be no negotiation or discussion that takes into consideration the independence of the Rifian State or any mention of the Treaty of 1912. It is possible to grant a kind of independence, economical and administrative, to the Rifian tribes, and also to confirm the position and rank which Si Mohammed ben Abdel Krim el-Khatabi (Abdel Krim) enjoys at present, also that of the Governors of the tribes who rule under the supervision of the Maghzen (Sultan's Government) and under the protection of the Spanish Government.

The negotiations shall be confined specially to the means of developing commerce, industry, and agriculture amongst the Rifian tribes and to the granting to them of material and moral assistance by the Maghzen and the Protecting Power.

If you agree to these conditions I beg you to send me a document signed by your chief (Abdel Krim) and the final negotiations will take place.

Finally, I beg you to consider me as being very desirous of bringing about a lasting peace, and of removing all your doubts that we are trying to deceive you. We desire to act with you in good faith and to prevent bloodshed. It is our hope and wish that the Rif should progress in wealth and in enlightenment, not in the interests of Spain alone but also in those of the Rifians themselves.

Above all, I must inform you, by orders of the Spanish Government, that your reply to our terms must be in our hands *within forty-eight hours* from the time that you receive this letter. I shall regret if you turn a deaf ear to propositions that are all to your benefit and if you refuse what is to your advantage, taking instead a road which will bring calamity upon you. If you continue in error, Spain will adopt every means to put down this rebellion in a way that is less her choice than her duty to the civilized Powers that entrusted her with this mission. If you are sincere in your expressed desire for peace, choose without hesitation the road that leads to rectitude and progress.

When you have duly considered these words, and when all suspicion is removed from your minds, send your reply, and may peace be upon all.

DIEGO SAAVEDRA.

To this letter the 'Foreign Minister of the Rifian Government' replied on July the 24th as follows :

## (*Translation.*)

AJDIR (RIF), 24 *July*, 1923.

Praise be to God.

From Sid Mohammed ben Mohammed Azerkan to Señor Diego Saavedra, salutations and regards.

\*     \*     \*     \*     \*

Your letter resembles a final ultimatum, and as such its contents have caused us much surprise.

Being as I am the Minister of Foreign Affairs to the Rifian Government I feel bound to inform you that our terms are as follows:

That the Rifian Government, established upon modern ideas and on the principles of civilization, considers itself independent politically and economically—privileged to enjoy our freedom as we have enjoyed it for centuries and to live as other people live. We consider that we have the right to enjoy the possession of our territory in preference to any other nation, and we consider that the Spanish Colonial Party have transgressed and violated our rights, and that they have no justification for their pretence of a claim to make a Protectorate of our Rifian State. We have never recognized this Protectorate, and we never shall recognize it. We refuse it once and for all. We desire to be our own rulers and to maintain and preserve our legal and indisputable rights.

We shall defend our independence by every means in our power, and we protest to the Spanish nation and its intelligent people, who, we believe, do not dispute the legality of our demands.

We state—before the Spanish Colonial Party sheds the blood of more of the children of Spain in order to promote their private ambitions and their imaginary pretensions—that if only they will take count with their consciences they will realize that they are greatly at fault, and that they have caused their country great losses through their colonial ambitions, (a policy) that is contrary to Spanish interests. Let them remedy their error before it becomes still more entangled. We protest against the wicked actions of the Colonial Party. We protest to the civilized world and to humanity. We are in no way responsible for the blood that has been shed nor for the money that has been wasted.

We are surprised that you ignore the interests of Spain herself in not making peace with the Rif by recognizing its independence, and thus keeping up neighbourly relations and strengthening the bonds of union with our Rifian people, instead of infringing our rights, of humiliating our people, and ignoring all the humane and legal doctrines of universal law such as are contained in the Treaty of Versailles, which was drawn up after the Great War.

This war taught mankind the penalty of ill-doing, of violation and of pride, and by it the world has learned also that no man is to be despised, and that it is a natural duty to leave every people to manage its own affairs. Power and force fail before right. The Treaty (of Versailles) was drawn up by the chief men of great nations who had taken part in the war and experienced its terrible consequences. In the end they could not fail to recognize the truth, and they gave to all nations, even the smallest, the rights of self-government. Yet politicians have said that treaties are only ink upon paper and that power rests with the sword. But truth is truth; otherwise the world would remain always in trouble and in perplexity. Peace will not come till every nation is at liberty to defend its rights. It would be no disgrace to Spain if she were to live in peace with the Rifians after recognizing our Government and its independence, and thus increasing the common interests of the two countries. On the contrary, it would be a noble action and an honour to her. It would form a magnificent record in her history, and we Rifian people are prepared to welcome a change (of policy) in the Spanish Colonial Party, for their present attitude is unjust. We sincerely hope that the misunderstanding will be removed. The cause of it is due to the wrong methods that they adopt, to their violence and to their failure to look ahead or to appreciate the consequences that must ensue.

The Rifian Government will be truly sorry if the Colonial Party persists in its transgression and in its tyranny. Imagine yourselves to be the party that is being invaded, your homes in the hands of foreigners intent upon the possession of your property. Would you submit to the invaders because they merely claimed certain rights and asserted their pretensions? I think that you, and even your womenkind, would defend yourselves and refuse to accept the humiliation of submission. Your history in this respect testifies for you that this is so. Know that the Rif and all its people are ready to die and, believe me, they will die in the cause of truth. They will defend their honour to the last, and nothing will shake their determination unless the Spanish Colonial Party will abandon its wicked motives—otherwise the Rifians will die to a man.

I must declare once and for all that the Rif will not change its attitude, nor give up the principles upon which we act—that is to

say, we will not reopen negotiations for peace except upon the
condition of the recognition by Spain of the independence of the
Rif.

MOHAMMED BEN MOHAMMED AZERKAN.

This reply to the Spanish invitation to reopen negotiations was sufficient to render it evident that it was
useless to continue the correspondence.  The Independence of the Rif neither the Sultan nor Spain nor
France could grant, not only for reasons that touched
their own position and their own prestige, but also
because it would be entirely outside their powers to
do so under the terms of international treaties.  Nor
was this all.  The Rif itself was in no condition to
profit by independence.  The tribes that inhabit much
of that country are certainly the most primitive in
Morocco.  Their history has been one long period of
anarchy, one continual succession of tribal and intertribal warfare and family blood-feud.  It is a boast
in the Rif that scarcely a Rifi reaches old age ; comparatively few survive the early years of manhood.
Many are murdered in their youth.  The family quarrel
passes on from generation to generation, leaving its trail
of blood behind it.  Sometimes the origin of the feud
is forgotten, whether it was a question of water rights
for irrigation or the love of a woman.  The vast majority
of the tribesmen have not even benefited from the
civilization that accompanies the acceptance and practice
of Islam, for they maintain the inherited traditions of
their Berber origin, and, although they have adopted
the Mohammedan Faith as a religion, they disregard its
social and juridical aspects.

Living in great poverty, cut off from the rest of
Morocco by race and the physical features of their

country, with no opportunity of learning or improvement, the Rifis of the remoter districts have remained almost barbarians. Hardy, courageous and moral, they are not without many good qualities, but important as good qualities are they do not by themselves suffice for a government of independence. Where, on the contrary, the Rifi has been brought into contact with civilization, he develops quickly while not abandoning as a rule his own characteristics. He learns foreign languages with ease and adopts the little comforts of life, but by nature he remains suspicious and grasping and cruel. He is himself the first to confess it, and I have scarcely met a Rifi who, after the difficulties and complications of even the most simple form of Government have been explained to him, has not recognized and acknowledged that self-government in the case of the Rif would be impossible.

Abdel Krim had gained experience during the period when he had been employed by the Spanish Government, and probably had a better idea of what administration meant. He was not without doubts, notwithstanding his confidence in his own capacities—and they were of no mean order—as to whether independence was feasible. I had no little communication by letter and through trusted messengers on this subject. I never hesitated to let him know that in my opinion, apart from all political difficulties, independence in the Rif was impracticable owing to the backward state and the inexperience of the country and its people. At first the Rifi leader insisted that their country was capable of self-government, and that the intelligence of his people was remarkable; but later he seemed to realize that intelligence, important as it might be, was not sufficient for the introduction and carrying on of an Administration, and that experience, in which the Rifis were completely lacking, was a more valuable and more necessary asset. Yet he never abandoned his claim to independence, even in the last days of the Ujda Conference. · He did, however, acknowledge that any independent Rif Government would require foreign aid and assistance, and made no secret, if his campaign was successful, of his intention to employ Europeans in his administration. He stipulated, however, that they were to be his paid servants and subject to his control, and not agents of foreign Governments. He would retain, he said, the absolute and unquestioned right to engage and dismiss them. Often during the Rif war and since I have been accused, particularly in the French press, of urging Abdel Krim to obtain independence and helping him to do so. As a matter of fact, as has been clearly proved by Abdel Krim's correspondence published in *The Times*, I never held out the least hopes or gave the least encouragement in a direction of which I entirely disapproved. Had Abdel Krim obtained the independence of the Rif, it would not have lasted more than a few months.

The only policy that he ought to have pursued, and which I strongly advised him to pursue, was to deal direct with the French and Spanish Governments—in both of which he could have had confidence—and to treat for peace without seeking any foreign aid or intervention. He could have obtained all that the Rif was capable of enjoying, a measure of Home Rule under the protection and control of France and Spain. Even that solution would have offered great difficulties. Constant and vigilant supervision would have been necessary, and control of any kind the Rifis were not

prepared to accept. A great many of the next generation of the people of the Rif will be in all probability
as intelligent and as advanced as any of the other
inhabitants of Morocco, for they have a remarkable
capacity for adaptation and aptitude for acquiring
knowledge. They are, it must not be forgotten, a white
race, and when they have come into contact with Europeans they can more than hold their own. In time
the development of their country, the education of
their children, and their natural capacities will render
them an important federation of intelligent tribes.
They have much to learn, and a good deal to unlearn,
but they have everything in their favour, race, health
and strength and considerable mental ability. They
will either prove a great asset or a great danger to
Morocco. Everything depends on the way Spain and
France govern them.

With the failure of the peace negotiations of July,
1923, all endeavours to come to an arrangement were
abandoned, and it was not till the following year that
rumours were once more current that another attempt
would be made. The French were not yet at war with
the Rif and the question of peace was still one that to
all intents and purposes only interested directly Spain,
though the French and the Sultan could not remain
indifferent to what was occurring in the neighbouring
zone. Communications passed between Tetuan and
Ajdir, but matters went no farther than that. Abdel
Krim continued to demand a guarantee of independence
as a preliminary to any overtures for peace, and in this
Spain naturally could not acquiesce. But he also
maintained a campaign of peace propaganda principally
in the columns of the European press. Not a few

journalists succeeded, at great risk and still more discomfort, in visiting him at Ajdir.  In putting forward
to them his views and ideas, Abdel Krim was quite
evidently influenced more by a desire for successful propaganda than for any direct assistance in the interests
of peace.  He knew that most of the terms he proposed
could never be accepted by Spain, but this important
fact did not deter him from constant publication of his
proposals.  He even went so far as to charge one or
two of his visitors to the Rif, who had gone in search
of 'copy,' of adventure, or of more material benefits,
to put forward his proposals in official circles, and to
obtain the views of the French or Spanish Governments,
but the story he told to each of his guests differed to
such an extent that there was no knowing what were
his real intentions or proposals.

Probably he was himself in doubt as to what he could
eventually hope to obtain.  At times he asked for the
total abandonment of the Spanish zone of Morocco, at
others he seemed to be prepared to allow the Spaniards
to retain certain districts as well as the ' Presidios ' of
Ceuta and Melilla.  In some of his proposals he mentioned large indemnities, in others he said he was
prepared to be reasonable and to forego obtaining even
what he thought he could legally claim.  It is impossible
to say how far it was the suggestions of his visitors that
influenced his demands, for each new arrival in the
Rif forwarded home a new set of propositions.  No
doubt he was not a little affected by the persuasion of
friends in Europe, who were able to keep up a desultory correspondence with the Rif.  There were several
organizations in France and in England and elsewhere
which did not hesitate to furnish him with much bad

advice, probably from the best of motives. There were
as well, as there always must be in these cases, politicians
and adventurers who sought little except their own
interests. The Rif cause was one that appealed to
sympathy, for here was a little race of plucky people,
whose independence had never been destroyed, striving
to maintain their freedom against terrible odds. Deprived of all medical aid, blockaded by land and by
sea, they held out with admirable tenacity. Was it
any wonder that groups arose in Europe who took up
their cause—though the assistance they rendered was
remarkably small—and openly encouraged resistance ?
In the end this sympathy and encouragement only
helped to prolong the war, for the moral support, and
the misguided advice that accompanied it, could have
no effect beyond raising hopes that were destined to
disappointment.

Would a Rifi victory have really benefited the country ? I doubt it. It would have meant the supremacy
of Abdel Krim and his Beni Uriaghel tribe, and despotism. He had talked of a Rifian Republic—it was good
propaganda—but he knew that the only form of government which could hold the wild tribes in check was
despotism. His rule was absolute. He promoted and
degraded, and killed, when he thought it was necessary,
his fellow Rifis, and probably it was at that period the
only course that he could have pursued. It was necessary to crush the tribal jealousies and feuds, and to
crush feuds in the Rif meant that men must be crushed
first. In a country that is split up into a number of
rival tribal factions only absolutism, or a government
that owes its origin to none of the local parties, is
possible. The Rifis will never consent to the predom-

s

inance of any one of their tribes. Abdel Krim they
chose as their leader and for a long time he had their
affection and their respect, but they regarded with
suspicion and displeasure the power that his tribesmen
of the Beni Uriaghel were usurping. The Rif was
prepared to accept a member of that tribe as their
leader, but they refused to recognize the authority of
all its members, whose arrogance toward the end became
distinctly unpopular.

On more than one occasion, notably to one of his
American visitors, an able and enterprising newspaper
correspondent, Abdel Krim stated that to govern the
Rif absolutism was a necessity, that it must be a ' one
man show,' and that he was the ' one man.' He was
right. The Rif was held together during those strenuous
years of fighting by Abdel Krim's forcible personality,
backed by the fighting qualities of his Beni Uriaghel
tribesmen. His prestige was immense. The Rifis disputed no order that he gave, no matter what it was ;
he used and abused the powers of life and death. The
tribes recognized not only his ability in native affairs
but equally the experience of European administration
which he had acquired during his employment by the
Spaniards in Melilla. His learning they believed to
be great, in that he was a proficient scholar of Islamic
studies. Above and beyond all he had been successful.
With a handful of followers and a rabble of ill-armed
tribesmen he had annihilated a Spanish army. That
was enough. Yet in the end it was from these very
people, who had suffered and died at his command,
that he fled by night and crossed the French lines to
surrender.

In all these negotiations for peace it was with Abdel

Krim alone that Spain had to deal. He pretended that he must consult the tribes, for it was good propaganda, but he never had the least intention of doing so. In only one respect was he responsible to them. He had promised them independence, and on this point his hands were tied. When the French and Spanish Governments insisted that the tribes should be represented at Ujda, he merely ignored the demand and charged one of his own three personal delegates with that mission. He allowed no native intervention whatever between himself and the enemy Powers. That he had reached a position in which he was able to do so was no mean accomplishment, but Abdel Krim was no mean man.

At various periods toward the end of 1924 and in the early months of 1925 there were rumours of peace, but no result was forthcoming nor does there seem at any moment to have been any serious attempt at negotiation on the part of either side. From time to time both protested their desire to arrive at a settlement, but matters went no farther and nothing materialized.

In the spring of 1925 the Rifis renewed hostilities in the Western part of the Spanish zone, and it became evident that co-operation between the Spanish and French armies was a necessity. It was a waste of energy and of life that two unco-ordinated campaigns should be waged against the Rif, which left the initiative largely in the hands of the enemy. At the end of May the Spanish posts in the Lukkus valley were attacked and there was fighting on the Tangier-Tetuan road and in the vicinity of Tetuan itself.

Looking back over the history of the past few years in Morocco, there is no fact more surprising perhaps

than the almost total absence of any co-operation either
in policy or in war between the French and the Spaniards.
The relations, though outwardly friendly, were certainly
not cordial. There was much jealousy and more
criticism. There was an inclination on the part of the
French press to ridicule the Spaniards' want of success
in their zone, and to point out the difference between
the results of French and Spanish administration—a
difference that was very marked. Nor had the two
armies ever come into contact, for nearly the whole
region of their frontier was country into which neither
had penetrated. Both had been fully occupied elsewhere,
and the Great War had retarded the occupation by the
French of the Northernmost regions of the Protectorate.
But it was quite apparent in the spring of 1925, when
both France and Spain were at war with a common
enemy, that a political arrangement and a combined
plan of campaign were essential to success. It was to
Monsieur Malvy that the French Government entrusted
the task and he was sent to Madrid to propose an
exchange of views between the two Governments.
His first visit was merely to explore the ground, but
so cordial was his reception and so prepared did he
find the Spanish authorities to accept the general
principle of an understanding that immediately after
his return to Paris at the end of May negotiations were
decided upon. At Paris, Monsieur Briand, the French
Foreign Minister, and Señor Quinones de Leon, the
Spanish Ambassador, put the finishing touches to the
programme, and on June the 6th a Franco-Spanish
Conference was announced, the subjects being stated
as limited to the suppression of contraband and the
co-ordination of military action.

The Conference met at Madrid on June the 17th, and General Jordana, who was the President, welcomed the French delegation. After the usual compliments he stated : ' We are called here to lay the foundation of a Franco-Spanish entente in Morocco, an entente of intimacy, of indispensable co-operation, of solidarity in front of the enemy, all rendered necessary by a community of interests and by the neighbourly ties of brotherhood. This solemn hour is one for decision. An unique occasion for an understanding is before us. Let us not allow it to escape us. With all our energy, with all our hearts let us realize a work that ought to have been taken in hand earlier.'

Monsieur Peretti de la Roca, the French Ambassador, replied in fitting terms and the Conference began its labours. The deliberations were kept secret, but it was known that the opening sessions were occupied by a discussion on the subject of the suppression of contraband, a matter of common interest, by land and by sea. This naturally brought Tangier and its little zone to the fore. The Spaniards have always claimed that Tangier formed one of Abdel Krim's principal sources of supply of arms and ammunition, but this was not the case. It would no doubt have been so had it not been far easier to land contraband directly on the Spanish zone coast only a few miles away. The landing of contraband at the Tangier zone was beset with many difficulties, for the organization of the zone, though by no means perfect, was at all events far superior in its policing and control to that of the neighbouring part of the Spanish sphere. Tangier was however the centre of Abdel Krim's propaganda and political activities and intrigue, and as such formed a very serious obstacle to the success of Spain's task across the frontier. Various projects were put forward at Madrid with regard to Tangier, but some at least met with a direct refusal in London, to which they were, very correctly, submitted. The British Government, however, consented that the British Navy should participate with France and Spain in the duty of patrolling the Tangier Waters for the prevention of contraband.

There was, however, one kind of contraband in constant practice at Tangier the suppression of which was, it would have been thought, within the power of the Spanish authorities. It has been the custom for Spanish soldiers—generally, but not always, native soldiers in Spanish employ—to sell cartridges. In the districts round Tangier it was difficult for these men to get into direct touch with the tribesmen and carry on individually this petty trade, which however on the aggregate was by no means restricted, and the number of cartridges which changed hands was considerable. On this account they brought their cartridges into Tangier and sold them to intermediaries, Christian, Moor or Jew, who in turn resold them to Spain's enemies, the tribesmen. So constant and so open was this trade that I myself was taken to a café where I saw a Spanish soldier in uniform sell several dozen rifle cartridges to a native Jew of Tangier across the table—both bargaining aloud and without the least attempt at concealment. The facility with which the cartridges came into the possession of the soldiers was a question which, it would have been thought, could have been controlled at the Spanish Posts, but this constant trickle of cartridges into Tangier and out again into the hands of the enemy was unceasing.

It is incontestable that Tangier has proved a very

serious drawback to legitimate Spanish interests in
Morocco. Not only its geographical position—an enclave in the Spanish zone—but also its political status,
have largely hindered Spain's work of pacification
in Morocco. It has cut her off, too, from the most
practical point of access to her zone. It was impossible
at Madrid to avoid a discussion of this thorny question.

The Conference terminated its labours on July the
25th, and was followed by a declaration on the part
of General Primo de Rivera, President of the Spanish
Directory, that Spain had decided to undertake a military
expedition in co-operation with France. He added that
he was himself proceeding to Morocco to carry out the
necessary measures. The Conference terminated in an
atmosphere of mutual optimism.

The principal points that had been discussed and
settled were the questions of contraband by land and
sea, the maintenance of Tangier's neutrality and the
measures necessary to safeguard the same, and Franco-
Spanish political collaboration for the purpose of restoring peace in Morocco. It was also decided that the military commands should decide upon a plan of combined
action on the front. It was further agreed that neither
Government should engage in any separate negotiations
with the Rif. The terms on which peace could be
offered to Abdel Krim were also discussed, and the
following essential conditions recognized : respect for
international treaties ; the proviso that any peace must
be of a nature to ensure its permanent character, and
that the honour and prestige of the Spanish army be
taken into account. The right of pursuit of the common
enemy into each other's zones was granted, but was to
be of a temporary nature. As far as military action

was concerned, it was agreed that it was to be rather simultaneous than combined, each Government retaining the right to initiative. The final agreement was for the future delimitation of the frontier between the two zones and the adoption of a *modus vivendi* for the present, based on the treaty of 1912.

This Franco-Spanish agreement for collaboration in Morocco naturally brought to the fore again the question of peace with the Rif and Jibala. At once there emerged into the open a number of Europeans and natives, one and all of whom pretended to be in possession of Abdel Krim's sole and only terms. Many had obtained their information direct from the Rif leader, for he received no few visitors at this time. But Abdel Krim seems to have provided each with a different programme, and an amusing and noisy discussion arose between them as to each other's credentials and sincerity of motives. Some put forward the most exorbitant demands based no doubt on Abdel Krim's boasts in his days of victory, while others represented the Rifis as ready to make peace on reasonable terms, and as prepared to accept a measure of Home Rule. Some of the propositions were so surprising as to cause little but amusement. The Rif was to receive the same status as Afghanistan or Canada or Ireland, with Abdel Krim as Emir. Spain was to abandon the Rif with the exception of the Presidios of Ceuta and Melilla, which have been Spanish territory for centuries. Whatever ideas the Spanish Government may have had at times of abandoning the Rif, it was not likely to do so as the price of peace with Abdel Krim. But all these propositions which were put forward as emanating from Abdel Krim, whether they originated at Ajdir, Tangier, London or Paris, were little more than a flight of *ballons d'essai* launched by the many people who from different motives desired to bring about a peace favourable to the Rif. It was no secret at this time to those who knew Abdel Krim's intentions—in so far as he had any fixed intentions, for his opinion often changed—that he had abandoned all idea of obtaining Laraiche, Tetuan or Arzeila, and now limited his pretensions to the Rif and Jibala districts. There had been moments when he had aimed much higher—Fez and the Sultanate,—but those days were over. He hoped, perhaps, that in abandoning his often avowed claim for Tetuan he might obtain some compensation in money. His argument was ingenious. He was aware that when the Spaniards, after their Moroccan war of 1859–60, had agreed to evacuate Tetuan the Sultan paid them an indemnity of 15,000,000 pesetas—about £600,000. The Spaniards in return for his indemnity undertook to abandon the town in perpetuity—and they had now returned. The money should be refunded. Abdel Krim informed me of his intention of claiming it, and I made the natural reply that as it was the Sultan who had paid the indemnity it should be refunded to him, and that I could not see what claim he, Abdel Krim, could put forward to it. In due season he replied that as he was performing the duty that the Sultan ought to have undertaken, of defending Morocco against a Christian invader, he considered that his claim to the money was indisputable. As there was never the slightest likelihood of its ever being taken into the smallest consideration, I did not continue the argument.

Abdel Krim was informed that the terms of peace drawn up by the French and Spanish Governments were at his disposal at Tetuan and at Melilla should he choose to send for them. It would have been much better if a copy of these terms had been officially placed in his hands, but *amour propre* forbade a proceeding so simple. The French and Spanish Governments considered that in sending the terms to Abdel Krim they might put themselves in the position of seeming to sue for peace, while Abdel Krim, on the other hand, was convinced that if he asked to see them he might be thought to have submitted. The result was confusion. At the long delay which naturally ensued public opinion in France and Spain grew restive and demanded to know what was going on. In the face of this unrest both the French and Spanish Governments decided to disclose to Abdel Krim unofficially the terms they were prepared to grant, instead of waiting for him to send for them, which by the way he had already declared he was determined not to do. Accordingly the terms of peace were communicated by the French and Spanish Governments, in both cases unofficially, to the Rifi leader.

These terms were briefly as follows :

1. The French and Spanish Governments are conjointly agreed to guarantee to the Rifi and Jibala tribes such autonomy as is compatible with the existing international treaties.

2. The two Governments are conjointly agreed to open at once negotiations with a view of arriving at the re-establishment of peace and for the purpose of putting into effect the new régime.

The essential points which are to be observed in these negotiations are the following :

(1) Release by French, Spaniards and Rifis of all prisoners.

(2) Reciprocal and complete amnesty, to date from 1 January, 1921.

(3) Definition of the districts to fall within the new régime.

(4) Agreement as to the geographical extent of the above-mentioned districts.

(5) Agreement as to the formation and number of the police force which would be required to maintain order and security in those districts.

(6) The recognition of commercial liberty in the territories in question according to the International Customs and other Treaties.

(7) Recognition of the illegality of all trade in arms and ammunition.

(8) Choice of a position on the Rif coast to be by common consent occupied by the Spanish forces after the cessation of hostilities.

Could anything have been more generous?

At almost the same moment—the middle of July—as these terms were brought to the knowledge of Abdel Krim, negotiations were tentatively opened at Tetuan by Rifi emissaries. A confidential messenger had brought letters and verbal communications to his agents at Tangier, authorizing them to discuss the question of peace both with the French and Spanish authorities, but with stipulations as to the preliminary recognition of Rifi independence, and that any eventual negotiations should take place at Tangier. The contents of these letters were at once communicated to the French and Spanish authorities at Rabat and Tetuan, and on a telegraphic invitation from General Primo de Rivera, who was arriving at Tetuan from Madrid the following day, the Rifi delegates proceeded to that place. They were courteously received, and in the course of a long and friendly conversation with General Primo de Rivera were able not only to put forward the Rifi views but also to learn what the Spaniards considered to be the most essential points in the peace terms, in so far as the interests of Spain were concerned. The Rifis, however, would not abandon the difficult point of a preliminary recognition of the independence of their country.

This visit of the Rifis to Tetuan led to the accusation that the Spanish authorities were attempting to negotiate a separate peace. This was entirely erroneous, and General Primo de Rivera made it clear to the Rifi delegates that no peace could be made either by France or Spain alone. All that he did was quite legitimately to explain the details of the terms which most closely interested the Spaniards. Although Abdel Krim publicly made statements to the contrary (particularly in his letter to myself of August the 29th), maintaining that he had never received the French and Spanish terms, he was as a matter of fact in possession of them. The French had sent Monsieur Gabrielli, the French ' Controller ' at Taurirt, to the Rif with a copy of the proposals, while the Spaniards again made use of Señor Echevarrieta, who had been largely instrumental in obtaining the release of the Spanish prisoners in 1923, for the purpose of conveying the terms to Abdel Krim. Monsieur Gabrielli had strict instructions not to discuss with Abdel Krim the details of the French peace proposals, while the Spanish delegate seems to have been fully authorized to do so.

The Rifi emissaries who had proceeded to Tetuan had before doing so communicated Abdel Krim's instructions as to their mission to the French authorities at Tangier, who had immediately transmitted them to Rabat. Considerable hesitation ensued and time was lost, and it was not till August the 5th that the Quai d'Orsay issued a communiqué which began : ' Abdel Krim has lately manifested through his agents at Tangier and in the Press his desire to see an end of hostilities.' The mention of the Press referred to a communication the Rifi leader had addressed to me on the subject which had appeared meanwhile in *The Times.* On August the 14th Monsieur Painlevé, Prime Minister and Minister of War, made public for the first time the generous terms which France and Spain were prepared to offer. In Monsieur Painlevé's own words the French Government agreed to ' guarantee the Rifi and Jibala tribes administrative, economic and political autonomy under the reserve of the sovereignty of the Sultan and subject to the delegation of the Khalifa.' He explained that the Independence of the Rif was internationally impossible as contrary to existing treaties. An attempt to cede on that point would only reopen the whole question of Morocco in a dangerous form. There was also another and very excellent reason to refuse independence to the Rif which Monsieur Painlevé did not state. However intelligent Abdel Krim might have been—and no one denied his ability—however patriotic his aims and intentions, the introduction of an independent Government into the Rif would only have been beset by so many difficulties and dangers that it could not have escaped certain and perhaps immediate failure. Even the large measure of autonomy proposed by France and Spain would have necessitated, if it had ever been adopted, a protracted period of delicate initiation. It is no exaggeration to state that no settlement within the possibilities of the circumstances then existing, no matter on what lines, could have been looked upon as really permanent.

Monsieur Painlevé's statement created a good impression, and the Rifi emissaries who had returned to Tangier at once sent copies to Abdel Krim, recommending that negotiations be opened on the basis of these proposals. It was Abdel Krim's great opportunity— and he missed it.

On August the 16th the Spanish Government issued at Madrid a communiqué almost identical with that which had been published in Paris. It clearly demonstrated the Spanish readiness for peace. In one respect the Spanish communiqué went further than the French, for in speaking of the Sultan's authority over the proposed Rif state the word ' nominal ' was employed. No more definite term could have been used to make known to the Rifis how large was the measure of autonomy that it was proposed to confer. Abdel Krim's intransigence was manifest. He never applied, as he had been invited to do, for the French and Spanish terms, and when they were communicated to him unofficially he denied that he had ever received them. He ostentatiously began the reorganization of his army and obtained further arms, ammunition and other war material from Europe and from Algeria. He was clearly making every preparation to renew the campaign. It was at this moment that he wrote me an important letter of which the following is a translation. It is dated Ajdir, August the 29th, 1925. After the usual salutations he continued:

Facsimile Letter from Abdel Krim to the Author.

' We have received your letter of August the 18th, in which you offered us your advice to accept the negotiations of peace in accordance with the conditions which the newspapers have published. Certainly. But up to the present we have not been formally informed of the conditions which are proposed, and therefore I can neither accept nor refuse them. And this being so I beg of you to be so good as to publish what I have told you—namely that I have not received anything in spite of what has been published in the newspapers. I am aware that this is a political manœuvre in order to prejudice public opinion and to deceive the French and Spanish people by leading them astray and thus bring them to calamity and war.

' I conclude, begging you to accept my cordial salutation and peace.

'MOHAMMED BEN ABDEL KRIM EL-KHATABI.'

My letter of August the 18th referred to above had contained copies of both Monsieur Painlevé's and General Primo de Rivera's official declarations on the terms the two Governments were offering to Abdel Krim.

The contents of Abdel Krim's letter were far from true, except in that perhaps he was justified in saying that he had not ' formally ' received the terms, if by ' formally ' he meant officially. Both Maréchal Lyautey and General Primo de Rivera gave me verbally the most solemn assurances that at the date in question copies of the terms were in Abdel Krim's possession. General Primo de Rivera told me that the letter containing the terms sent to Abdel Krim by the Spanish authorities was signed by himself.

Why did not Abdel Krim accept the proffered proposals ? What was his reason for refusing to negotiate on terms that were far more generous than anything he might ever have been led to expect ? The answer is clear. He was advised to continue the campaign by his friends in Europe, he was promised assistance and the support of public opinion, and he was told that he must have no confidence in either the French or Spaniards. The people who gave him that advice are responsible for much.

On September the 5th a Spanish army successfully disembarked on the West point of Alhucemas Bay. This action, striking as it did at the heart of the Rif, changed the whole aspect of the situation and brought all immediate questions of peace to an end.

# CHAPTER XII

## THE UJDA CONFERENCE

On April the 5th, 1926, *Le Temps* published the following note :

' Monsieur Aristide Briand presided this morning at the Quai d'Orsay at a new conference on the subject of Morocco, in which took part Messieurs Painlevé, Minister of War, Steeg, Resident-General, Marshal Pétain and his Chief-of-Staff General Georges, and Ponsot, Assistant Director of African Affairs at the Ministry of Foreign Affairs.

' During the deliberations an examination was made of the situation in Morocco, from the dual point of view of military operations and of the means of realizing peace. On these subjects General Simon, who had arrived from Morocco and was present at the meeting, furnished the Prime Minister and his collaborators with the latest information.

' The eventuality of the opening of official negotiations can be looked forward to hopefully. Conversations are at this moment taking place between properly authorized emissaries of Abdel Krim and representatives of the Spanish and French Governments. They can be considered as serious, and favourable results are expected to ensue.'

The publication of this Note caused not a little surprise. There had been so many false starts in the past which had led to nothing, that the public had almost abandoned hope of any possibility of peace. Yet peace was generally and sincerely desired by the majority of all the interested parties, though there were doubts as to whether the moment was appropriate. It was realized, however, that both in Spain and in France there existed a military party that wished to continue the campaign and to arrive at the desired result by a triumph in the field. The Spanish army had never forgotten and never forgiven Anual, and was intent upon at least one signal victory in Morocco to wipe out the stain of that disaster. Nearly five years had passed since a few thousand tribesmen had annihilated the Spanish army in the Rif and no victory had as yet come about. On the contrary, there had been a great retirement, that of the autumn of 1924, which, wisely conceived and skilfully carried out as it was, could not be looked upon as a compensation for the bitter memory of the past. It was, therefore, only natural that the Spanish army should show no great satisfaction at the possibility of a peace obtained at a conference, more especially when it was known that the proposed conditions would contain some at least of the demands put forward by Abdel Krim. It put out of the question the Spanish dream of a military conquest of the Rif and the defeat of the hardy tribesmen who for so many years, and so successfully, had kept the Spaniards at bay. Peace would mean, too, the withdrawal of a large portion of the Spanish officers and soldiers from Morocco and a diminution of active employment on double pay, to say nothing of the cessation of opportunity for promotion, decorations and glory. There were other interests also that compensated for the discomforts of a campaign in Africa, and, although the opportunities of acquiring wealth had largely diminished owing to the Marqués de Estella's vigorous reforms, they still existed.

The Communiqué, which appeared at Madrid at the same date as in Paris, announcing that peace negotiations were on the point of being opened, met with an unfavourable reception in Spain. The fact was not disguised that there existed divergences between the views of the Spanish and French Governments. It was even hinted, and it was no doubt true, that the Spanish Cabinet, although pacific, was not in favour at that precise moment of any negotiations at all. It was considered that Abdel Krim's prestige was still too great, and would continue so until he had received the blow that it would be necessary to inflict before any serious consideration could be advisedly given to the question of peace. However, the Spanish Government, acting in conformity with the Franco-Spanish policy of common action which had been accepted during Monsieur Malvy and Marshal Pétain's visits to Madrid, did not hesitate to acquiesce in the French proposals and issued a communiqué to that effect. It stated, after announcing the approaching conversations :

'The cordiality existing between the two Governments is in no way affected by this divergence of views, for Spain is as desirous as is France to conclude peace as quickly as possible, but with the certitude of not being forced into embarking upon a further military campaign.'

There was no doubt whatever, in spite of what has been written to the contrary, that the people of Spain were desirous of peace in Morocco. The officers of the army, and perhaps not all of them, were almost the only exceptions, but the army, under a régime which

was upheld principally by military power, counted for
much. That the Marqués de Estella had always been
pacifically inclined is certain. He had already risked
unpopularity in this endeavour on more than one occasion. I was in Tetuan when, less than a year after the
founding of the Directorate, he announced the coming
retirement of the Spanish troops in the field to their
bases on or near the coast. There was no mistaking
the painful impression this decision made upon the
Spanish officers, and the Marqués de Estella himself
could not have failed to detect in the surrounding atmosphere a breath of intense opposition. But it would
take more than a threat of unpopularity to deter him
from carrying out what he considered to be necessary
in the interests of his country. It required only a short
space of time to prove how right he had been. The
retirement necessitated heavy losses, but had it not been
effected at that precise moment there would have been
another and still more disastrous Anual. The whole
object of this movement of the army toward its bases
was due as much to the President of the Directory's
desire to inaugurate a new and peaceful policy in Morocco
as to his determination to escape from a danger that he
perceived to be imminent—the danger that arose from
the installation of small isolated military posts scattered
far and wide over the country.

When the immense cost in life and wealth that Spain
has incurred in her adventure in North Africa is taken
into account, can one be surprised that public opinion
amongst her population was almost unanimously in
favour of any move that might tend toward the termination of the campaign ? Yet it was Abdel Krim who
had proposed these conversations. To have refused to

entertain them would have been difficult after the continual protestations emanating from Paris and Madrid that both Governments were intent on peace and would neglect no legitimate or serious proposition to secure an understanding with the Rif. The position of France with regard to that country was, however, very different from that of Spain. The whole Rif falls in the Spanish zone and therefore the ultimate responsibility was Spain's. Briefly France's task was to protect the tribes of the French Protectorate from the incursions and attacks of their Rifi neighbours. She had, it is true, also to suppress the revolt of her own tribes, but that was already partly accomplished and everything was ready for its completion. It is clear then that the question of the Rif was for Spain one of vital importance, while to France it meant little more than furthering the means by which a turbulent neighbour was to be rendered innocuous. From this it will be seen that the whole idea of a conference, and what it might lead to, far more deeply affected Spain than France.

Both Governments showed undoubted wisdom in accepting Abdel Krim's proposals to seek an end of the unhappy war. There existed in Europe—even in France itself and certainly in Spain—a strong sentiment of opposition to the whole campaign, and a general suspicion that neither at Madrid nor Paris was peace really desired. The reasons given were the old story of French imperialism. Though the Spaniards could hardly be accused under that heading, other reasons for their desiring a continuance of the war were not difficult to discover, or to invent ; and in the case of the army they were no doubt justified.

This spirit of opposition to France and Spain's action

in Morocco owed its origin to many causes.  It was only natural that the foreign military occupation of any small country, and the deprival of what any small race considered to be its birthright, should awaken sympathy far and wide.  In this case sympathy, which was in principle justified, was increased by skilful propaganda. The material was there, it needed only the match being put to it to raise a little blaze of pity and commiseration for the victim of two great Powers.  The match was applied by little groups of people in various parts of the world, more especially in England and in Paris. Publicity was given to the whole Rif question, and Abdel Krim and his Rifis, with a natural instinct for propaganda, as well as having a cause the justice of which it was easy to assert, lost no opportunity of winning over public opinion far and wide.  His various attempts to open peace negotiations before this period have already been recounted, but no account of the situation on the eve of the Conference at Ujda would be complete without these brief references to the past. They render it clear why France and Spain, even had they not been desirous of peace, could have ill afforded to refuse Abdel Krim's invitation to discuss the question. Not only would their action have been severely criticized but the Rifis themselves would have been given an undeniable opportunity of protesting against the military intentions of the two Governments.  There is, however, no doubt that, totally apart from the question of advisability, both France and Spain went to Ujda genuinely prepared for peace and with the best intentions.  The French believed it possible.  The Spaniards did not.

On April the 9th, 1926, an official communiqué was

issued at Paris stating that the negotiations were on the point of taking place.

' The French and Spanish Governments having decided to accept Abdel Krim's offer to negotiate, have to-day nominated the delegates who will represent them at the conversations with the representatives of the dissident tribes of the Rif which will open at Ujda on April 15.'

' The French delegation includes General Simon, in command of the 11th Division, who directed for several years the Intelligence Department in Morocco ; Monsieur Ponsot, director of the African Department at the Ministry of Foreign Affairs, and Commandant Duclos, Director of Native Affairs at the French Residency.

' The Spanish delegates are Monsieur Lopez Olivan, director of the Moroccan Department at the Madrid Ministry ; Commander Aguilar, Chief of the Bureau of Native Affairs (' Intervencion ') at Ajdir, and Captain Miguel.

' The dissident Moorish tribes will be represented by Si Mohammed Azerkan, the Rifi Minister of Foreign Affairs ; Si Mohammed Hitni and Si Ahmed Sheddi, these last two designated by the tribes.'

As a matter of fact Si Mohammed Hitni did not attend the Conference, owing to ill-health, and was replaced by Kaid Haddu El-Kahal.

On April the 12th an official communiqué was published at Paris which stated briefly the outlines of the conditions of peace. They were : (1) the recognition of the Sultan of Morocco by the Rifis ; (2) the disarmament of the Rifi tribes ; (3) the release of the French and Spanish prisoners ; (4) the expatriation of Abdel Krim. In return the Rif would enjoy a state of autonomy compatible with existing treaties. The tribes

could not, of course, be permitted to enter into direct
relations with Foreign States, France, and to a lesser
extent Spain, being alone qualified by treaty to do so.
Such autonomy as could be granted must keep within
the bounds of all existing international agreements, of
the treaty of the Protectorate and the Algeciras Act.
It was to be understood that so long as peace was not
definitely established the military preparations of France
and Spain would continue. Already, as a matter of
fact, in anticipation of the Conference, fighting had
by mutual consent ceased upon the various fronts.

The scene of interest now passed from Paris and
Madrid to Ujda, a little town, chief of the province of
that name, lying in the extreme East of Northern Morocco
near the Algerian frontier. Ujda was no doubt chosen
as the seat of the Conference on account of its accessi-
bility from the Rif. It lies in the plain of Angad, 2,000
feet above the level of the sea. Its population numbers
slightly over 21,000, of whom over 7,000 are Europeans,
13,000 Moslems and about 1,500 native Jews. The town
itself, surrounded by old Moorish walls, offers no particular attractions and has been much Europeanized, but
the public gardens, which extend for some length along
the outside of the ramparts, are very charming. The
surroundings of the place consist of several thousands
of acres of olive-groves and orchards profusely watered
by the natural springs of Sidi Yahia. Close outside
the town walls the Europeans have built a small modern
quarter. Ujda's trade is due to its position and consists
largely of goods in transit between Algeria and the districts of Eastern Morocco. It was altogether a suitable
place for such a Conference. Its inaccessibility kept
away any crowd that might by curiosity have been

attracted to the spot, while the accommodation was ample for the Delegates and the correspondents of the Press. Living was by no means expensive, and the people of Ujda, of all races and religions, extended to the strangers within their gates a friendly and disinterested welcome. All those who were there were unanimous, I think, in recognizing the extreme courtesy and cordiality with which the inhabitants treated the visitors. It was much appreciated, and by no means universal in Morocco.

I reached Ujda on April the 18th, from Southern Morocco. It was impossible to imagine while travelling by motor over the 320 miles of excellent roads that unite Marrakesh and Fez that there was war anywhere in the country, such was the sense of security and peace. From Marrakesh, lying in its great groves of palm trees, to the moment when the minarets of Fez appeared on the horizon, I do not remember to have seen a single soldier, or in the towns passed through en route, a policeman. Everywhere extended the great fields of cereals, sparse and yellow from the want of rain, until, nearing the coast, there were signs of better crops. For the most part the country is monotonous and bare, and almost the only trees passed on all that distance are those of the forest of Mamora between Rabat and Meknes. Here and there, generally well away from the road, are villages, which, according to the districts in which they lie, vary from mud hovels to thatch huts, and from thatch huts to low black tents. Herds of cattle and sheep and goats pasture in the fields in the open country tended by half-naked children. Everywhere the spring flowers formed bright patches of colour, red, yellow and blue, a very carpet of blossom. On the roads were motors and camels and little donkeys, and groups of peasants. The plains appear limitless. The French have done much for Morocco, but they have done nothing better than to construct these vast roads and to provide, for the European and native alike, the facilities of travel. Nothing had helped more in creating and preserving the tranquillity of Morocco than these routes and the means of transport.

Fez was reached on the second day of travel and presented an aspect of eternal peace. Its gardens were full of flowers and spring reigned supreme. It was the second day of the Feast that celebrates the end of Ramadan, the month of fasting, and the flat terraces of the houses were aglow with gaily-dressed native women. The streets were full of men who seemed to have forgotten that, in spite of the tacit armistice which had already been some days in existence on the front so short a distance away, the war would quickly break out again if a basis for peace was not found by the delegates of France, Spain and the Rif at Ujda.

From Fez to Ujda is 210 miles. The first part of the way after crossing the Wad Sebu is over pleasant, hilly country till a descent is made to the rich valley of the Wad Innawan. After following the river for some time the road ascends steeply to drop once more into the valley which at this spot opens out in a rich circular plain surrounded by mountains. Taza, 73 miles from Fez, is left high up on the right, a mile away from the road, picturesquely crowning its hill, with a range of rocky peaks rising behind it. Then on through Safsafa to Msun and into dreary country, which though sometimes green in winter and early spring is desert for the rest of the year. Then Guercif with its few colonists and its military post and, 30 miles beyond, Taurirt. From its strategic position at the crossing of two important caravan routes—Algeria to Fez, and Tafilet to the Mediterranean at Melilla, by the valley of the Mulaya and Northward across the Rif—Taurirt has always been a place of importance and the scene of many fights. The fortifications date from the fourteenth century. The little town of to-day is of modern construction and contains about 1,600 inhabitants, of whom over 300 are Europeans. High above the hill tower the high posts of the wireless telegraph installation. The narrow cultivated valley is well irrigated and intensely green, forming a curious contrast with the surrounding barrenness. From Taurirt to Ujda is 60 miles, through burnt-up country parched at this particular period by want of rain.

It was at Taurirt that the Rifian delegates Si Mohammed Azerkan, Si Ahmed Sheddi and Kaid Haddu were awaiting the opening of the Conference, for the most convenient road from the Rif to Ujda passed that way. Already preliminary conversations had begun, and General Mougin and Monsieur Gabrielli, the 'Controleur' at Taurirt, were busily engaged in preparing for the more serious business that was to follow. On April the 15th, General Simon, President of the French and Spanish delegations, arrived at Ujda and lost no time in visiting his Rifi colleagues at Taurirt. On April the 18th the French and Spanish delegations met the Rifi delegates for the first time at Camp-Bertaux, a French post situated a few miles to the North, chosen for this first reunion because of its retirement and tranquillity. At this meeting two new demands were put forward by the French and Spanish delegates. The first was that

the release of the prisoners, which was one of the four
conditions to be discussed at the Conference, must take
place at once as a *preliminary* to the Conference. The
second was the insistence that, in order to guarantee
the strategic security of the French and Spanish troops
at several points on the front, an unresisted advance on
several kilometres should be permitted them. Both
were made essential to the holding of a Conference.

In putting forward these totally unexpected demands
the French and Spaniards were in error, and their action
in so doing caused a little surprise even amongst their
own people, and some criticism. The impression made
upon the Rifis was most unfortunate. They had been
told what were to be the conditions that would be
discussed at the Conference, and they were prepared
to discuss them, and now at the last moment they found
themselves confronted with demands the acceptance of
which they were informed was essential to there being
a Conference at all. They were naturally indignant.
That the French and Spanish delegations realized their
mistake in putting forward these surprise conditions
was clear, for after a quite unnecessary and unwarrant-
able delay had been caused, they were forced, in the
face of Abdel Krim's refusal, to withdraw them and
to allow the Rifi delegates to come to Ujda without
their acceptance.

The Rifian delegates had been expected to arrive at
Ujda with their French and Spanish colleagues on the
night of April the 18th after this first meeting, but their
demand, a reasonable one, to consult Abdel Krim on
these new questions, rendered their continued stay at
Taurirt a necessity. Everything had been prepared
for their arrival, and it had been announced to the Press

that the first official sitting of the Conference would take place in Ujda the following morning, April the 19th. It was clear, therefore, that the French and Spanish delegates had hoped to persuade Azerkan and his Rifi colleagues to accept the new conditions. They were known to be very anxious to reach Ujda, as their continued stay at Taurirt had been unpleasing to Abdel Krim and to the tribes. Their deliberate refusal to subscribe to the new conditions without the sanction of their Chief and of the tribes they represented was no doubt a surprise. The whole story of the preliminary terms was not very edifying and savours of an attempt to bluff. In any case it was a mistake. It must be allowed that the French and Spaniards eventually withdrew from the position they had taken up, but it would have been much better never to have adopted it.

So Azerkan and Sheddi remained at Taurirt while Kaid Haddu was taken in a French aeroplane to Targuist, to discuss the situation with Abdel Krim. Meanwhile on the evening of April the 19th a Rifi communiqué was distributed to the Press correspondents at Ujda which threw some light upon their intentions and views. It stated :

'On April the 18th we met the French and Spanish delegations at Camp-Bertaux. A few moments after the presentations had been made by General Simon, the President of the Conference, the first sitting was opened and the conversations on the six principal points were begun. Amongst them were four conditions the acceptance of which is impossible without certain modifications. Our agreement to the first two has already been announced in the Press. The two other conditions are the following :

' (1) The liberation, before any official conversations take place, of the prisoners.

' (2) The advance of the French and Spanish troops to stated positions actually in Rifi occupation ; and this advance to be allowed to take place pacifically.

' These two conditions were the object of a laborious discussion.

' The acceptance of these two preliminary conditions cannot be considered, in our opinion, before the opening of official conversations. Should we deliver over the prisoners immediately and should we accept the advance of the French and Spanish troops in the zone as stated without offering resistance, in the case of peace not being reached we should have been tricked. In any case we have asked for a delay in order to consult the Amir Abdel Krim.

' We may add that we believe that these conditions will never be accepted unless concessions are granted by the (French and Spanish) Governments.'

The adoption by the Rifian delegates of communiqués as a means of making known their views to the Press and to the public, caused no little stir amongst the members of the Conference at Ujda. The French and Spanish delegates had already adopted this system of publicity and it was difficult to insist that the Rifis should not do likewise. However, General Simon expressed to them the general disapproval of the members of the Conference at the publication of details which should, he said, have been kept secret. Si Mohammed Azerkan, however, took a directly opposed line. He had not come to Ujda for secrecy. The Rifis desired that everything should be public, and it was, they said, their intention to put their case before the whole world.

Azerkan even proposed that the correspondents of the Press be invited to the meetings, a proposal that caused consternation amongst the diplomats. But there is no doubt that the publicity given to the conversations at Ujda was not a little owing to this intention of the Rifis, an intention they did not abandon. ' We have,' Azerkan told me, ' no secrets. We do not understand diplomatic methods and intend to have everything out in the open,' —and they did.

On April the 20th Abdel Krim's reply was received. He refused to agree to the new conditions, and insisted on the original programme of the Conference being maintained. The four conditions he was prepared to discuss were, as he had already announced, these :

(1) The recognition of the Sultan.
(2) The expatriation of Abdel Krim.
(3 The disarmament of the tribes.
(4) The release of the prisoners.

In return the Rifis were to be granted autonomy.

Surprise has sometimes been expressed that the terms offered by the French and Spanish Governments at the Conference at Ujda were less advantageous to the Rifis than those that the same Governments had proposed, and been ready to accept, in July of the previous year (1925). It must, however, be remembered that the situation had changed since the day when Abdel Krim, acting on the unwise advice of foreigners, refused to negotiate and so foolishly disregarded the generous conditions which had been proposed to him. The Spaniards were now installed at Alhucemas and at Ajdir, Abdel Krim's capital, while the French had reoccupied practically all the territory they had lost during the last year's campaign.

On April the 24th, in company with several other correspondents, I motored 60 miles to Taurirt, where the Rifi delegates still remained awaiting the termination of the preliminary discussions before being invited to proceed to Ujda.

We were received by Monsieur Gabrielli, the ' Controleur ' of Taurirt, who had played so leading and so useful a part in bringing about these negotiations for peace. He introduced us at once to the Rifi delegates in the drawing-room of his official residence. I found myself in the presence of three typical Rifis—Si Mohammed Azerkan, still a young man, with the frank sympathetic Berber type of countenance ; Si Ahmed Sheddi, almost a youth, good-looking and rather shy, and Kaid Haddu, middle-aged with a beard turning grey and an expression of much astuteness—keen and intelligent. It was not difficult to perceive that, while Azerkan and Sheddi were almost untouched by European influences, and could be expected in their methods to follow with dignity the traditional policy of the Berber race, Haddu was capable of any flights into the regions of intrigue and opportunism.

The three delegates were dressed in the ordinary clothes of Rifi tribesmen—brown woollen ' Jelabas ' reaching a little below their knees, worn over simple long white cotton shirts. On their heads they wore narrow white turbans which exposed the shaven crowns. They received us very courteously, and a general conversation, frank and unrestricted, ensued. While Kaid Haddu and Sheddi spoke to my companions, Si Mohammed Azerkan took me aside and engaged me in a long and intimate conversation on the whole subject of the negotiations. He first of all impressed upon me the

real desire of Abdel Krim to arrive at peace and recalled
the long letter that the Rifi Chief had sent me to this
effect, which was published in *The Times* of March the
17th, 1926. He then referred to the subjects mentioned
in the communiqué that they had issued on April the
19th, and confirmed to me that the Rif was prepared
to recognize the *temporal* and *spiritual* authority of the
Sultan, which was almost more than the French and
Spanish Governments had asked for. He stated that
the immediate expatriation of Abdel Krim was not in
the interests of France, Spain or the Rif. It might, he
said, be left over and reconsidered when Abdel Krim's
presence in the Rif was no longer required for the introduction of the new form of Government. Disarmament
of the tribes he recognized as necessary, but before it
could be carried out without danger, a military police
must be introduced and guarantees given to the tribes
that they should enjoy autonomy. The exchange of
prisoners, Azerkan insisted, could not be made until
peace was arrived at. The Rifis were, however, prepared
to allow a French and Spanish medical mission to visit
the prisoners at once and to remain with them during
the negotiations for peace, at the conclusion of which
the prisoners would be handed over.

Si Mohammed Azerkan spoke very strongly on the
subject of the introduction at the last moment into the
programme of the Conference of the two preliminary
conditions of which mention has already been made.
The armistice, he stated, had been religiously adhered
to by both sides, and would be scrupulously observed
by the Rifis in the future, but they could never permit
that the relative strategic positions of the two armies
should be radically altered by an advance of the French

and Spanish troops. He was astonished that such a demand should ever have been made, and if the French and Spanish delegations were awaiting its acceptance before allowing the Rifis to proceed to Ujda, then the sooner the Conference was countermanded the better. He explained that this proposed advance, particularly in the Spanish zone, meant the cession to the Spanish troops of fortified positions actually in the hands of the Rifis. These unexpected conditions and the fact that the Rifi delegates had been detained so long at Taurirt had much annoyed Abdel Krim, whose suspicions had not unnaturally been awakened, while at the same time there was a danger that the tribes' confidence in their delegates—himself, Sheddi and Kaid Haddu—might be seriously shaken.

This conversation with Si Mohammed Azerkan lasted over an hour. It was friendly, intimate and honest. He told me frankly exactly how the situation lay in the Rif, and I informed him that if he was looking for out-side political intervention none would be forthcoming. I informed him that it was well known that Abdel Krim, and he himself, had constantly held out to the tribes this hope, this expectation, of ultimate British inter-vention. It was useless. The Rif enjoyed in England a certain and admissible sympathy, but great exaggera-tion had been given to its importance. I pointed out that such sympathy could only be platonic, and that neither officially nor unofficially could the British Government, even had it been desirous of doing so, which was certainly not the case, intervene in any way whatever. I reminded him of the very definite reply Abdel Krim had received to a demand for intervention. I regretted the folly of the Rifi in not having negotiated with the French and Spanish Governments on the basis of the terms those two Governments had so generously offered in the previous July. In reply to this remark Azerkan assured me that it was only in deference to advice from England and from the Communists in France that they had refused to do so. Abdel Krim and the Rifis, Azerkan assured me, had been told that no confidence should be placed in the word of those two Governments, whose sole desire was to catch the Rifis in a trap. They were advised to continue the fight by every method in their power, and hopes were deliberately held out of the overthrow of the Government in Paris and of intervention on the part of England. They had known too late that the opportunity offered them in July could never be repeated. It had gone for ever.

In the presence of the French ' Controleur,' who spoke Arabic fluently, and in that of my French, English and American colleagues of the Press, I again repeated to Azerkan that the question of the future of the Rif lay between themselves and France and Spain, and that no foreign intervention could under any circumstances be forthcoming. I regretted that any such idea should have arisen from any action of any group of English people, who, I pointed out, were totally unauthorized.

There was no doubt that my remarks caused disappointment to the Rifi delegates, but I felt it necessary for their sakes, and also because rumours of British intrigue in the Rif were current in other quarters at Ujda, to make in the presence of French officials and the members of the Press, a definite and very clear statement. It certainly cleared the atmosphere.

On April the 26th the French and Spanish delegations issued the following communiqué :

' The French and Spanish Governments, fully informed by their delegations of the course of the negotiations with the Rifi delegates since April the 18th, consider, in their desire to arrive at the establishment of a complete and durable peace, that it behoves them to continue to advance the negotiations on the basis of the conditions which were brought to the notice of Si Mohammed Azerkan on April the 11th.'

This communiqué, the wording of which was rather unnecessarily vague, really meant that the French and Spanish Governments had withdrawn the two unacceptable preliminary conditions and had reverted to the original four terms proposed in the first agenda of the Conference. Many days had been wasted through the insertion in the programme of these preliminary conditions, for the Rifi delegates had been detained at Taurirt pending Abdel Krim's hoped-for acceptance. But Abdel Krim had refused to budge, and only one course had been left open, their withdrawal. This was done, and on the afternoon of the same day (April the 26th) the Rifi delegates arrived at Ujda. They were received at the French Consulate General by Monsieur de Witasse in the presence of the French and Spanish delegations and the journalists. The reception was devoid of any official character and was marked by a general spirit of cordiality. The Rifis were quite evidently pleased to be in Ujda at last and conversed freely with the officials and guests. Their arrival passed almost unnoticed by the public.

There was some doubt at this moment as to what was the policy of Spain in regard to the Rif. Should peace be reached at the Conference what were the intentions of the Spanish Government ? It was a question of no little importance, not only to the Rif but also to the

French, with their long frontier with the Spanish zone.

Five months earlier, in November, 1925, the Marqués de Estella, in the course of a long and frank conversation on the subject of Spanish Morocco, had given me a clear and definite outline of Spanish intentions. At Ujda the delegate of the Spanish Government confirmed this policy and informed me that there had been no change whatever since that date.

It was the desire of the Spanish Government to restrict Spanish action in Morocco within the limits of national interests in complete conformity with international agreements. In order to carry out this policy the Government intended to confine its action in the Rif and Jibala districts to the continued possession of the Presidios, which had long been Spanish territory— Melilla, Alhucemas, Ceuta and the other smaller fortresses—and to the occupation of certain other points of strategic value to be decided upon in due time. The Spanish Government was most anxious to avoid any new adventure in the interior of the zone, or any military occupation of any of the outlying regions, but hoped, by a policy of friendship, assistance and sympathy to live on terms of close amicable relationship with the tribes. It was the intention of the Spanish Government to grant financial, technical and medical assistance to the natives, and by this means it was hoped to bring about the pacification of the country. Public works, especially roads, and the encouragement of trade relations would form a large part of this programme. The Government believed that a period of peace and prosperity would result. The Spanish authorities would not exercise direct control over the tribes of the interior, but the inhabitants would be invited to seek at the hands of competent officials advice and arbitration in their local affairs. Every encouragement would be given for the maintenance of law and order amongst the tribes, and the Spanish Government would be prepared to place competent police officers and technical advisers at the disposition of the tribesmen, should they so desire.

The Spanish Government considered that such a policy of sympathy and pacification was the best suited to its own and the tribesmen's interests. But in order that this policy might be successful they realized that not only must the existing state of war be terminated but, for their own security in the future, serious and adequate guarantees must also be forthcoming from the tribes. It was the desire to secure these guarantees, on which the future policy of pacification so largely depended, that influenced the Spanish attitude at Ujda. Every precaution had to be taken to render Spain's garrisons and civil population in her zone immune from surprises in the future. The desire of the Spanish Government in this particular comprised interests other than those of Spain alone. Should anarchy continue in the Spanish zone the neighbouring French Protectorate would equally feel the effects, and would be liable at any moment to incursions from over the border. Even more, a prolonged state of anarchy might threaten to reopen the whole Morocco question, which in the interests of European concord and peace, was very far from desirable. The Spanish Government and their delegates at Ujda were, therefore, very earnestly intent that any solution of the Rif question that might be arrived at should be of a satisfactory and permanent character.

The path of the Conference was strewn with thorns

and hedged in on one side by Abdel Krim's intransigence and on the other by the exigences of France and Spain. Perhaps all were exaggerated in detail. The meeting of April the 28th disturbed the Rifi delegates, less from the tenor of the Franco-Spanish proposals than from their impracticability in the existing circumstances. The conversations were confined to questions of security in the Rif and the guarantees that must be given by the Rifis for the maintenance of that security. Under these headings some mention was made of the complicated international situation that had always to be kept in mind. The first step toward security was, it was agreed, disarmament. Proposals were put forward that included the collection of tribal arms by French and Spanish columns to be sent into the Rif for that purpose. The Rifis argued that it was Abdel Krim, and Abdel Krim alone, who had distributed these arms amongst the tribes and that only he was capable of confiscating them again. Even in that case, they said, the task was not an easy one. To send European columns into the Rif would inevitably be destined to failure. Disarmament required strong moral persuasion rather than actual force. The Rifi delegates did not dispute the necessity of disarmament, but they raised the strongest objections to the manner in which it was proposed that this measure should be carried out. They went so far as to insist that the presence in the Rif of Franco-Spanish columns for the purpose of disarmament would only render the task impossible. The suspicions that such a measure would awaken amongst the tribesmen would either tempt them to secrete their arms for protection on future occasions or drive them to acts of hostility. The Rifis accepted the principle of disarmament by their own people, to be carried out in the presence of the French and Spanish Commissions, but they demanded at the same time, in order to protect the population, the installation of some kind of native military police.

At the next meeting, held the same afternoon, the question of autonomy was discussed both from a technical and practical point of view. The explanation was a long and difficult one and tired both the propounder and the Rifi audience.

No one expected the Rifi delegates to accept the French and Spanish proposals in the form in which they were presented. A long discussion and some amendment were evidently necessary, but it was clear from the beginning that Abdel Krim's instructions to his representatives left but little chance of a successful issue. It had been he who had proposed the calling of a Conference and who had protested his readiness to treat on terms which, in principle, he had already accepted as a basis of negotiation. But when these terms came to be discussed the divergence between what he was prepared to accept and what France and Spain could offer was a very wide one. Outside the Conference every effort was made to persuade the Rifi delegates to adopt a more reasonable attitude, but it was obvious that they dared not exceed the instructions that they had received from Abdel Krim.

What appeared to be the first and principal error of the Rifis was their refusal to release the French and Spanish captives in exchange for the Rifi prisoners. It was only later that the reason was known—when the Conference was over. Most of the prisoners were dead and Abdel Krim dared not disclose this fact! To have released the survivors would have brought upon the scene a band of miserable sick and broken men, with a few women and children. The Rifi delegates could not face the outcry that would have arisen at this evidence of the barbarity with which these wretched people had been treated. It was only on the last day of the Conference that Si Mohammed Azerkan gave me this reason for their stubborn refusal to release this band of sufferers. 'We cannot,' he said, 'their plight would horrify Europe.' Even then he did not confess that not one Spanish officer was left alive—much less that they had died under the most suspicious circumstances. There is no doubt that the Rifis must at this moment have deeply regretted their cruelty. To have been able to release the prisoners, even if in poor condition, would have won them some sympathy and eased the path of negotiations ; but they realized how impossible it was to do so and refused, not because they had any desire to retain them, but because they knew that such an exhibition of suffering, after their many protestations that the prisoners were being well treated, would have been fatal to their cause.

I had written on more than one occasion during the previous two years to Abdel Krim about the prisoners, and had, at the request of certain personages, attempted to intervene in order to obtain some alleviation of the captivity of the two Franciscan friars and their two or three boy pupils who had been captured while walking near Tetuan. With reference to the treatment of prisoners Abdel Krim wrote to me that they were being as well provided for as his own Rif soldiers ; that there was a scarcity of food-stuffs, but that all he could do was being done for them.

A little later on I was assured that the Franciscans were in security at the Zawia of the Shereefs of Akhamlich, that they were living apart from the other prisoners, and that the two or three schoolboys were with them. I was told they had planted a little garden and were teaching the Rifis horticulture and that they were much respected. This message reached me direct from Abdel Krim. At that moment the priests and boys were all dead, victims of barbaric treatment. At Ujda the principal Spanish delegate, Señor Lopez Olivan, appealed to me to ask the Rifi delegates to do all in their power for a Spanish prisoner officer who was reported ill. He was in need of some kind of surgical appliance for an injured arm, and I was particularly requested to see if I could assure its being sent to the Rif. His mother, broken down with her long sorrow—her son had been a prisoner two years—was at Ujda. I spoke at once to the Rifi delegates. Kaid Haddu gave me a solemn assurance that he himself had sent, by aeroplane from Taurirt, the surgical appliance, and that it had been delivered to the sick man—who had been separated from the other prisoners and was being well looked after in a room by himself. He was receiving every attention and was better. Azerkan confirmed this information and told me that, ever since my first letter to Abdel Krim on behalf of this officer, written at the desire and in the name of two of the most distinguished ladies in Europe, he had received a special treatment. It was a most deliberate untruth. At the moment that these assurances were given me at Ujda the officer in question had been dead of ill-treatment for several days and the Rifi delegates were perfectly aware of it. Not only was he dead, but there is every reason to believe that he was, with many others, done to death in the most cruel and brutal manner.

Shocking as such revelations are, they are little to be wondered at. The cruelty of the Rifis, not only to outsiders, but amongst themselves, is proverbial. The perpetual blood feuds leading to constant murder have inured this hardy race to every kind of suffering, and what they perpetrate on others they bear themselves with wonderful endurance. All through these five years of continual warfare they had had none but the most primitive native medical aid and, in spite of their terrible sufferings from artillery fire and bombing from the air, they had never given in. The Rif had been devastated by war, by sickness and by famine. In almost every village the wounded lay without treatment and without medicaments—with nothing to alleviate their suffering or to ease their pain beyond the very primitive remedies of the country. Is it to be wondered at they treated the French and Spanish prisoners badly ? Nor had cruelty been confined to their side alone. There had been reprisals on more than one front, and reprisals as base and as barbarous as those practised by the Rifis themselves. In one respect at least they were worse, for they were perpetrated by a European army engaged, under what amounted to a mandate from Europe, in restoring peace or order in a distressed country. What is more, until the Marqués de Estella issued in November of last year stringent orders to put a stop to those reprisals once and for all, they had received official sanction. Happily his orders were obeyed and the cruelties have ceased, one may hope for ever.

The Governments that accept the great responsibilities of restoring order and introducing civilization into such countries as Morocco are aware as a rule of the nature of the people amongst whom their work will lie. They

must realize, if not by their own experience at least
from that of others, that should warfare ensue it must
be carried on under great difficulties and at great loss,
and with people whose ideas of war are totally opposed
to those of Europe.   The Rifis, a sturdy people, renowned
throughout Morocco for their morality and endurance,
were equally well known to be treacherous and cruel.
They could be counted upon to resist the invaders by
every means in their power and to massacre them if
ever they got the chance.   After the fall of Anual in
July, 1921, the chance presented itself, and the Rifis
perpetrated every possible horror and committed every
possible act of treachery.   They slew and tortured and
mutilated wholesale.   Was it to be expected that they
would do anything else ?   They did it because fate had
given them the opportunity and because they thought
it the best method to treat an alien and—to them—
' infidel ' army that had threatened their independence
and their country.   It was horrible, but natural.   Their
treatment of the prisoners was equally horrible, but not
surprising.   All warfare is cruel, and those who engage
in it must expect to reap cruelty.   The Rifis ill-treated,
and no doubt in some cases deliberately murdered, the
Spanish and French prisoners.   The French and Spanish
dropped hundreds of tons of high explosive bombs upon
the villages of the Rifis and Jibala.   The Spaniards
used gas.   But in my opinion the most cruel, the most
wanton and the most unjustifiable act of the whole war
was the bombing of the open town of Sheshuan in 1925
—when every male inhabitant capable of bearing arms
was known to be absent—by a squadron of volunteer
American airmen with the French Flying Corps.   A
number of absolutely defenceless women and children

were massacred and many others were maimed and blinded.

By April the 30th the negotiations at Ujda had reached what can only be described as an impasse. This unfortunate situation had arisen over the question of autonomy. For two days the French and Spanish delegates had been putting before their Rifi colleagues the views of their Governments on the measure of autonomy which the Rif should enjoy. It was pointed out to them that the Rif was inseparable from the rest of Morocco, in so far as all treaties were binding on the entire country, and that the Sultan was sovereign of the whole Moorish Empire. The French and Spaniards proposed, therefore, an autonomy which, while granting a large measure of Home Rule to the Rif, included the controlling right of the Sultan or of the Government or individual to whom the Sultan might delegate his authority. Such a state of autonomy could only be granted after the recognition by the Rifis of the Franco-Spanish Treaty of 1904—the original agreement by which France and Spain came to terms as to their respective zones. The international situation necessitated also the recognition of the Algeciras Act of 1906, which amongst other things regulates the 'open door' and commercial equality in Morocco, and of the Mining Law of 1914, which equally applies to the whole country. It is quite evident that neither the French and Spanish Governments nor the Sultan could grant any form of autonomy to the Rif that did not include formal recognition of these existing international arrangements. This recognition was therefore insisted upon by the French and Spanish delegates and refused by the Rifis.

Many details of the system of the proposed Rifian

autonomy had already been discussed and on the whole the Rifis considered the French and Spanish proposals generous but complicated and likely to give rise to misunderstandings. It was clear to every one, except the Rifis themselves, that they were quite incapable, from want of experience and education, of organizing or directing an independent Government except under close supervision and with the assistance of trained European advisers ; a system they certainly did not desire to accept, for they realized, and justly, that it would mean ' control.' They therefore refused to accept any form of autonomy that included the possibility of foreign supervision or recognition of existing treaties. In fact, if not in words, they returned to Abdel Krim's original demand for entire independence.

The Rifi reply to the other points was as follows: On the subject of Abdel Krim's withdrawal from the Rif they accepted the principle that it might be advisable for him to retire into private life after the introduction of the new régime. Under very considerable pressure they agreed to hand over at once the women and children prisoners, and the sick, but insisted on retaining the rest—the ' rest ' including those whose deaths they had not dared to divulge ! They were prepared to recognize the Sultan's authority on all religious questions and to send deputations on the various Feasts, as is the custom of all the tribes of Morocco, to the Sultan's Court, with expressions of loyalty and the presentation of tribute in the form of gifts. On disarmament they maintained their demand that the tribes should be disarmed by Abdel Krim and the Rifi authorities and not by French and Spanish columns sent to the Rif for that purpose, as was proposed. Pending the installation of a military police sufficient arms must be left in each tribe for defensive purposes. The arms when collected could be counted and destroyed by the French and Spanish Commissions.

The Rifi reply embodying these views was presented to the French and Spanish delegates at the following day's meeting. It was looked upon as bringing matters to an impasse, and the atmosphere of Ujda was charged with pessimism.

On May the 2nd Si Mohammed Azerkan and Kaid Haddu left Ujda for the Rif to consult Abdel Krim once more and to ask for his definite decision, more especially to the demand by the French and Spanish Governments for the immediate release of the prisoners. This journey of the two Rifi delegates was undertaken after two official statements had been issued on the evening of May the 1st by the French and Spanish delegations conjointly.

The shorter of these two official communiqués stated that the French and Spanish delegates had informed the Rifi delegation that an acceptance in principle of the conditions which had previously been notified to them, together with the liberation of all the prisoners detained in the Rif, was required before May the 8th. The French and Spanish Governments reserved full liberty of action if these conditions were not complied with by that date.

The second and longer document restated the original conditions of April the 11th, and the preliminary condition embodying the strategical rectification of front which ' in a spirit of conciliation ' had been withdrawn but was again now put forward.

The Rif delegates travelled to Nemours, a little port

on the Algerian coast, whence a French torpedo boat conveyed them to the Rif coast near Alhucemas, where they landed. A ride of 25 miles brought them to Targuist, Abdel Krim's headquarters since the Spanish occupation of Ajdir. It was there that the final decision of the Rifis was taken. Abdel Krim refused to accept the conditions.

The return of Azerkan and Kaid Haddu to Ujda without the prisoners was deplored. It had been hoped up to the last moment that at least on this point Abdel Krim would yield. It was still not known that all the Spanish officers had died, nor was the terrible state of the survivors realized. The refusal to release them was put down to intransigence on the part of Abdel Krim. The real reason was fear.

# CHAPTER XIII

## SURRENDER OF ABDEL KRIM

The Ujda Conference was over and the little town that had for a few weeks worn an unaccustomed air of movement and animation retired once more into its habitual state of peaceful inactivity. The Spanish and French delegations proceeded home via Fez and Rabat, and the Rifis had already left for the Rif.

There are some who claim that neither France nor Spain really endeavoured to arrive at peace and that the Conference was held merely to give satisfaction to the anti-war parties at home. This is certainly not true. The French Government, beset with every kind of annoyance, responsibility and worry in Europe, was undoubtedly anxious to come to terms with Abdel Krim. The Spaniards were in any case prepared to accept peace, though perhaps less anxious to obtain it, but it was unjust to suspect that either Government was influenced by anything except a real desire to put an end to the war in Morocco. That they failed was not their fault.

It had been clearly stated to the Rifi delegates that the French and Spanish Governments reserved their entire liberty of action should Abdel Krim refuse the terms offered. It was, therefore, no surprise when, immediately after the Conference had broken up, the campaign was reopened. Everything had been prepared

for an advance before the Conference met, and these
preparations had only been countermanded in order that
one last attempt should be made to obtain peace before a
renewal of hostilities took place.

The situation in May, 1926, was very different from
that which existed a year before, when the tribes had
attacked the French posts and were sweeping over the
whole frontier district.  The French had then been
caught almost unawares.  They had failed to realize
the strength of the Rifi forces and the spirit of nationalism that animated them.  They had attributed the discomfiture of the Spaniards rather to Spanish incapacity
than to the fighting abilities of the Rifis.  There had
been a tendency both in France and England to consider
the difficulties that Spain met with in Morocco as largely
due to her state of unpreparedness and inefficiency.
No doubt the Spanish campaign had been prolonged
by these causes, and had anyone of the spirit and
energy of Primo de Rivera come forward in the past,
the reforms which he introduced might long before
have been carried out with no little advantage to Spain.
But this knowledge of the want of organization which
existed in the Spanish army gave rise to a general estimate
of the situation that was certainly at fault.  There is
no doubt whatever that the French authorities, from
the General in command to the youngest officer of the
Service des Renseignements, believed that the French
front could easily hold back an attempted invasion of
Protectorate territory by the Rifis.

A year had passed since the tribesmen swept over
the frontier necessitating the abandonment of Post after
Post, and during that year, except for the unaccount-
able delay in the despatch of troops in the spring and

early summer of 1925, everything had been done to remedy the state of affairs. The French had discovered that these Rifi warriors, whom they had until then looked upon as bands of untrained tribesmen, were a foe whose prowess and fighting capacity were of a very high order. They had been attacked here, there and everywhere—often far behind the line of Posts—by an enemy whose mobility was extraordinary and who was practically invisible, and it was realized that an entirely new system of warfare must be adopted if success was to be achieved.

The winter of 1925–26 was one of strenuous preparation, not only in military matters, but also in the political relations with the frontier tribes whose sudden fall into ' dissidence ' had been one of the great surprises of the previous spring and summer. These conversations between the French Authorities and the tribesmen were carried on with the thoroughness and skill that render the French so successful in this kind of negotiation. The result was that at the moment at which the Ujda Conference broke down, both France and Spain were prepared, and well prepared, to take the field. The Spanish disembarkation at Alhucemas Bay in the previous September had given the Spaniards a new base from which to advance within easy striking distance of Targuist, Abdel Krim's headquarters. From the South the road lay open to the French, while Spanish columns were in readiness to march Westward from the Melilla front. Thus Abdel Krim and his stronghold were threatened on three sides and his only outlet for escape lay in the mountain district to the West.

On May the 8th two French Divisions commanded by Generals Ibos and Dosse advanced to the valley of

the Wad Kert, where they were joined by a Spanish force from the East. On May the 19th these two French Divisions and a Third Division under General Vernois occupied Jibel Rokdi and Jibel Zineb. Continuing their march they both took up positions on the Wad Nekor and the Wad Guis, two small rivers which eventually reach the sea in Alhucemas Bay. Meanwhile the Spaniards had reached Tamassint about half way between Ajdir, their base, and Targuist, Abdel Krim's headquarters. The suddenness and the success of these converging movements spread panic amongst the tribes and Abdel Krim himself abandoned the district. On May the 23rd Targuist was taken and the Beni Kassim and other tribes submitted. Meanwhile on other parts of the French front the troops were successfully advancing and tribe after tribe submitted.

It was at this time that Abdel Krim realized that he was defeated and that the moment had arrived to sue for peace. He accordingly wrote two letters—to Monsieur Steeg, the French Resident-General, and to General Sanjurjo, the Spanish High Commissioner—asking for a cessation of hostilities and a reopening of the negotiations which had been abandoned at Ujda. These letters he entrusted to Monsieur Parent, a French gentleman who in the interests of the welfare of the Christian prisoners in the Rif had gone to Targuist with Doctor Gaud. There is no doubt it was largely owing to Monsieur Parent's ability, reputation and advice that Abdel Krim offered his submission. Here at last was an intermediary whose intervention in the interests of peace had no connection with mining concessions or personal benefits ! His mission undertaken solely for the purpose of bringing hope and relief to the ill-treated prisoners was admirable and led to results beyond expectation, for it was to him that Abdel Krim turned for advice when he realized that further resistance was useless. But his first communications were too indefinite for action to be taken upon them and, after due consideration, the French and Spanish Governments decided that no cessation of hostilities could at that moment be conceded. This wise decision brought about the almost immediate surrender of the Rifi leader.

There are many opinions as to why Abdel Krim refused to accept at Ujda terms that were generous and which would have secured for the Rif a considerable measure of Home Rule. There is probably some truth in all these versions, but after consulting many Rifis who enjoyed the confidence of their leader, in so far as he confided in anyone, I believe that Abdel Krim's refusal to accept the terms was due to the following reasons. On the one hand he argued that there was a decided want of unanimity amongst the French themselves as to what policy to adopt in regard to the Rif. Abdel Krim was aware, and at Ujda it was very apparent that, while there was a genuine desire to arrive at peace by negotiation on the part of the French Government and the French Residency in Morocco, there was also a military party anxious to put an end to the situation by a crushing defeat of the Rifis. Both these parties were genuinely convinced of their respective policies, but these divergences of opinion no doubt encouraged the Rifis to run the risk of refusing the French terms. The Rifi delegates at Ujda were probably also convinced that the relations of the French and Spanish Governments were not sufficiently close and intimate to allow of any actual united action. They did not believe that

the French forces would invade the Spanish zone, not
so much from any hostility on the part of the Spaniards
as from the opposition that such an adventure would
arouse in France.   Abdel Krim looked too for intervention—perhaps the intervention of England or America,
so rashly held out to him as more than a bare possibility
by certain of his English admirers—and still more
certainly he looked to the intervention of the French
Socialists.   Such were the Rifi views in as far as they
concerned the outside world.   But Abdel Krim had also
to consider his position in the Rif and his relations with
his own people.

Apart from all question of the possibilities of Franco-
Spanish disinclination to continue the war, from whatever reason it might arise, it would have been difficult
for Abdel Krim to have accepted the peace terms offered
at Ujda.   Generous as they were, they fell far short
of what he had promised.   The Rif was not yet beaten,
and there was no doubt that the tribes, whatever may
have been the opinion of some of the more intelligent
amongst their members, still believed that the fastnesses
of their country could never be invaded by Christian
troops.   They were prepared, weary though they were
of warfare, to continue the struggle.   They were convinced that they could hold the Spaniards on any advance
that might be attempted from their base at Alhucemas,
and they doubted whether the French would pass the
frontier of the Protectorate.   Abdel Krim, and his delegates at Ujda, on the other hand, realized that should the
campaign be continued, which they doubted, the Rif
could not resist beyond a very short period of time.
They were aware of the vast preparations that had been
made for the advance and that the French Army had

learned by experience the manner of warfare that the situation required. His plan was to await the advance of the French and Spanish troops until the danger of the situation was realized by his tribesmen. Then declaring that all was lost he hoped to win the tribes over to accepting the peace terms, which he, too sanguinely, imagined would be those he had refused at Ujda. He would in this way not only make peace with his enemies, but by acting with the consent, and on the authority, of the tribes maintain his own position of supremacy in the Rif. Had he accepted the terms offered at Ujda, when the French and Spanish columns were still some distance from the heart of the Rif, he ran the risk, and it was a great risk, of his tribes turning against him. He played his cards accordingly. If anyone, he decided, was to invade his country, it must be the French, because the Rif was in the Spanish zone and the Spaniards would be likely to remain in any part of the country that they occupied. Not so the French; for once peace was made they would retire back again across their frontier, leaving the country, Abdel Krim hoped, in his own hands, to govern under some generous form of Home Rule. He therefore resisted the Spanish advance from Targuist far more stubbornly and more effectively than he did that of the French columns advancing Northward from the Protectorate.

Yet there is no doubt that the Rifi tribes had been desirous that peace should be reached at Ujda. The long campaign had played havoc with their lives and with their property and they were weary, ill-fed and decimated by warfare and disease. But the peace they demanded and expected was the peace Abdel Krim had promised and was still promising them, by word of mouth and in manifestos,—the absolute independence of their country. When the negotiations at Ujda broke down and the tribes learned that once more they were to enter upon a period of renewed hostilities, there was an undoubted wave of discouragement and disappointment. They would fight again but not with the same dogged determination, for their spirit was breaking. These years of war and misery had eaten deeply into their hearts, and now they had gained neither peace nor victory. The wheel of Abdel Krim's fortune was turning. He had become cruel in these last days. There had been many executions. He was still respected, but the respect was due to fear and no longer to affection.

With the occupation of Targuist, his headquarters, by the French the moment to carry out his plan had arrived. He meant to obtain the consent of the tribes to the terms of peace by pointing out the presence of the enemy in their very midst. He had held the Spaniards back on their march from the coast; the French would retire to the Protectorate once peace was made. He would still be master in his own house. It was a bold game and skilfully conceived —but it failed. He had not counted upon the effect the presence of the French columns in the very heart of the Rif would have upon the tribesmen. It was almost instantaneous. In spite of all Abdel Krim's promises in spite of all their sufferings, the tribes realized that the Rif was lost. The unimaginable had happened; their unconquered race was beaten. The tribes turned against the man whom they now accused of having deceived them, and when on May the 26th Abdel Krim crossed the French lines in the early morning and gave himself up, he was a refugee fleeing from the revenge of his own people.

At the last moment, within a week of his surrender, Abdel Krim had made an appeal for British intervention, for the third time.

The first occasion was on June the 15th, 1925, when a confidential messenger brought me a letter from Abdel Krim for publication in *The Times*, which stated the objects and aims of his campaign. His messenger, who enjoyed his master's full confidence, at the same time made a fervent appeal on his behalf for the good offices of the British Government. Naturally this was impossible. There were no grounds upon which British intervention could have been offered. It was, of course, refused.

The second occasion was on July the 22nd, 1925, when another confidential messenger brought me a long written statement of Abdel Krim's policy and intentions. He again asked for the good offices of the British Government. This messenger, like all those of whom Abdel Krim made use, was well trained and well instructed. His long request, based on many arguments, had been learned by heart for the risk of passing such a request through the Spanish lines was too great for it to be committed to writing. It stated that Abdel Krim was fully aware that the British Government could accept no responsibility in the matter, and that all he requested was its initiative and good offices. He asserted that it was the only chance for peace and begged that the matter might receive consideration. He appealed to British feelings of humanity and Great Britain's sense of justice. Abdel Krim said that he would accept any terms from France and Spain to which Great Britain agreed. His request was naturally refused. It could not be otherwise. It was evident that the British Government could in no circumstances intervene in a question that was essentially one between France and Spain and the Rif, and even if its good offices had been possible the situation in the Rif and uncertainty as to its future would have rendered any form of intervention undesirable.

On this occasion Abdel Krim made a curious confession. He stated that he was alone and had no one to turn to for advice and did not know what terms he ought to accept or offer. He did not, he said, consult his Rifi chiefs on these questions nor any European in the Rif. Politically he was at a complete loss what to do. Such Europeans as were with him, he said, were adventurers or deserters and, beyond teaching his soldiers to drill and to dig trenches, were useless to him. It was the only confession of weakness Abdel Krim ever made to me till his letter published in *The Times* of March the 17th, 1926.

The reasons why his request for intervention could not be considered were communicated in writing to Abdel Krim in a letter which at the same time advised him to negotiate with the French and Spaniards direct on the advantageous terms which they were offering him. This desire of Abdel Krim for British intervention was communicated at the time to the French authorities, together with the reply.

Abdel Krim was much distressed at this failure to obtain intervention, and undeterred, he turned his efforts in other directions. He received, from other sources, encouragement to maintain the fight against France and Spain, and was advised in no circumstances to negotiate with those two Powers, which were described as incapable of good faith and desirous only of obtaining a cessation of hostilities in order to catch the Rifis in a trap. In these communications every hope was held out of ultimate intervention. Confident that certain important names connected with this correspondence carried great weight, Abdel Krim decided to continue the struggle and refused to negotiate on the basis of the generous terms then offered. My message published in *The Times* of April the 5th previous to the Ujda Conference, called attention to the cruel injury done to the Rifis by this raising of false hopes.

The French and Spanish Governments would have been well advised to include in the conditions of peace the demand that all Abdel Krim's correspondence with Europeans be handed over to those two Governments for examination and publication. Some astounding documents would be found, to which not a little of this last year's bloodshed and devastation is due. The possible existence of mines in the Rif, the awakening of cupidity in the Rifis, and the action of foreign financial interests have resulted in the sacrifice of a vast number of lives—French, Spanish, and Rifi.

On the approach of the French columns Abdel Krim had abandoned Targuist and proceeded to Snada, a Zawia of the Shereefs of Wazzan, as the guest of the respected Sidi Ahmedo. Here at least he was safe from any attempt on the part of his tribesmen, because these Zawias are ' sanctuaries ' in the eyes of the natives. It is said, and no doubt truly, that Sidi Ahmedo el-Wazzani had never abandoned his respect for the Maghzen and the Sultan's dynasty and that he had never been a very firm supporter of Abdel Krim nor of the

Rifi movement.  No doubt Abdel Krim himself was fully aware of this, but he had respected the venerated Shereef's opinions and had always treated him with deference and respect.  It was to him, as a useful mediator, that he went in this moment of crisis, and his assistance that he demanded.  It was not refused.

At Snada, Abdel Krim learned of the growing defection of the tribes and that village after village and district after district were submitting to the Christian invaders.  Only a small portion of his own tribe, the Beni Uriaghel, remained still faithful to his cause. He determined, in a last hope of being able to maintain the struggle, to attempt to reach a safer part of the Rif and there with the tribesmen who remained loyal, and Jibala contingents, to hold out.  But he was told that any attempt to leave the region in which he was would certainly end in his own arrest by the tribes. Realizing that the critical situation could not be protracted, he authorized Sidi Ahmedo to enter into direct relations with the commander of the nearest French column, Colonel Corap.  On receiving the important intelligence that Abdel Krim was prepared to come to terms, Colonel Corap sent two officers, Capitaine Suffren and Lieutenant de Vaisseau Montagne, with a small escort, to Snada.  They were bearers of a letter by which France promised to protect the Rifi leader and his family, but which at the same time contained a demand for the immediate release of the Christian prisoners.

It was on the afternoon of May the 25th that the two officers reached Snada and were introduced by the Shereef into the presence of Abdel Krim.  The conversation was difficult and contentious, and the Rifi leader defended

himself and his cause with acumen and with dignity.
He spoke very bitterly of the Spaniards and did not
disguise the hatred in which he held them.   He realized
that they would demand revenge and probably his death
or punishment.   He heaped recriminations upon the
French and Spanish alike, and it was not until after three
hours of heated conversation that he consented to
address a letter to Colonel Corap in the following terms :

To Colonel Corap.
My compliments and my respects.
I have received the letter by which you accord me
security.   I have decided at this moment to come to
you.   I ask for the protection of France for myself and
for my family.   As to the prisoners I have requested
that they be set at liberty to-morrow morning.   I will
let you know the hour of my arrival ; it will be before
or about midday.

Mohommed ben Abdel Krim el Khatabi.

The following morning, accompanied by Monsieur
Parent and Doctor Gaud, the prisoners, a band of broken
sick men, crossed the French lines and were free.

Abdel Krim on horseback paid a hasty visit to his
family at the neighbouring village of Kemmum in order
to prepare them for their departure.   He returned to
Snada distressed and exhibiting every sign of depression.
It was not unnatural.   Once or twice during the morning
he announced his intention of abandoning his promised
surrender and of continuing the struggle.   He was still
free, he argued, and at liberty to take what course he
pleased.   While he held forth on the history and independence of the Rif a Spanish aeroplane bombarded the
outskirts of Snada and three Rifis were killed.

Before daylight the following morning (May the 27th) Abdel Krim mounted his horse at the doorway of the Shereef's house and, surrounded by the little escort of Spahis that had accompanied the French officers, set out. On the way, soon after leaving the Zawia, in the clear moonlight a little group of Rifis approached their leader and kissed his stirrup. They asked for his orders, but he rode on in silence. At sunrise Targuist was reached and Abdel Krim's surrender was accomplished. It was the exit from the Moorish stage of a very remarkable man.

It was, as has been seen, the French who struck the final blow. Abdel Krim had never disguised the fact that his real enemy was Spain, and that he had been brought into war with the French Protectorate solely by the fear of the invasion of the Rif by French forces. He seems always to have considered that at almost every moment of the campaign it was possible to come to terms with France. He felt that the war was unpopular, and it was always his intention, though he more than once threw away the chances of putting it into practice, to make peace with the French and turn with all his forces against the Spaniards. He never believed in the possibility, or at least the practicability, of the Franco-Spanish entente, and was convinced that he was capable of keeping his two enemies apart. There is no doubt that in this he was for a time successful. By skilful propaganda, for the publication of which he had no difficulty in finding agents amongst the journalists of all countries ; by appeals to the sympathies, political or humanitarian, of the public ; by promises of concessions to international adventurers, Abdel Krim was able to keep the world informed of his aims, his movements and his intentions and to obtain sympathy. He certainly succeeded in attracting an immense amount of attention to these Northern districts of Morocco. Nor was this attention ill-placed. The struggle of the Rifis for independence—for on the part of the tribes it was a struggle for independence—obtained a merited sympathy, and was full of interest. It mattered little if behind the scenes there were ulterior and less patriotic motives—the existence of mines of supposed enormous wealth, a craving for power. Of that only very few Rifis were aware and the tribes were genuinely struggling, as they were bidden to struggle, for the independence of their country, for the freedom of their race. They did not realize that had Abdel Krim been successful they would in reality have obtained neither. They would have remained under a despot—a capable and clever despot it is true,—who would have never ceded his rights of life and death and whose intention it was to rule as an autocrat. Perhaps he knew the Rifi tribes well enough to be convinced that it was the only manner in which they could be governed.

It is not easy to judge the personal motives of Abdel Krim, from the moment when, after Anual in 1921, he took command of the Rifi forces and became the national hero of his country. No doubt his ambitions increased with his successes. There seems every reason to believe that his first motive, after he escaped from imprisonment in Melilla, was almost solely revenge. His hatred of the Spaniard was intense, unreasonable, though in his case comprehensible. He had worked with them apparently to his own and their satisfaction. If he complained of their corruption he was certainly guilty of having participated in it. It is possible that at the termination of the Great War he saw many of his hopes dispersed. His close relations with German mining groups, encouraged by the Spanish authorities, had led him to look forward to a future of prosperity and wealth. But the victory of the Allies rendered necessary a change of policy on the part of Spain and a discontinuance of official protection and encouragement to German interests in the Spanish zone.

There is no doubt that Abdel Krim had looked with no disapproving eye upon the advance of the Spanish troops into the Rif in 1918, for it meant the eventual, and he may have hoped speedy, opening up of the rich mineralized district from which he intended to extract his full measure of profit. For him the Spanish advance merely freed the way to German industry. But when in 1919 Spanish policy changed, the German influence waned and Abdel Krim's visions of fortune faded. He quarrelled with the Spaniards and was imprisoned. He escaped imbued with an intense hatred of Spain and an all-absorbing desire for revenge. What had passed between him and General Silvestre has never been disclosed. All that is known is that they had quarrelled and that words had been uttered that could neither be forgotten nor forgiven. Probably it was nothing more than [conflict between two men of deep feelings and little restraint. The quarrel may have been of itself of little importance, but its consequences were great.

That no national sentiment stirred Abdel Krim to resist the Spaniards in their invasion of the Rif has often been stated. It is erroneous, and there is no doubt that as time went on the Rifi leader was largely influenced by a desire for the freedom and independence of the Rif.

It is probable that this patriotic sentiment might never have come to the fore had it not been for the more personal aims that originated his campaign. I should be inclined to put the successive phases of Abdel Krim's motives in the following order—Revenge, the acquisition of wealth, personal ambition, the independence of the Rif. The latter was owing not a little to the contagion of the enthusiasm that he had succeeded in awakening amongst the tribesmen, as well as a means to an end. But there seems no doubt that, genuine as may have been Abdel Krim in his protestations of patriotism, it was his hatred of the Spaniard and his personal desire for revenge, so typical a characteristic of the Rifi people, that originated, underlay and influenced all his actions.

With the surrender of Abdel Krim the war in the Rif came to an end. It had been his personality alone that had held together the federation of the tribes and spurred them on to such prolonged resistance. His courage, his endurance, his handling of a situation that was always precarious and often appeared hopeless, had brought the Rif through five years of almost unceasing war, unparalleled in colonial history. With the exception of certain arms purchased in and introduced from Europe and Algeria, the Rifis had fought throughout with weapons captured from their enemies. When the surrender came about, the Rifi and Jibala tribesmen were in possession of 135 cannon, over 40,000 rifles, 240 machine-guns and large quantities of bombs and ammunition. All cannon, the machine-guns, and most of the rifles and other material they had captured

from the Spanish and French armies. By the end of
1926 the whole of this vast accumulation had been
handed over to the Spaniards, with the exception of
about 10,000 rifles which yet remained in the hands of
the Jibala tribes.

The endurance of all these mountain tribesmen,
ill-nourished, ill-clothed, practically unpaid and without
medical assistance, can only be described as admirable.
There was no situation however desperate, no suffering
however severe, that they did not face without com-
plaint and without hesitation. If their methods and
their reprisals were open to criticism, their spirit was
above all praise, but the task was too great. With the
disappearance from the scene of their leader, whose
surrender and escape gave rise to unanimous disapproval amongst the tribes, they disbanded and
returned to their own districts. For a few months
they remained sullenly watching the Spanish advance
as the army occupied their country. The massacres
and outrages they had expected never occurred; and
instead of being imbued with a feeling of hatred and
revenge, they found the invading army carrying out
its work with every consideration for the welfare of the
population. The Spanish soldiers' lot—and many of
them were natives—was a happy one compared with
what they themselves had suffered in Abdel Krim's
service. Fighting was now rare, and the principal duty
of the advancing columns was the restoration of order
and the introduction of peace. One by one the Rifi
soldiers of Abdel Krim came down from their mountain
fastnesses, and by the end of 1926 Spain possessed in
Africa no finer body of men than the picked 1,500 Rifis
of the Beni Uriaghel tribe, who only a comparatively

few months ago had formed the backbone of their enemy's forces.

During the autumn months this Rifi contingent has fought brilliantly against their former allies, the Jibala, in the interests of Spain. Obedient, cheerful, courageous and well trained in Abdel Krim's harsh service, they form ideal troops. The hopes of peace for the Rif which they once reposed in their own leader have now been transferred to the Spaniards, whom they have learned to trust. God had given the victory to the strongest, and the Rif had been bled white. That last advance of the French and Spaniards, and the ensuing surrender, had left them abandoned and disheartened, but with a sense of duty done. They had held out until the very end. To settle down to work in their devastated and abandoned fields was impossible. The spirit of the warrior was paramount. They enlisted in the Spanish Army, a band of volunteers ready to fight as valiantly for Spain and for the restoration of order as they had fought in resisting the Spanish invasion. There could be no better proof that the pacification of the Rif by the Spaniards is not any longer an insurmountable problem, and that already the co-operation of the people is won. The Rifi is laborious and intelligent. In a generation he will be on a par with the Spaniard of Morocco, in two generations it is more than probable that he will be ahead of him, for he comes into the field after centuries of the survival of the fittest, hampered by inexperience, but the offspring of white ancestors, and with a mentality on a par with that of the races of Europe. His strength and stamina leave nothing to be desired. As long as the Rifi race survives there is hope for Morocco.

Y*

While in the North the Rifis were enlisting in the
Spanish Army and settling back on to their lands, those
of the South, suffering still from the famine which this
long period of warfare had caused, were migrating into
the French Protectorate with their families. Long
straggling lines of tired immigrants—men, women and
children, with a few donkeys, and now and again cattle
—marched southward towards Fez, to be received with
every kindness and assistance by the French authorities.
Collected at first into large camps, for they had no
shelter or means of procuring any, they were gradually
given work on the farms and agricultural estates of the
Northern districts of the French Protectorate. It says
much for the reputation of the French that almost
immediately after the termination of war these wild
tribesmen ventured with their women and children to
throw themselves upon the hospitality of their enemies
of yesterday, knowing no harm would befall them.
Horrible, cruel as had been the whole period of the Rif
War, it seems that it has led to the advent of happier
days. The hatred of race and religion seems to be
stamped out and a mutual goodwill, a mutual desire
for peace and for a better understanding, to have taken
its place.

Meanwhile Abdel Krim was removed from the front
to Taza, where his family and belongings, conveyed
on over 200 mules, arrived a little later. With him
were his uncle, his brother Sid Mahammed, who had
been his commander-in-chief, Sid Mohammed Azerkan,
the Foreign Minister, and Sid Ahmed Sheddi. They
all received from the French authorities a courteous
and respectful treatment. It was the desire of Monsieur
Steeg, the able Résident-Général of France in Morocco,

that the Rifi Chieftain should be ' neither exalted nor humiliated—but in time forgotten.'

Abdel Krim remained at Taza till June 5, when he and his companions were brought to Fez and lodged in a sumptuous residence which had been prepared for their reception. The question of his legal status and the plans and proposals for his future caused very considerable discussion, particularly between Paris and Madrid. It was no secret that the Spanish Government desired a full judicial inquiry to be held into Abdel Krim's past actions, more particularly his barbaric treatment of the Spanish prisoners, but the terms on which he had surrendered to the French had to be taken into account. He was a prisoner of war whose personal security, and that of his family, had been guaranteed. That he could be put upon his trial was out of the question. It was even reported that at one moment the Spanish Government was prepared to demand his being handed over to the Spanish authorities, on the grounds that he was a rebel against Spain, which was true to the extent that he had been in Spanish service ; but if such was ever the intention of Madrid, wiser counsels prevailed. The only safe and certain policy to pursue was, as Monsieur Steeg proposed, to allow Abdel Krim to be forgotten.

It was not until Abdel Krim had arrived in Fez that the tribesmen of the remoter parts of the Rif, of Ghomara and the Jibala began to realize what had happened. The surrender had been so sudden, so unexpected, that the reports which spread quickly through the tribes were discredited and considered as enemy propaganda put abroad by the Spaniards and the French.

On June 7 the Spanish Government announced that

it was its intention to carry out the occupation of the whole Spanish zone, and no longer to limit its activities to the districts lying behind the ' Primo ' line and to the newly acquired districts of the Rif. This decision simplified the whole question as between France and Spain and was the origin of a common policy in both zones. At the same time it was decided in principle to delimit the frontier between the French Protectorate and the Spanish zone with as little delay as possible.

It is a curious fact that though the Jibala tribes had been slow to adhere to Abdel Krim's campaign, and had awaited the downfall of Raisuli before doing so, they were the last to abandon their fallen chief. They hesitated, showing none of the readiness of the Rifis to accept a *fait accompli* even when they were certain that Abdel Krim was a prisoner. In this was apparent the difference in the characteristics of the two races. The Rifi, hard-headed, practical, and influenced by a sense of his own welfare, perceived at once which course to pursue. The Jibala, excitable, ready to follow any leader on almost any crusade however impracticable, clung to the lost cause and refused to see reason. It was the Rifis who had led them to acknowledge the supremacy of Abdel Krim. That the Rifis themselves had surrendered to the Spaniards, that Abdel Krim had, as they now knew, passed over to the enemy, that the Spaniards would concentrate all their forces against themselves, did not deter the Jibala from continuing the struggle. They should have realized how ineffectual in the end their resistance must prove, deprived of the Rifi *bloc* on their flank, and of their supplies of arms and ammunition which all came from the Rif. Yet they determined to maintain the struggle alone, and added to their Spanish enemies their former Rifi allies. They drove Abdel Krim's representatives and contingents from the country and threw off the recently imposed Rifi yoke. At Sheshuan a native of the Akhmas tribe, by name Uld el-Far, seized the town in the name of the Jibala and proclaimed its independence. He was unable to maintain his own ascendancy, but his action put an end to the Rifi domination in that district. But the Jibala tribes were no longer united ; the stern restraining hand of a Raisuli or an Abdel Krim was lacking. For the purpose of choosing a leader a meeting of the tribesmen was called in June at the sacred tomb of Mulai Abdesalam ben Mashish in the Beni Aros. Uld el-Far was not confirmed in his position as chief of the federation of the tribes, in spite of the fact that at that moment he virtually held Sheshuan, the key of the Jibala position. The gathering, after several days' deliberation, chose, in order to escape worse confusion, an almost unknown personage as their leader, the Shereef Sid Abdesalam ben Hassan, a man of holy descent but of no political or military importance. His election was, in fact, a compromise amongst the several claimants for the leadership of the tribes. Any other choice would have led to dissension and possibly to intertribal war.

Meanwhile rapid progress was being made in the pacification of the Rif. The Spaniards were occupying the country without resistance, and by the end of June the tribes had delivered up over 12,000 rifles and other arms. The people were invited to nominate their own Kaids and officials, and lands confiscated by Abdel Krim were restored to their rightful owners. The Rif seemed to have entered upon a period of peace with every promise of prosperity, such as it had never known in the past. Under Abdel Krim the intertribal and inter-family blood feuds had been suppressed ; under the Spaniards there were no signs of their renewal. They had existed from time immemorial for the reason that a state of anarchy had always prevented the introduction of any form of Justice capable of executing its judgments. The only remedy was self-protection, and self-protection is easily misunderstood. It not unnaturally gave birth to almost universal feud. But under Abdel Krim there had been a central administration to which appeals for justice could be made, and there is no doubt that, arbitrary as were his acts, a very fair measure of justice existed under his régime. The Spaniards, on their occupation of the Rif, had only to take advantage of this situation. They inherited the Rifi Government's place as supreme arbiter and, accepting the customs of the country as a line of conduct, continued to administer justice. The disputants who had appealed to Abdel Krim found an even more equitable form of justice being administered, which, though its origin was Christian and foreign, yet complied with the unwritten laws and customs of their country where the Koranic code has only been partially adopted.

The Jibala tribesmen remained on the alert, but with the exception of small attacks upon convoys and now and again resistance to the Spanish advances, they attempted no action of any real importance. In early August the Spaniards were back in Sheshuan without having to fight a single battle. The same tribes that had so furiously attacked the Spanish troops during the costly retirement in 1924 now watched their return with apparent complete indifference.

Two facts explain the facility of the Spanish occupation of the Rif—the victory of the combined Franco-Spanish forces and the new policy and attitude adopted by the Spanish authorities themselves in their relations with the natives. It is impossible to exaggerate the importance of this change of policy. General Primo de Rivera's orders for the total suppression of all forms of reprisals on the enemy—and there had been many in the past—and for the treatment of the natives with kindness and consideration under all circumstances, bore immediate fruit. The moment the Rifis realized that they could submit with safety, that their lives and property—and their women and children—would be respected, they hesitated no longer to come in. The Spanish soldier is by instinct and nature of kindly disposition. The excesses of which the troops had been guilty, until General Primo de Rivera put a stop to reprisals, were due undoubtedly to a sort of hereditary tradition that seems to have been innate in the Spanish Army at all periods of its history from the time of the invasion of America. How superficial it was has now been demonstrated. One severe order issued by the President of the Spanish Directory put an end to it, and Spain has gained in every way by his act. There is no reason whatever why the good relations between the Spaniards and the Rifis should not be permanently maintained.

On August 28, Abdel Krim left Casablanca for the island of Réunion, which had, by mutual agreement between the French and Spanish Governments, been chosen as his place of exile. Twenty-three members of his family accompanied him, including his brother and uncle. His departure left the Moors indifferent.

In a country where everything is considered as directly ordained by God, a fall from power means a fall from memory. The man whose name had only a few months before been world-known, who had played so important a part in the recent history of Morocco, passed into exile and oblivion.

The autumn brought no untoward incident to mar the progress of pacification. Small bands of Jibala tribesmen still caused annoyance to the Spaniards and to the French in the districts near Wazzan, but these purely local affairs were of no real import and were the natural consequence of events. Large districts in those regions had never been explored, much less occupied, and the physical difficulties of the country prevented any immediate advance. But little by little, by military measures and by political preparation, the Spaniards penetrated the wild mountains of Ghomara, and to-day, in the last week of 1926, their work of occupation is practically accomplished. There are still Jibala tribes to disarm, and Jibala bands to disperse, but the future is full of hope.

Early in November Ahmedo Heriro—Abdel Krim's lieutenant in the Northern Jibala districts—was killed while resisting, with his followers, the advance of a Spanish column in the Beni Idir country. He had been a staunch follower of Raisuli until a quarrel drove him over to the Rifi side, in the days before the Jibala had recognized the Rifi supremacy. It was he who had been instrumental in bringing about the federation of the Jibala and Rifis, and it had been at his invitation that Abdel Krim had sent Rifi authorities to govern the Western tribes. His first act had been the capture of Tazrut and the surrender of his former master Raisuli.

Of all the Jibala tribesmen Ahmedo Heriro had been Spain's most energetic and capable enemy. Young— he was under 30 when he was killed—honest, energetic and courageous, he was a born leader of men, and no undertaking was too venturous for him to engage in. It was he who had brought the famous Rifi gun to the heights overlooking Tetuan, and for a long time carried on a desultory bombardment of the capital of the Spanish zone. The Spanish authorities had done their best to come to terms with him, and negotiations had more than once been opened, but his demands were exorbitant. Nothing less than a position little short of that which Raisuli had at one time occupied would satisfy him. He asked to be made a practically inde- pendent Kaid of the Jibala, with an army of his own to be armed and paid by Spain. Naturally such terms were impossible to grant.

He was shot at the front of his men, fighting desper- ately to resist the advance. He died within an hour or two, and the Jibala contingents, bearing the body of their young chief, retired into the mountains of Beni Aros. Near the sacred tomb of Mulai Abdesalam ben Mashish they buried him. His loss was a great blow to the tribes and has facilitated not a little the Spanish task. The disappearance of such a leader could not but cause great damage to the cause he had so stubbornly defended. He was one of the most romantic and most courageous figures of the war.

The winter rains had already begun to fall, and although the Spaniards continued to occupy suitable positions in the Jibala country, all possibility of a general 'clearing up' campaign in that region was out of the question. Not only do the rivers and streams become unfordable at this period of the year, but the mud and wet render any progress very difficult. The cold, too, this winter has been extreme, and at the end of December much of the Jibala highlands was under snow. There were heavy falls on Christmas Day at Tetuan and at Fez, a very rare occurrence.

The situation in both the French Protectorate and the Spanish zone at the end of December (1926) was eminently satisfactory. The Spaniards still had some work to do amongst the Jibala, where certain of the tribes had not yet been disarmed. In the Rif the tranquillity was absolute, and there Spain's task seems at long last satisfactorily accomplished. Should the present policy of pacification and goodwill be continued, there should be no change in the situation.

In the French Protectorate there is peace. After the surrender of Abdel Krim the military authorities turned their attention to the Taza district, occupying after a short and brilliant little campaign the high mountains of that region. Further South, near the valley of the Wad el-Abid, a little movement of revolt was easily suppressed. Within a few weeks of the end of the Rif campaign large numbers of these hardy tribesmen, with their women and children, came down from their mountain districts to find food and work in the French zone. They were kindly received, looked after, and distributed over the neighbouring districts where work in the fields was found for them. Their confidence in the French was manifest and warranted. The enemy of yesterday has become the friend and protector of to-day.

# INDEX

Lightning Source UK Ltd.
Milton Keynes UK
UKHW011314190320
360610UK00002B/637

9 781783 310456